RODIN
A Magnificent Obsession

RODIN
A Magnificent Obsession

MERRELL
in association with the
IRIS AND B. GERALD CANTOR FOUNDATION

Published by Merrell Publishers Limited
42 Southwark Street
London SE1 1UN

in association with the

Iris and B. Gerald Cantor Foundation
1801 Avenue of the Stars, Suite 435
Los Angeles, California 90067

First published 2001

Distributed in the USA and Canada by Rizzoli
International Publications, Inc. through
St. Martin's Press, 175 Fifth Avenue, New York,
New York 10010

British Library Cataloguing-in-Publication Data:
Rodin : a magnificent obsession
1.Cantor, B. Gerald 2.Rodin, Auguste, 1840–1917
3.Sculpture – Private collections 4.Sculpture –
France
I.Varnedoe, Kirk, 1946– II.Iris and B. Gerald
Cantor Foundation
730.9'2

ISBN 1 85894 143 1 hardback
ISBN 1 85894 144 x paperback

Produced by Merrell Publishers Limited
Edited by Iain Ross and Anthea Snow
"Rodin's Studio" by Antoinette Le Normand-
Romain translated from the French by Brian
Brazeau
Designed by Tim Harvey

Printed and bound in Italy

Front jacket/cover:
Rodin, Auguste
Marsyas (Torso of Falling Man, Enlargement)
c. 1882–89, Musée Rodin cast 4/12 in 1970
Bronze
Georges Rudier
40½ × 27½ × 18½ in.
(102.9 × 69.9 × 47 cm)
Iris and B. Gerald Cantor Collection, promised gift
to the Iris and B. Gerald Cantor Foundation

Back jacket/cover:
Rodin, Auguste
The Cathedral
Original stone version executed in 1908,
Musée Rodin cast in 1955
Bronze
Georges Rudier
25¼ × 12¾ × 13½ in.
(64.1 × 32.3 × 34.3 cm)
Iris and B. Gerald Cantor Foundation

Frontispiece:
Rodin, Auguste
The Thinker
1880, enlarged in 1902–03, this cast about 1960
Bronze
Georges Rudier
79 × 51¼ × 55¼ in.
(200.7 × 130.2 × 140.3 cm)
Iris and B. Gerald Cantor Foundation, promised
gift to the Iris and B. Gerald Cantor Center for
Visual Arts at Stanford University

*In the captions to the plates, the name following
the medium is that of the foundry.*

CONTENTS

FOREWORD

This book was created to document the Rodin collection held by the Iris and B. Gerald Cantor Foundation, including promised gifts from Iris Cantor. The Foundation's collection was very purposefully assembled by B. Gerald Cantor to be an active and educational tool. For over 30 years it has been seen by countless individuals in hundreds of venues around the world in the form of individual loans, small focus shows, and blockbuster exhibitions. Except for the necessary shipping containers, darkened storage areas were never a part of Mr. Cantor's plan.

Newlyweds Iris and B. Gerald Cantor launched the Foundation in 1978. Its formal mission was, and is still, as Iris Cantor would say, to support the body and the soul. More specifically, it exists to promote and encourage recognition and appreciation of excellence in the arts and medical research, through the support of exhibitions, art scholarships, medical research centers and hospitals, and through the endowment of galleries at major museums around the world. The main thrust of the Cantor Foundation's support focuses on the art of Auguste Rodin and women's health issues. The Foundation's efforts are concentrated primarily in California and New York.

RIGHT: 2. B. Gerald Cantor (center) with Albert Elsen (left) and Kirk Varnedoe (right) at the Coubertin Foundry in Saint-Rémy-lès-Chevreuse, France, for the lost-wax casting of Rodin's *The Gates of Hell*, 1979

LEFT: 1. Rodin, Auguste
Eve
c. 1887
Marble
30¼ × 11½ × 13 in.
(76.8 × 29.2 × 33 cm)
Iris and B. Gerald Cantor Collection, promised gift to the Iris and B. Gerald Cantor Foundation

Since the loss of the visionary Mr. Cantor in 1996, Iris Cantor has carried on this mission. Slowly at first, and then galvanized by the vitality of his legacy, she undertook bigger and more significant projects. The exhibition program continued and expanded. Two special exhibitions, *The Hands of Rodin: A Tribute to B. Gerald Cantor* and *Rodin's Monument to Victor Hugo*, were organized and circulated. Both were shown at the Los Angeles County Museum of Art and traveled to the Portland Art Museum, Oregon. The former was then mounted at the Philadelphia Museum of Art, the Brooklyn Museum of Art, the Museum of Art at Brigham Young University, Utah, and the Arkansas Arts Center; and the latter at the Cummer Museum of Art and Gardens, Florida, the Metropolitan Museum of Art in New York, and the Iris and B. Gerald Cantor Center for Visual Arts at Stanford University. Iris Cantor also confirmed her support of exhibitions of American sculpture by sponsoring many at the White House and in accompanying publications, and she placed eight of her monumental Rodin bronzes in the Channel Gardens at Rockefeller Center in New York. It is estimated that over 4 million people visited these last two exhibitions alone. All this has been in addition to the Foundation's support of other art exhibitions and scholarly research on Rodin, as well as its contributions to women's health care, medical research, and the endowment of new patient facilities on both coasts.

During nearly 20 years of marriage the couple contributed millions of dollars toward the arts and medicine and gave more than 450 works from their 750-piece Rodin collec-

3. The B. Gerald Cantor Sculpture Gallery at the Metropolitan Museum of Art, New York

tion to institutions around the world. They also collected and donated the work of other sculptors, including Emile-Antoine Bourdelle, Jean-Baptiste Carpeaux, Albert-Ernest Carrier-Belleuse, Camille Claudel, Aimé-Jules Dalou, Jean-Alexandre-Joseph Falguière, Malvina Hoffman, Georg Kolbe, Gaston Lachaise, Wilhelm Lehmbruck, Aristide Maillol, and Medardo Rosso; paintings from the Impressionist, Post-Impressionist, and Expressionist periods; and work from various areas in the decorative arts.

The Cantors' names can be found gracing museums and galleries, sculpture gardens, auditoriums and theaters, special exhibitions, plazas and rooftops, endowed curatorial positions, educational books and films, hospitals and research laboratories and, as a consequence of all these acts of generosity, their names are also etched upon numerous awards and honors. In 1995 President and Mrs. Clinton presented them with the National Medal of the Arts. In 2000, perhaps to complement Mr. Cantor's earlier Arts and Letters award, Iris Cantor was appointed a Chevalier of the Legion of Honor by the French government.

In 1946, when Bronx-born Bernie Cantor made his first purchase of a Rodin sculpture, he was blissfully unaware that Rodin was out of favor with the art world. Not that it would have made any difference to him, determined as he was to become a titan in the worlds of both business and philanthropy. In his youth he had worked the grandstands at Yankee Stadium, selling hot dogs during double-headers (and only double-headers, because that's where the real money was). He quit New York University to become a broker and served as a paratrooper during World War II. After the War he found his niche in business and made a fortune on Wall Street, but discovered his true purpose in collecting and sharing his love for Rodin. He told the writer Richard Shepard: "I am not a frustrated artist. I never even cared for the visual arts when I was at school—I was always good at math."

Cantor frequented Paris's Musée Rodin from the 1950s, when he met the director, Cécile Goldscheider, the keeper of its vast archives and of the artist's clay and plaster works at Meudon. She became his cherished friend and advisor and introduced him to Rodin's lesser-known sculptures, to the artist's interest in partial figures and hands, and to the complexities of bronze casting. Later, Cantor's friendship with Stanford University professor Albert Elsen served to increase not only his own knowledge but also that of Elsen's students, some of whom became Cantor Fellows and went on to write and teach in major museums and academic institutions worldwide.

As Cantor's interest in Rodin grew, his fiscal prosperity also increased and he was able to accelerate his purchasing. His securities brokerage company had been a financial success from its start in 1945, and for over two decades it experienced steady growth. In 1972 Cantor Fitzgerald Securities purchased a controlling interest in the company Telerate. The merger produced a major breakthrough: the revolutionary practice of live market, screen-based brokerage in U.S. government securities. Bernie Cantor changed the way Wall Street did business.

For the exuberant Mr. Cantor it was a natural inclination to blend his passion for business with his passion for art. He displayed his collection throughout his offices, incorporated *The Thinker* into his company's image, was a founding member of the Business Committee for the Arts, and encouraged his employees to give to the arts and other important causes through his company's matching gift program. He gave many of

4. The B. Gerald Cantor Rodin Sculpture Garden at the Iris and B. Gerald Cantor Center for Visual Arts at Stanford University, Stanford, California

his early purchases to business colleagues and friends; as a result, he often had the need and the desire to purchase more than one cast of the same work. He lived in a perpetual state of excitement, planning for his next purchase, making endless notes with yellow and pink highlighters in his leather-bound copies of George Grappe's catalogues of the Musée Rodin. As he became more involved, Cantor encouraged the Musée Rodin to open its records to scholars, which it did in 1975 under the guidance of curator Monique Laurent. He commissioned many Rodin bronzes to be cast under the Musée Rodin's official auspices, while he simultaneously sought to purchase, from private sales and auctions, fine-quality casts made during Rodin's lifetime.

In the late 1960s Mr. Cantor set aside a small room in his Beverly Hills office as a gallery to show some of the bronzes. The question of what to do with his growing collection was becoming pressing, and he knew of the distinguished tradition established by several earlier American Rodin collectors. The significant collection of the dancer Loïe Fuller was shown in 1903 at the National Arts Club in New York. Fuller had also interested Alma de Bretteville Spreckles and Samuel Hill in Rodin's work. The Spreckles collection formed the core of the California Palace of the Legion of Honor in San Francisco, and the Hill holdings were the basis for the smaller Maryhill Museum collection in Goldendale, Washington. There were also Kate Seney Simpson, whose acquisitions went to the National Gallery of Art in Washington, D.C., and Thomas Fortune Ryan, who donated a number of Rodins to the Metropolitan Museum of Art between 1910 and 1913. And finally there was a man who, like Mr. Cantor, was inspired by one of Rodin's sculptures of a human hand and made it his first purchase: Jules E.

Mastbaum, a film magnate in Philadelphia. His collection was formed quickly and vigorously during the 1920s and today is housed in an independent Beaux-Arts structure administered by the Philadelphia Museum of Art.

Cantor decided that he wanted actively to share his collection, and he began by embarking on a series of organized exhibitions that toured the United States. The first exhibition was the Los Angeles County Museum of Art's *Homage to Rodin* in 1967, which was followed immediately by an eight-city tour managed by the newly established American Federation of Arts. A story in the Mobile, Alabama *Press-Register* reported on the visit of 50 sight-impaired students, aged 7 to 19, who traveled six hours by bus to the Mobile Art Gallery for a special "touch and see" experience. This was the first of many such programs that allowed people with little or no vision to experience Rodin's sculptures with their hands.

By 1974 Cantor's collection had toured 53 cities in 23 states. Internationally, smaller portions had been sent to Tel Aviv, Beirut, Tokyo, Helsinki, Prague, Stockholm, Athens, Munich, Kyoto, London, and Rome. Cantor found himself in the habit of leaving behind gifts of sculpture at each of these venues as mementos and to express his thanks for the institution's interest in Rodin. Also in 1974, he announced three major gifts to American museums totaling 127 works by Rodin: 29 went to the Los Angeles County Museum of Art, 88 to Stanford, and 10 studies for the *Monument to Balzac* to the Museum of Modern Art in New York.

That same year, in recognition of these gifts, which represented just the first of those he planned to make, Mr. Cantor received a crate from the directors of the Musée Rodin

5. Rodin, Auguste
The Hand of God
1898
Plaster
28¾ × 26¾ × 38 in.
(71.1 × 67.9 × 96.5 cm)
Iris and B. Gerald Cantor Collection

containing a plaster model of *The Hand of God* (pl. 5), the composition that had inspired his first purchase. On a flat side of the plaster base was a personal inscription: "*The Hand of God* offered from the Musée Rodin to Mr. B. Gerald Cantor." The gift was accompanied by a note that read: "For the magnificent effort that you made and continue to make to assemble the most important collection ever achieved of the works of the great French sculptor. You are always ready to exhibit or even to donate these works, which you selected with so much competence and love."

Shortly thereafter, Mr. Cantor began to discuss with the Musée Rodin his dream of commissioning a bronze cast of Rodin's most ambitious monument, *The Gates of Hell*, using Rodin's preferred technique, the *cire-perdue* (lost-wax) method. This was the process that most accurately replicated the artist's model, but it was also the most labor-intensive and time-consuming method, and it had not previously been attempted with the *Gates*. The casting project was begun in 1977 so that the work could be included in the 1981–82 *Rodin Rediscovered* exhibition at the National Gallery of Art in Washington, D.C., the largest Rodin exhibition ever mounted. After this *The Gates of Hell* went on a national tour and was then given to Stanford University. During formative discussions for the casting project, Iris Cantor proposed making a film that would document this

6. The Iris and B. Gerald Cantor Art Gallery at College of the Holy Cross, Worcester, Massachusetts

complex undertaking, which was to be guided by Jean Bernard at the Coubertin Foundry in Saint-Rémy-lès-Chevreuse, France. *Rodin: The Gates of Hell* became Iris Cantor's own work of art (she co-produced the film with David Saxon), and today it accompanies the Cantor Foundation's exhibitions to help visitors familiarize themselves with the life of Rodin, his major monuments and themes, and the complex technical aspects of the lost-wax *cire-perdue* casting process. Mr. Cantor later commissioned the Coubertin Foundry to make several small models showing the 10 stages of the casting process; these models also accompany Cantor Foundation exhibitions.

Aside from the traveling shows, Mr. Cantor established a major exhibition space of his own. In 1981 he opened the B.G. Cantor Sculpture Center, a 4000 square-foot (3700 square-metre) gallery on the 105th floor of the World Trade Center in New York. At the time it was the "highest museum in the world," according to the *Guinness Book of World Records*. In the end it became cumbersome to schedule visits to such an extreme elevation, and it also became necessary to return the space to his company. However, having the gallery did allow Cantor the chance to create an exhibition (in 1983–84) on Rodin's practice of reductions and enlargements. Albert Elsen wrote a concise booklet examining Rodin's relationship with his "perfect collaborator," Henri Lebossé, who used the Collas machine to produce reductions and enlargements for the master. It had become important to Mr. Cantor to emphasize to the public that Rodin's studio was operating at the dawn of the age of mechanical reproduction, which included much experimentation and was not concerned with the modern-day concept of limited editions.

In the years to come, additional gifts went out to large and small museums around America. To the Los Angeles County Museum of Art Cantor gave a total of 117 objects. At LACMA, the Cantors also endowed the B. Gerald Cantor Sculpture Garden, the Cantor Plaza, and the Iris and B. Gerald Cantor Gallery. In Worcester, Massachusetts, the College of the Holy Cross received 46 gifts of art and the endowment of the Iris and B. Gerald Cantor Art Gallery. The Brooklyn Museum of Art (Iris Cantor was born in Brooklyn) received a total of 69 gifts of art, the Iris and B. Gerald Cantor Rotunda, and the Cantor Auditorium (designed by Arata Isozaki and James Stewart Polshek). The Metropolitan Museum of Art received 34 gifts of art and the endowment of the Iris and B. Gerald Cantor Chair of the Department of European Sculpture and Decorative Arts. The Metropolitan also received the Iris and B. Gerald Cantor Exhibition Hall, the B. Gerald Cantor Sculpture Gallery, and the Cantor Roof Garden—well known in New York for its spectacular view of Central Park (and for being one of the city's greatest cheap dates).

Ultimately Mr. Cantor chose Stanford University to be the recipient of his largest gift: over 250 Rodin-related objects, including bronzes, plasters, clays, ceramics, drawings, memorabilia, portraits of Rodin (by Bourdelle, Troubetskey, and Soudbinine), and the collector's own personal reference library, making Stanford the largest Rodin research center in America. Cantor also established a fellowship program under Albert Elsen and created the B. Gerald Cantor Rodin Sculpture Garden. In 1999, funded by the Cantor Foundation, the University's museum completed a major renovation (by Polshek and Partners) and became the Iris and B. Gerald Cantor Center for Visual Arts.

During the more than five decades since B. Gerald Cantor's first purchase, there have been hundreds of projects, hundreds of exhibitions and acquisitions, and an untold number of helpful friends and associates who have made the Iris and B. Gerald Cantor

OVERLEAF: 7. The Iris and B. Gerald Cantor Rotunda at the Brooklyn Museum of Art, Brooklyn, New York

Foundation what it is today. Founders Iris and B. Gerald Cantor and their Foundation's Board of Directors would be the first to acknowledge the care and management by the professionals at the Musée Rodin in Paris, beginning with its first curator, Léonce Bénédite, and continuing through Cécile Goldscheider, Monique Laurent, Jacques Vilain, and Antoinette Le Normand-Romain (the last two having both contributed greatly to this publication).

The Foundation also acknowledges and thanks the other authors of this catalogue: Aida Audeh, Mary Levkoff, Daniel Rosenfeld, and Kirk Varnedoe. A special note of thanks is due to Ruth Butler for her wise counsel during the preparation of this book. The Foundation's staff would like to express gratitude to Iris Cantor and its Board of Directors for their immediate enthusiasm for and support of this project and for allowing it to take precedence in daily operations.

Preparation of this catalogue has required hard work, patience, dedication, and meticulous attention to detail by Cantor Foundation staff members. It must be noted that this project was a complicated one, primarily because the Foundation adheres at all times to the wishes set forth by B. Gerald Cantor and keeps the collection as a working educational tool, which is perpetually moving around the world. The sculptures documented in this catalogue were on view at multiple locations outside the Foundation offices, and it was therefore a challenge for the staff to verify casting dates and numbers, measurements, and inscriptions, and to achieve complete photographic documentation. There are many people to thank for their assistance. In-house, Judith Sobol, my successor, for continuing the project. Danna Freedy Kay, the Foundation's Associate Curator and Registrar, deserves recognition for her work in helping to conceptualize the project and for her diligent attention to the checklist and the supervision of many aspects of the production. Amy Silvey, Art and Education Coordinator, took responsibility for all photography, and her insightful organizational contributions to the checklist are greatly appreciated. Rina Brill, Assistant to the Executive Director, managed the rights and reproductions permissions and facilitated communications and contracts between the various authors involved in the project. Outside the Foundation staff, Steve Oliver took the majority of the photographs in this book; they are both beautiful and accurate. The Foundation is pleased to have his collaboration and privileged that his pictures grace our publication. Thomas Frick provided preliminary assistance in editing and Brian Brazeau carefully provided translation services. A significant portion of the Foundation's collection was on view at two primary locations while this project was underway and the Foundation greatly appreciates the assistance of Helen Moss at the Dayton Art Institute; of Larry Wheeler, David Steel, and Carrie Hedrick at the North Carolina Museum of Art; and of William J. Hennessey, Jefferson Harrison, and Catherine Jordan Wass at the Chrysler Museum of Art.

Above all, this project is dedicated to the memory and the achievements of Mr. B. Gerald Cantor, the Foundation's founder, benefactor, mentor, and visionary leader. His memory endures.

Rachael Blackburn
Director, Kemper Museum of Contemporary Art, Kansas City, Missouri
Executive Director, Iris and B. Gerald Cantor Foundation,
Los Angeles, California, 1998–2000

8. Rodin, Auguste
Cybèle
c. 1890, enlarged in 1904. Musée Rodin cast 3/8 in 1982
Bronze
Coubertin
65 × 34 × 56 in.
(165.1 × 86.4 × 142.2 cm)
Iris and B. Gerald Cantor Collection, promised gift to the Iris and B. Gerald Cantor Foundation

The Collector and the Scholar

Is it a contradiction—or in retrospect does it seem somehow logical—that a man who lived his professional life in the unforgivingly hard-headed but also essentially abstract and mathematical world of electronic finances, would build another, parallel life devoted to the heatedly emotive and physical art of Auguste Rodin? This was the case with B. Gerald Cantor. With the fortunes he made in modern investment trading, Bernie became not only the most avid collector of Rodin's work, but also the patron who undertook the most dedicated and effective campaign ever mounted to further the sculptor's representation in museums worldwide and to advance scholarship related to his achievement.

The origins of the connection between the financier and the form-giver are known to me only by legend, in the frequently told story of Bernie's "epiphany," when he was "touched" by the hand of God. That is to say, when Rodin first seized his imagination through the sculpture *The Hand of God* (pls. 5, 130, 133). Here the seeds of humanity, personified by a sensuously adrift Adam and Eve, are cradled in a disembodied, monumental hand—divine creation envisioned as the transmission of life through the fingers of a modeler. That huge caress also shaped, in effect, a good deal of the remainder of its admirer's life. Cantor went on to enlarge its metaphor by himself giving life, through his patronage, to an unprecedented expansion of Rodin's teeming family of human forms, by the commissioned casting and donated dissemination of virtually every aspect of the master's sculpture.

I came to know Bernie years later, when his collection had already grown, but when his involvement with the artist's legacy was at a new and decisive turning point. At that moment, in the late 1960s, the seemingly irresistible, headlong force of Bernie's acquisitive energies seemed poised for a potentially disastrous collision with the utterly immovable and temperamentally pugnacious obstacle of my mentor, the Rodin scholar Albert Elsen. The two men did not know each other when Al delivered himself of a scorching review of the Cantor collection, so there was nothing personal in the broadside. Instead, that blast might better be understood, at least in part, as a venting of Elsen's long-standing frustrations with the Musée Rodin in Paris, which had done every bit as much to starve his efforts as a research scholar as it had done to feed Bernie's urge to acquire newly cast bronzes. Bernie, understandably, did not immediately take a detached, analytical view of the critique, and but for the counsel of a prudent curator, might have found himself meeting Al for the first time in court, over a lawsuit for libel.

Instead, Bernie sent out, via his curator, a dove of peace. Elsen, whose complaint was in part that Cantor's embrace of the Musée Rodin's posthumous casts had up to then been ill-advised and undiscriminating, responded that he was—perhaps—willing to share advice and guide discrimination. However, playing hard to get, he tested

9. Rodin, Auguste
Toilette of Venus
c. 1886, Musée Rodin cast 4/12 in 1967
Bronze
Georges Rudier
18 × 9½ × 8½ in.
(45.7 × 24.1 × 21.6 cm)
Iris and B. Gerald Cantor Collection, promised gift to the Iris and B. Gerald Cantor Foundation

10. Rodin, Auguste
Eternal Idol
c. 1889, Musée Rodin cast 7 in 1971
Bronze
Georges Rudier
29 × 21 × 15 in.
(73.7 × 53.3 × 38.1 cm)
Iris and B. Gerald Cantor Collection,
promised gift to the Iris and
B. Gerald Cantor Foundation

Bernie's resolve (and doubtless his temper as well) by asking for an initial gesture of affirmation. I was—or more precisely the initial push in my scholarly career was—that gesture. Elsen's request was for a fellowship in support of Rodin studies at Stanford, where he taught; and I, a first-year graduate student, was the initial recipient of that grant, the first in what was to become a long line of Cantor Fellows. I was doubly fortunate because the grant not only sent me to Paris for the summer of 1969, to fight my own battles with the Musée Rodin, but it also allowed me to witness from the inside the coming-together of these two formidable men.

It was perhaps an unlikely scenario: two boys from the Bronx finding each other in the sunshine of 1960s California, with little common ground in their present-day lives. The relationship worked in part, however, because they were alike in what they treasured from the past and in how they wanted to enrich that treasure for posterity. It also worked because of their singular natures. I knew Elsen was no ivory-tower academic, but a born crusader with a broad knowledge of and commitment to art's role in society; and I discovered that Cantor was equally unconventional in his role as investment tycoon. He never stood on ceremony, as was driven home to me the first time I encountered him, in a vivid-blue sweatsuit and sneakers, fresh off the exercise cycle he kept next to his desk in his Beverly Hills office. This was an expert in calculations and strategies, but also a man attracted to passion, whether it appeared to him in the twining of bronze or marble bodies, or in the form of a scholar's burning determination to improve and expand a sculptor's legacy. He had both respect and affection for Elsen, whose sometimes prickly manner was balanced by an always tenacious and demanding drive to reform, and he grew to trust and enjoy this partnership, which was to transform both the Cantor collection and the life of art at Stanford. Together, too, they eventually encouraged—by slow suasion and with Bernie's humane loyalty to the old guard always honored—important changes in the direction and professional standards of the Musée Rodin itself.

The last time I saw Bernie Cantor was at the memorial service that followed Al Elsen's sudden and unexpected death. It took place at Stanford, in the Rodin sculpture garden that Bernie had endowed and Al had designed, in the shadow of the cast of *The Gates of Hell*, which had crowned Bernie and Iris Cantor's many gifts to the museum—a museum that would soon be named in their honor. The great collector, himself in badly failing health, sat at the rear of the crowd, shaded by a tree from the press of the California sun. All but blind, his eyes could not take in the scope of the monument that surrounded him, but only fill with tears. Cautioned by his doctor's advice, Bernie should not have been there; instructed by his heart, he had to be. Life twins friendship with loss as surely as it binds passions and tragedies, and the emotional depth of what Bernie had lost, like the impressive concrete evidence of what he had fostered, was never more evident than in this scene. Cantor and Elsen had shared, with regard to Rodin, a paradoxical combination of the desire to possess and own and the drive to share and give away. Bernie was as set on being the artist's leading collector as Al was on dominating scholarship in the field. They both succeeded. And yet for each this meant not simply personal gratification or power, but an increase in the ability to spread the word and share the wealth—to endow museums and form students, to send out exhibitions and create publications. Each man fulfilled and empowered for the other an aspect of this two-edged quest that would have been immeasurably weaker for either on his own. And they loved it: loved the art, loved the dialogue, loved the joint mission. It is evident to all how much was achieved, and what great good things were done. It is a personal privilege to have known at first hand the human satisfaction and fun they enjoyed in doing it.

Kirk Varnedoe
Chief Curator, Department of Painting and Sculpture, Museum of Modern Art, New York

The Legacy of B. Gerald Cantor

In 1974, B. Gerald Cantor asked: "Why not give it while you're alive and can see people enjoy it?" In this sense, the collector is like the sculptor. In 1916, one year before his death, Rodin gave to the French state all his works, sculptures, and drawings, as well as his rich collections of antiques and photographs, and his books and exhaustive archives, the basis for any research on Rodin.

Rodin wanted his work to be shown in public; unfortunately he did not live to see the museum that bears his name, which opened in 1919, two years after his death.

Generosity and ubiquity are the key words that characterize Rodin's donation; B. Gerald Cantor understood its spirit quite well, respecting the wishes of the Master of Meudon, and even expanding and magnifying them, being a knowledgeable collector who by chance was born the same year Rodin made his donation to France.

In 1945, B. Gerald Cantor, a young businessman just out of the army, discovered the marble of *The Hand of God* at the Metropolitan Museum of Art in New York. A few months later, he purchased a small bronze of the same work from a dealer on Madison Avenue. Thus began the long and faithful love affair between collector and sculptor. Let us look at the results.

B. Gerald Cantor purchased, mainly from the Musée Rodin in Paris, more than 700 of the artist's bronzes and gave more than 450 of them to museums and institutions throughout the world.

LEFT: 11. Rodin, Auguste
Young Girl with Serpent
No date. Musée Rodin cast 4/8 in
1988
Bronze
Godard
13⅜ × 4¾ × 5⅝ in.
(34 × 12.1 × 14.3 cm)
Iris and B. Gerald Cantor Collection,
promised gift to the Iris and
B. Gerald Cantor Foundation

RIGHT: 12. Rodin, Auguste
Amour and Psyche
Before 1893
Marble
9 × 27½ × 17¾ in.
(22.9 × 69.9 × 45.1 cm)
Iris and B. Gerald Cantor Collection,
promised gift to the Iris and
B. Gerald Cantor Foundation

When one sees the incredible group of antiques and objects in the Rodin collection in Paris and Meudon, one must think again of these two men linked by their insatiable appetite for accumulation. B. Gerald Cantor was by far the world's greatest Rodin collector, both quantitatively and in terms of the eye and taste that made him choose pieces that at the time were truly underappreciated. Thus, through the generosity of Iris and B. Gerald Cantor, both in the United States and in other countries, the public has been able to admire a significant and complete body of Rodin's work, since the consistency of the collection is matched by the consistency of the Cantors' generosity.

The exhibition *Rodin Rediscovered*, at the National Gallery of Art, Washington, D.C., which included works from the collection of B. Gerald Cantor, marked a decisive turning point in the history of the understanding of Rodin's work. The casting of *The Gates of Hell*, today at Stanford, was central to this understanding. However, in hindsight, it is surely the resumption of Rodin studies, led by Albert Elsen, who is much missed, and by Ruth Butler, that is remarkable. Their work is fundamental to our knowledge of the master's œuvre and remains the foundation of studies currently being conducted.

To the delight provided by this huge body of work (it is not by chance that in 1900 Rodin was compared to the German composer Richard Wagner), B. Gerald Cantor has added scholarship and understanding. And it is this comprehensiveness that constitutes his true glory as collector and patron.

Jacques Vilain
Director, Musée Rodin, Paris
General Curator of French Patrimony

Rodin's Studio

Antoinette Le Normand-Romain

16. Weisser, C.
Rodin's Studio
1888
Oil on canvas
31½ × 25 in.
(80 × 63.5 cm)
Musée de Nogent-sur-Seine

15. Rodin, Auguste
The Spirit of War
1883
Bronze
Griffoul & Lorge
44½ × 22½ × 15 in.
(113 × 57.2 × 38 cm)
Iris and B. Gerald Cantor
Foundation

Numerous artists and craftsmen passed through Rodin's studio (pl. 16), spending various amounts of time there. Rodin is possibly the last artist to have had a studio akin to those of the masters of the Middle Ages and the Renaissance. It was organized like a business, one that employed over 50 people after 1900. Each member of the studio had a well-determined task to perform. In Meudon, according to Rodin's long-time friend Camille Mauclair, "He leads a life that fully suits his tastes, among beautiful trees and flowers, with a majestic landscape before him … . He spends his mornings in his garden or in his light and cheerful studio drawing or superintending his workmen."[1]

At the beginning of his career, and even after his return from Belgium, Rodin himself had worked for others. One such person was Albert-Ernest Carrier-Belleuse, who produced large quantities of busts with intricate accessories (hair, flowers, lace, ribbons), the precise detail of which made them very lifelike. Rodin wrote of this period: "Those who have been poor like myself, without state help or a pension, worked for everybody else. This constituted a sort of disguised apprenticeship; one moment I made earrings for a goldsmith, the next I was making decorative torsos three meters high. Thus, I was able to learn all parts of the trade."[2]

Rodin acknowledged having acquired great skillfulness in this way, commenting to Henri-Charles-Etienne Dujardin-Beaumetz: "I was, starting in my youth, prodigiously quick with my hands, like Albert-Ernest Carrier-Belleuse, like Jules Dalou." However, he also had the dexterity of a modeler, as the sculptors Alfred Boucher and Paul Dubois would proclaim during the *Age of Bronze* scandal. As soon as possible, then, he limited his activity to modeling and left certain other tasks to outside hands. An example of this is marble work, which is difficult and tiring: it was Léon Fourquet, one of his oldest friends, who produced the marble bust of *The Man with the Broken Nose* shown at the Salon of 1875. Rodin lived in Brussels at the time. He had associated himself with the Belgian sculptor Joseph van Rasbourgh, but he was still partly based in Paris, home of the founders, detailers, and craftsmen with whom he worked. For example, in October 1874, the founder Demax gave the mold, a clay copy, and a plaster copy of a bust to Henri Tréhard in Paris, who then wrote to Rodin: "I don't think it is possible to make anything of it unless you touch it up," adding, "Let me know what you wish to do with it."[3] Almire Huguet was then in charge of the hairstyling for the decorative female busts that generated the majority of Rodin's income at the time. On September 9, 1874, he wrote:

As I promised you, I am sending you the case containing the bust of the *Petite Alsacienne*, the one with the vine hair, as well as four other hairstyles: one of roses, one of lilacs, one of wheat, and lastly one of poppies. I hope you will find that they are consistent with the program you gave me. I divided them as much as possible, so

17. Rodin, Auguste
The Age of Bronze (*Reduction*)
1876, reduction *c.* 1903–04. date of
cast unknown
Bronze
Alexis Rudier
26 × 8½ × 7 in.
(66 × 21.6 × 17.8 cm)
Iris and B. Gerald Cantor
Foundation

18. Unknown photographer
Rodin by the studio at the Dépôt des
Marbres
c. 1900
Gelatin silver print
Paris, Musée Rodin

19. Unknown photographer
View of the studio, Pavillion de
l'Alma, Meudon
after 1900
Gelatin silver print
Paris, Musée Rodin

OVERLEAF: 20. Bernes & Marouteau
The Pavillion de l'Alma (Rodin's
Studio at Meudon)
after 1917
Gelatin silver print
Paris, Musée Rodin

that you could cut them and style them as you wish. I even avoided molding difficulties as much as possible. You will surely encounter some, but the parts that
protrude made it impossible to avoid this. The founder will simplify things by
making a few cuts. It is not my role to criticize or promote the work. I can only say
one thing: I have done all that I could in order to satisfy you.[4]

Evidence of their collaboration comes in the form of the bust of Mme Huguet: it is
signed "Rodin 74," but the base, which is relatively large and decorated with apple
branches, is probably the work of Huguet rather than Rodin.

In Belgium, Rodin had acquired a certain financial independence. However, upon
his return to Paris, in 1877, he was faced with a difficult period during which he was
forced to spend large amounts of money defending himself against accusations that he
had molded on the body in the creation of *The Age of Bronze* (pl. 17).[5] "I am not sure
what to do, I have many expenses and no more money," he wrote to Rose Beuret, probably in May of that year, "… Life is going to be difficult, for my money will go towards
another attempt, and let us hope I will make some more! The future is dark and surely
full of poverty."[6] Rodin was therefore forced to work on several projects: he made
masks for the fountain of the Trocadéro Palace constructed for the 1878 World's Fair; he
went to Nice in August 1879 and then to Strasbourg in order to carry out decorative
work; and he worked for the Manufacture de Sèvres between 1879 and 1882. During this
time the Ministry of Fine Arts acquired *The Age of Bronze*, but at a low price. The same
institution ordered a large decorative door, *The Gates of Hell*, which led to his being
given a studio at the Dépôt des Marbres. The *Gates* were paid for only incrementally,

according to their progress, and therefore, on October 20, 1881, he asked Turquet, secretary of the Ministry of Fine Arts, to help him by ordering more work. If that were not possible, he noted, "then I will need to take into account the daily necessities of life, work outside and accept projects which are non-artistic but lucrative. This is not the goal you articulated, and does not reflect the desire you have always manifested, which is that of supporting me in this work of art and beauty that you have bestowed upon me."[7]

21. Unknown photographer
Pavillion de l'Alma and the Villa des Brillants
No date
Gelatin silver print
Paris, Musée Rodin

In conjunction with the enormous project of the *Gates*, Rodin soon had to attend to new orders: *The Burghers of Calais* (pl. 37) in 1884; the statue of Jules Bastien-Lepage in 1886; the monuments to Claude Lorrain and to Victor Hugo in 1889 (pl. 47), and to Honoré de Balzac in 1891 (pl. 30). After 1890 he set out to use figures he had created in the past; these became the point of departure for the making of marble work that was widely appreciated, especially after the exhibition at the Place de l'Alma had lifted him to the highest renown. These marble works were popular with members of a rich international clientele, who also wished to have their portraits done by Rodin. Naturally, he needed help to complete these numerous projects. It was therefore from the mid-1880s that a true "studio" was created around him, first at the Dépôt des Marbres (pl. 18), on the rue de l'Université, then at Meudon (pls. 19, 20) where, mainly after 1900, he installed assistants of all kinds in the buildings surrounding the Villa des Brillants (pl. 21). The number of specialized assistants multiplied as time passed.

In following the evolution of Rodin's work, one must acknowledge the primary importance of his models, as did the artist himself. He confided to Bartlett: "A model is, therefore, more than a means whereby the artist expresses a sentiment, thought, or experience, it is a correlative inspiration to him. They work together as a productive force."[8] He returns to the subject in his *Entretiens* (Conversations) with Dujardin-Beaumetz, which devotes an entire chapter to the model: "I can only work with a model ... I declare that I have no ideas when I have nothing to copy; but when nature shows me her forms, right away I find something worth saying and even developing."[9] We are aware of Auguste Neyt's role in the making of *The Age of Bronze*, and that of Pignatelli in *St. John the Baptist* (pls. 22, 23), and later that of the Abbruzzesi sisters. The most significant example is that of old Caira, who posed as toothless Fate for *Poverty* by Jules Desbois, as well as for *She Who Was the Helmet-maker's Beautiful Wife* (pl. 98) by Rodin, and for *Clotho* by Camille Claudel.[10] These are three works that show the fascination that a wrinkled, gaunt, aged body held for sculptors, who would not represent age in and of itself without the pretext of allegory or reference to literary or mythological sources.

22. Michelez, Charles
Rodin's *St. John the Baptist Preaching*
1878–79
Albumin print
Paris, Musée Rodin

In front of the model, the sculptor is alone: it is his hand that fashions the clay, and *The Hand of God* can be seen as the symbol of this creative process (pl. 24). For Rodin, the modeling hand is the creative instrument *par excellence*, such that, according to Judith Cladel, he arrived "at this central idea: the first thing God thought of in creating the world, if we can imagine God's thoughts, was the model. It is funny, isn't it, to make God a sculptor?"[11] All the same, once this stage is complete, different types of help are needed, the first of which is provided by the molder. Clay, which is the primary material of sculpture, can be conserved only if it is constantly dampened. It is necessary, once the artist is satisfied, to make a mold of the work and from this mold to make a copy, which is called the original model, that is to say, the first conserved stage, the clay having been

23. Unknown photographer
Pignatelli in the pose of *St. John the Baptist*
after 1878
Paris, École Nationale Supérieure des Beaux-Arts

24. Unknown photographer
Rodin at the Dépôt des Marbres with
The Hand of God
c. 1910
Albumin print
Paris, Musée Rodin

destroyed during the molding process. However, whereas most sculptors had one copy only, Rodin, from very early on, had several made. As Kahn writes:

> When he feels he has found it, he has a mold made, starts over, and has another one made. These are approximations that will lead him to the definitive formula. When he attained great fame, all of these were sold as stages, as interesting as the final product. The molding process, which at first was only a trial, becomes an important date. From *The Gates of Hell* on, Rodin began calling his fragments and studies works … . He is more attached to some of his partial studies that he sees as successes than to some of his finished works.[12]

For Rodin, creation is much more than simply working with clay. From the late 1880s he returned to figures made earlier, undertaking work on them in which the processes of assembly and fragmentation held an increasingly important place: "The key grates and the door creaks," writes Gustave Geffroy in 1900. "None of the sculptor's favorite models expends any muscular effort, none constitutes a statue of quivering flesh. Rodin is alone, working at the assembly of groups, searching for arrangements and harmonies."[13] As early as 1886 *I am Beautiful* (pl. 81) was exhibited at the Galerie Georges Petit, and then, in 1889, *Dried-up Springs* (pl. 145); the first was the result of the juxtaposition of the *Crouching Woman* and *Falling Man* (pl. 102), the second brought together two versions of *She Who Was the Helmet-maker's Beautiful Wife* (pl. 98), one seen from the front and the other from the back.

The molders were therefore precious to Rodin, and he used several throughout his career: the two Guiochés, the father and, especially, the son who worked for Rodin from 1897 to 1915; then Paul Cruet, who assisted the artist in the final years of his life. It was Cruet who realized a new plaster model of *The Gates of Hell*, destined for the future Musée Rodin (transferred to the Musée d'Orsay in 1986), and who, from Rodin's death until 1946, was in charge of the molds left by the artist. The Guiochés were extremely deft: "Their work was distinguished by an extraordinary lightness," reports Jakov Nicoladze, a Russian sculptor who worked in Meudon for a year. "They could pour an enormous sculpture with such a thin layer of plaster that, for example, a single man could lift *The Thinker*."[14] The great plaster works that have been in so many exhibitions have an eggshell-like thinness equaled only by their fragility, but Rodin could send them throughout Europe without worrying about damage. If they were harmed, he simply destroyed the work and immediately replaced it with another. For example, the *Eve* acquired by the Boymans–van Beuningen Museum in Rotterdam after the 1899 exhibition in Brussels, Rotterdam, Amsterdam, and The Hague is not the touring copy, but a new and intact one. Rodin could also transform, fragment, and assemble the figures from this surplus of forms to his liking. This was quite efficient, all the more so because in general he did not take the time to erase the molding marks. Thus, in Meudon, one can see two Eves; they are identical save that one has visible seams and the other does not. *The Crouching Woman* is above them and they are completed by a type of sheet made from plaster, while a dead branch balances the whole.

Today we are very sensitive to this play of figures, which during his lifetime were part of the artist's private domain. It is only recently, after several contemporary exhibi-

26. Druet, Eugène?
Rodin and Lebossé at Meudon
No date
Aristotype
Paris, Musée Rodin

27. Bodmer, Karl-Henri (Charles)
Rodin's *Ugolino and Sons*
before 1893
Gelatin silver print
Paris. Musée Rodin

25. Claudel, Camille
Bust of Rodin
1888–92, date of cast unknown
Bronze
Alexis Rudier
15¾ × 9¼ × 11 in.
(40 × 23.5 × 28 cm)
Iris and B. Gerald Cantor
Foundation

tions, that our attention has been turned to this aspect of Rodin's work. The exhibition entitled *Rodin sculpteur. Œuvres méconnues* (*Rodin the Sculptor: Little-known Works*: Paris, Musée Rodin), in 1992, illustrated this using the leaning female figure sometimes (wrongly) called *Dawn*, of which there is a complete version and another that has neither head nor feet. This work can also be seen in the form of a bust with head and hands (as in the *Gates*), mounted on a small square base, or as a headless torso, cut at the knees and wrists. The piece can be positioned vertically, bending forward, or placed in an antique vase from the artist's collection from which it appears to be attempting to escape. We see the same torso, completed by the head of the *Slavic Woman*, with disproportionate hands carelessly attached to the arms, and with two small arms—similar to a mermaid's tail—in place of legs in the *Hand of the Devil*.[15]

When it was necessary to enlarge a piece, as for the vertical portion of the female torso discussed above (*Female Torso*, the so-called Victoria and Albert Museum *Torso*, bronze, London, Tate Gallery), or to make a reduction, Rodin called upon Henri Lebossé, beginning the association in 1894 (pl. 26). Lebossé's business was the "Reduction and Augmentation of all Artistic and Industrial Objects by a Perfected Mathematical Process," using a machine inspired by the reduction process invented by Collas and Sauvage in 1844. He went to great lengths to be a "perfect collaborator" for Rodin, who was a very demanding client, and who insisted that Lebossé be at his disposal at all times and would not allow him to work for others. This was insisted upon to such an extent that Lebossé was forced to give Rodin the assurance that he only "gave a few pieces of advice and made an appearance at deliveries … and kept only a few small clients in order to support my three or four workers who have been with us for many years (March 16, 1904)."[16] Speaking of a child of *Ugolino* (pl. 27), Lebossé stresses the amount of time he spent on the extremities, the head, and the torso, "so that you will have no reason to complain of my work, as I strive for perfection as much as possible in the reproduction of your masterpieces (February 7, 1904)." This care, judging from the correspondence left to us, called for enormous efforts. To enlarge a figure, and even more so a group of figures, he was forced to proceed piece by piece, and sometimes met with unpleasant surprises when it was time for the final assembly in the master's studio. In addition, the machine systematically enlarged everything. Proportions changed and Lebossé had to rework the entire surface so that it would faithfully reproduce Rodin's "particular touch." As he states: "It takes time, a lot of it, to obtain a large version of the beauty of your model (September 26, 1902)." *The Thinker* (frontispiece; pl. 73) is, surely, the most famous work carried out by Lebossé. However, the enlarged group of *Ugolino* (pl. 27), of which there is a bronze at the Musée Rodin and a plaster version deposited by the museum at the Musée d'Orsay that differ from each other, shows that Lebossé's work was in part the assembly of separately fashioned elements. One of the children of *Ugolino*, given the head of *Gwen John* in plaster and the *Head of Sorrow* in bronze, was moved from left to right when changed from plaster to bronze. An examination of the plaster allows us to see very clearly the hurried juxtaposition of each element; there was no attempt to hide the seams. For Rodin, enlargement offered a new way to explore space, an element that is an integral part of all sculpture. Some of his works, such as *The Thinker* and the *Walking Man* (pl. 134), in many ways find their true force of expression only in their enlarged versions.

At this stage Rodin needed assistants. Rose Beuret, who cared for the studio and the works that remained there when he left for Brussels in February 1871, was probably the first, while Camille Claudel is certainly the most famous. Rodin met the latter in 1883 and, struck by her talent, hired her with her friend Jessie Lipscomb, from 1884 or 1885, to work for him at the Dépôt des Marbres. Many others followed these young women, for although Rodin never had a large teaching studio like those of David d'Angers, François Rude and, closer to him, the teachers at the Fine Arts School, he readily agreed to give advice to certain young sculptors. One of these was Malvina Hoffman, who had interested Rodin because of the "character" she had given to her early busts. Many artists, young or rather less so, passed through his studio, especially after 1890. Their status was that of assistants or craftsmen; but Desbois, Bourdelle, Despiau, Schnegg, and Millès all gained from their daily contact with the master. The strongest proof of this inescapable influence was the decision by Brancusi and Maillol to keep away from the studio, despite the admiration they had for Rodin.

"It is difficult," responded Rodin on July 19, 1907, to Marie Curie after she recommended a young Polish artist, Gardecki, for work in his studio,

> to employ a man who knows how to see and compose, but who to be useful in my studio needs to know how to mold pieces, such as hands, feet, etc … . For it is this kind of work that is done at my place. Those people that I employ leave these elements to be done, and it follows that I have unfinished groups in this area; I will set your sculptor to this kind of work, which can be very fruitful for studies and expressions.[17]

Camille Claudel is the collaborator who met Rodin's criteria the most fully: "The joy of being always understood, to see his expectations always surpassed … was one of the great joys of his artistic life."[18] However, there were others who, although they were not as close to Rodin, participated intimately in the creation of his works. The hands of the large *Shade* are the work of the Czech sculptor Joseph Maratka. The smaller *Shade* of *The Gates of Hell*, which was the starting point for the enlargement, did not include hands, "as if they had been burned by the fires of hell, or as in Antiquity when the hands of the guilty were amputated or burned. After the enlargement, Rodin understood that this mutilation would be misunderstood by collectors, as the rest of the statue was very polished." Maratka therefore added hands to the seemingly fragmentary figure that had been exhibited in 1902. The work was left in this state by Rodin. "Rodin did not touch them. It was a noble gesture on his part, a silent reward for several years of service from Maratka. For the latter, it was an encouragement for life."[19] As a result, however, certain complications might have to be avoided, such as when Rodin allowed the Minister of Finance and his friend to believe that a hand modeled by Ottilie McLaren for a *Nebuchadnezzer*, which the minister was considering, was his own: "He is the kind of guy who would be furious if he knew he had made a mistake, so I did not dare tell him, and I am having two bronzes made for them, and they think it's my work!!!"[20]

Not all of these assistants received such proof of Rodin's trust. Their role, then, must have been comparable to that outlined by Gerald Kelly, a young Irish painter who spent some time with the master. He described a work session for the *Monument to Victor Hugo* (pl. 47): "There was the master, rather disheveled and obviously in a very bad mood, and there was the figure of Victor Hugo—I mean a huge beast of a thing, heroic—and there were three light cranes, carrying the swinging plaster women." Kelly suddenly found himself in charge of the left arm of one of the Muses. "I was therefore told to cut it—I must say that I did not dare take this liberty, so I asked one of the workers to come with a wire and he performed the amputation ..." and the entire day passed in this fashion, in attempting, unsuccessfully, to group the Muses with the poet seated.[21] The *Monument to Victor Hugo* is one of the works in which Rodin's creative process is the most clear: for the first project (Victor Hugo seated surrounded by his inspirations) there were four successive models that assembled figures used first for the *Sirens* (pl. 89) of the *Gates*, then for *Cybèle* (pl. 8) and *Meditation* (pls. 52, 53). In the second model Hugo rests his head on his right hand, while the left hand is outstretched; he is still clothed in this version, but the following step finds him relieved of his coat. Completely nude, or partially covered by a sheet, the poet's body would scarcely change from this point, with the exception of the left arm, which was raised little by little, and the neck, which was raised to give the head a more eminent position. The outstretched arm was conserved for the second project (in fact contemporaneous with the first), called *The Apotheosis of Victor Hugo*, which shows the poet standing upon the shore of Guernsey listening to the *Sirens*, while *Iris, Messenger of the Gods* (pl. 51) comes to crown him. From a horizontal position, the arm is placed in a vertical position and is then folded to embrace the rhythm of the body. In the models that show a seated Hugo, the elements taken from a mold—those that stay the same from step to step—are easily distinguished from the elements remodeled in fresh plaster, the whole being unified by a drape made from cloth soaked in plaster. This type of work, which is a search for the best possible positioning of pre-existing figures, would have been difficult for one man to perform alone. The help of assistants was indispensable for the larger pieces, but, if we are to believe Malvina Hoffman, Rodin also used assistants for smaller work. This happened later, it is true, for the young American met Rodin in 1910: "He would hand me little plaster figures, and ask me to cut off the arms and legs; then with white wax he would rearrange the groups, changing a gesture and adding action or some new suggestion of composition."[22]

Once Rodin was satisfied with the plasterwork, he still had to oversee the making of the final version. At the beginning of his career, almost certainly for economic reasons, but also probably out of curiosity and friendship, he attempted fleeting experiments such as the "galvanization" of a plaster bust of *St. John the Baptist* he was to exhibit at the Salon of 1879.[23] For this he went to J. Danielli, with whom he began working upon his return from Belgium. Danielli's business was that of "Hardening, Plating and Artistic Decoration of plaster, inalterable procedures," for which he had received several awards. He had also created a "malleable marble," which at an unknown date he showed to Rodin, although he could not convince him to try it. Rodin was, nevertheless, interested in various materials, an attitude characteristic of the end of the nineteenth century. This is shown later by his collaboration with ceramicists such as Lachenal and Jeanneney, and with Jean Cros, who transformed the masks of Hanako, Rose Beuret and Camille Claudel into glass.

These few works are nonetheless quite exceptional. The majority of his plaster models found their final versions in bronze or marble. Bronze is probably the best material for Rodin's sculpture as it reproduces the model very faithfully and brings out the audacity of form. Paradoxically, it is here that the artist was least involved, except in the choice of the founder, who from 1902 was usually Alexis Rudier.[24] The marble craftsmen, often excellent sculptors constrained by material necessity to work for others, were a large group who worked closely with the master; the majority of them worked in Meudon. The sale of marble sculptures was a large source of income for Rodin, and in the last years of the century he began to have large groups of modest size made, in order to show them to future clients. A study of the marble work acquired by August Thyssen between 1905 and 1909 shows that this great admirer of Rodin always chose nearly finished works that he could see and appreciate in the studio, even if the artist then delayed delivery for months.[25] We often encounter several versions of the same work, although they are never perfectly identical, since each block of marble presents peculiarities that dictate the piece's final appearance in some way. For instance, there are two marble statues of *The Death of Athens*: as soon as Rodin had sold the first to James and Betty Smith in 1904 (now in the Walker Art Gallery, Liverpool), he had a second carved from the mold he had made on the first. The first version is characterized by the asymmetry of its base, which sinks to one side and rises on the other, while the second version, acquired by Thyssen in 1905, is one-third larger and more symmetrical. Successful pieces were reproduced on numerous occasions, some up to eight or ten times, as in the cases of *Eternal Springtime* and *Fugitive Love* (pl. 80). This practice of making replicas was fully developed in the last years of Rodin's life, at which time he wished to reconstitute a series of marble pieces for his future museum.

The various copies were carried out indiscriminately by any one of the craftsmen surrounding Rodin. These workers represented the hand that was asked only to execute, while Rodin remained the creative spirit. Indeed, in the nineteenth century the sculptor was not a stonecutter, but rather a creator of models. Thus, the role of the sculptor ceased with the creation of a perfect plaster model, which the craftsman was then hired to reproduce as faithfully as possible in the block of marble. This was carried out after a worker had reduced the size of the marble block to the dimensions of the model, creating a piece 2 or 3 centimeters (1 inch) thicker than the desired dimensions. The worker proceeds by using a three-pronged compass fixed to the original plaster:

> By means of a steel needle about seven inches long, the heights of the surface are all registered by hand and the needle is set. The compass is then transferred to the stone, and hung on three identical points to correspond with those on the plaster model. The excess stone is cut away until the needle can be pushed into the same depth as the original. It is not unusual to take three or four thousand points, to prepare a portrait for the final surface. If the machine shifts, or the needle is not accurately set, the entire effect will be ruined by errors in the setting.[26]

The needle left marks, and it is not rare to see traces of them in the form of small holes on Rodin's marble works. The artist, it appears, often decided to execute his marble pieces in a volume slightly greater than that of the plaster model.

Indeed, the relationship between sculptor and craftsman is transformed with Rodin. The extremely short deadline given him for the creation of *The Kiss* (pl. 83) (ordered by the government in January 1888 for the World's Fair that was to open on May 6, 1889) led him to suppress the stage of the definitive model. He simply gave the craftsman, Jean Turcan (an artist whose works were in the Musée du Luxembourg), the group at its original size, as it was conceived for the *Gates*. *The Kiss* was then doubled in size at the same time as it was cut in marble (pl. 28).[27] This more expedient method pleased Rodin, and he proceeded in this fashion from then on.

For the works from the beginning of his career, we have examples of traditional models made from clay (*The Thinker, Crouching Woman*) or in wax (models for the *Gates*). As time progressed, however, Rodin had at his disposal an immense quantity of figures and an inexhaustible stock of small hands, legs, and feet (pl. 127). More and more, therefore, he assembled these elements to create his works, making his models from pre-existing pieces. He would then give the craftsmen more an outline than a model—an indication of what he desired. This implies, of course, a constant surveillance of the craftsmen's progress during the creation of the work. The form of the marble block, the personalities of the craftsmen, the suggestions he made, all played a role in the process. On the whole, the collaboration between Rodin and his craftsmen was one of interpretation. A famous example of this comes in the making of *Thought* (pl. 131), which was at first to be a bust of a young woman (Camille Claudel), for which Rodin hired Victor Peter. The inventory sheet in the Musée Rodin, probably written by Bénédite, the first curator of the museum, explains that, "assuming, from the hair, that Rodin could complete the costume by a collaret, Peter had kept the material intact from the bottom of the face. But Rodin, after seeing the produced effect, told him 'Don't touch it anymore, stop there!'—A friend cried, more or less jokingly, that it was Thought emerging from matter, hence this work's name." Nevertheless, Rodin's dealings with the craftsmen were not always easy. The artist often waited quite a long time to visit them, and then he demanded quick delivery. He sometimes reclaimed an unfinished work from one craftsman and gave it to another, or harshly criticized those who worked for him.

There were frequent misunderstandings. At times a craftsman could interpret a model in too personal a fashion. In one such instance in July 1909, Rodin reclaimed several works from Jean-Marie Mengue, with whom he was unhappy. He was also not satisfied with one of his most beautiful marble pieces, the bust of *Mme. Vicuña* (pl. 147) cut by Jean Escoula, "because it bears too much the impress of the superior marble cutter that executed it."[28] In order to be a good craftsman, one had to follow Rodin's style, to the detriment of one's own personality. Assistants such as Jean Escoula, Victor Peter, Jean Turcan, Jules Desbois, François Pompon, Antoine Bourdelle, Charles Despiau, and many others understood this, even though they went on to have individual careers. They all, at least at first, admired Rodin, but we can guess that much discontent, rivalry, and jealousy filled that little world. "I certainly do not need to re-cut the stone," wrote Bourdelle, concerning a group whose preliminary shaping had been poorly executed, "on the contrary I need to defend the smallest piece, for everywhere there are portions very dissimilar to your plaster, hollow portions, and my task is simple, to fill them by linking them together, which my unknown predecessor neglected ... . My only contributions to the master ... are my time and my limited experience."[29]

The Musée Rodin possesses over 6000 plaster works, the existence of which we now better understand. They are the result of the intense activity of a studio and represent the tip of the iceberg, the public facet of the artist's life. However, they also guide us toward the more secretive Rodin, the private artist, the contemplative and solitary master who at night meditated in the countryside at Meudon. This is the Rodin who was attentive to the language of shapes, the artist who made deliberateness a virtue and who enjoyed examining his plaster works, as he did his antique collection, by candlelight:

> Often a single figure takes form under his hands, and he cannot understand what the figure means: its lines seem to will something, and to ask for the completion of their purpose. He puts it aside, and one day, happening to see it as it lies among other formless suggestions of form, it groups itself with another fragment, itself hitherto unexplained; suddenly there is a composition, the idea has penetrated the clay, life has given birth to the soul.[30]

This Rodin, who wished to attribute to dreaming great importance (as he confided to Gsell concerning *The Kiss*),[31] fascinated Rainer Maria Rilke upon his first visit to Meudon in September 1902. Uninterested in the volume of activity suggested by the numerous molders, assistants, and craftsmen working around the Villa des Brillants, the poet was instead able to see the essential elements. For his wife, Clara, he described in great detail the vision of plaster works and fragments aligned

> side by side spanning entire meters ... Suddenly we realize that envisioning the body as a whole is more the work of the erudite. That of the artist is to create, using these

elements, new relationships, new wholes, larger, more legitimate, more eternal; this inexhaustible richness, this infinite inventiveness, this presence of mind, this purity and vehemence of expression, this youth, this gift of constantly having something else, something better to say, all are without equal in human history.

[September 2, 1902]

Notes

1   Camille Mauclair, *Auguste Rodin: The Man, his Ideas, his Works*, London: Duckworth & Co., 1909, p. 109.

2   Henri-Charles-Etienne Dujardin-Beaumetz, *Entretiens avec Rodin* [1913], 2nd edn. Paris: Musée Rodin, 1992, p. 81.

3   Letter from Henri Tréhard to Rodin, November 5, 1874, Paris: Musée Rodin.

4   Letter from Almire Huguet to Rodin, June 18, 1874, Paris: Musée Rodin.

5   See *Vers l'Age d'airain. Rodin en Belgique*, exhib. cat., Paris: Musée Rodin, 1997, pp. 246–67.

6   Letter from Rodin to Rose Beuret, 1877, Paris: Musée Rodin.

7   Paris: Archives Nationales, F21/2109.

8   Truman H. Bartlett, "Auguste Rodin," in *The American Architect and Building News*, IX, June 1, 1889, p. 262.

9   Dujardin-Beaumetz, *op. cit.* note 2, p. 63.

10 Anne Pingeot, *L'Age mûr de Camille Claudel*, Paris: Musée d'Orsay, 1988, pp. 5–12.

11 Judith Cladel, *Auguste Rodin pris sur la vie*, Paris: éd. La Plume, 1903, p. 77.

12 Gustave Kahn, *Silhouettes littéraires*, Paris: éd. Montaigne, 1925, p. 88.

13 Gustave Geffroy, *Auguste Rodin et son œuvre*, Paris: éd. de la Plume, 1900, p. 34.

14 Quoted by Frederick Grunfeld in *Rodin*, Paris: éd. Fayard, 1988, pp. 601–02.

15 Nicole Barbier, *Rodin Sculpteur. Œuvres méconnues*, exhib. cat., Paris: Musée Rodin, 1992–93, pp. 41–51.

16 Dossier Lebossé, Paris: Musée Rodin.

17 *Pierre et Marie Curie*, exhib. cat., Paris: Bibliothèque Nationale, 1967, p. 31.

18 Mathias Morhardt, "Mlle Camille Claudel," in *Mercure de France*, 1898, p. 719.

19 René Chéruy's notes, Paris: Musée Rodin.

20 Letter from Ottilie McLaren to William Wallace, Scottish National Library, McLaren collection.

21 BBC Television, *Sir Gerald Kelly Remembers*, no. 4, Rodin, p. 8 (X-23).

22 Malvina Hoffman, *Heads and Tails*, New York: Bonanza Books, 1936, p. 43.

23 Judith Cladel, *Rodin. Sa vie glorieuse et inconnue*, Paris: éd. Bernard Grasset, 1936, p. 67.

24 On the relationship between Rodin and his founders, see Monique Laurent, "Observations on Rodin and his founders," in *Rodin Rediscovered*, exhib. cat., Washington, D.C.: National Gallery of Art, 1982, pp. 285–93.

25 Antoinette Le Normand-Romain, *Rodin. Les marbres de la collection Thyssen*, exhib. cat., Paris: Musée Rodin, 1996.

26 Hoffman, *op. cit.* note 22, p. 96.

27 See Antoinette Le Normand-Romand, *Le Baiser/The Kiss*, exhib. cat., Paris: Musée Rodin, 1995, Musée d'Orsay, 1995–96, bilingual.

28 T.H. Bartlett, "Auguste Rodin," in *The American Architect and Building News*, VII, May 25, 1889, p. 250.

29 Letter from Antoine Bourdelle to Rodin, September 8, 1906, Paris: Musée Rodin.

30 Arthur Symons, "Rodin," in *Fortnightly Review*, June 1902, pp. 963–66. Compare Ruth Butler, *Rodin in perspective*, Englewood Cliffs, New York: Prentice Hall, 1980, p. 117.

31 Paul Gsell, "Propos de Rodin sur l'art et les artistes," in *La Revue*, November 1, 1907, p. 105.

The Monuments to *The Burghers of Calais*, *Victor Hugo*, and *Honoré de Balzac*

MARY L. LEVKOFF

ABOVE: 30. Rodin, Auguste
Monument to Honoré de Balzac
First modeled 1897, Musée Rodin cast
9/12 in 1967
Bronze
Susse
117 × 47¼ × 47¼ in.
(297.2 × 120 × 120 cm)
Los Angeles County Museum of Art,
Gift of B. Gerald Cantor Art
Foundation

LEFT: 29. Rodin, Auguste
The Spirit of Eternal Repose (with Head)
c. 1898–99. Musée Rodin cast 2/8 in
1982
Bronze
Coubertin
76 × 46 × 48 in.
(193 × 116.8 × 121.9 cm)
Iris and B. Gerald Cantor Collection,
promised gift to the Iris and
B. Gerald Cantor Foundation

Auguste Rodin's numerous efforts in the creation of public monuments are somewhat overshadowed by the immense popularity of his two best-known sculptures, *The Thinker* (frontispiece; pl. 73) and *The Kiss* (pl. 83), which Rodin originally conceived as elements of *The Gates of Hell*, his first important state project, commissioned in 1880. Yet Rodin was awarded many commissions for commemorative monuments until just after the twentieth century dawned, when his career entered its late phase. Several of these overlap in time, and not one that was important was received without some kind of dispute and public controversy. The schematic (and incomplete) list[1] below gives an idea of how these projects, of widely varying degrees of complexity, in fact dominated Rodin's career until 1898, when his *Balzac* was rejected by the literary society that commissioned it.

The Burghers of Calais	Commissioned January 1885. Second maquette accepted July 1885. Final model exhibited 1889. Delayed by financial crisis until 1893. Inaugurated 1895 (see text).
Jules Bastien-Lepage	Commissioned 1886. Unveiled 1889.
Benjamin Vicuña-Mackenna	Commissioned 1887. Not completed owing to cost.
General Patrick Lynch	Commissioned 1887. Not completed for unknown reasons.
Claude Lorrain	Preparatory work began possibly as early as c. 1879–82 or, more likely, 1884/86.[2] Formally commissioned 1889.[3] Model for pedestal ready 1890 but figure of Claude still incomplete 1891 (see text).[4] Unveiled 1892; pedestal modified soon after.
Victor Hugo	Commissioned 1889. First (horizontal) version rejected and second version (the vertical *Apotheosis*) begun 1890. Horizontal maquette finished 1895; marble version of the horizontal maquette finished 1901; unveiled in Jardin du Palais Royal 1909. Vertical example not executed in marble or installed (see text).
Honoré de Balzac	Commissioned 1891 (see text). Final model completed 1898 and rejected.
Domingo Faustino Sarmiento	Commissioned 1894; almost complete 1896. Unveiled 1900.
Monument to Labor	Commission transferred to Rodin 1894. Model completed 1899. Not realized.

31. Rodin, Auguste
Whistler's Muse
1907, Musée Rodin cast IV/IV in 1991
Bronze
Coubertin
88 × 35½ × 42⅞ in.
(223.5 × 90.2 × 108.9 cm)
Iris and B. Gerald Cantor
Foundation

Pierre Puvis de Chavannes	Commissioned 1899. Partial maquette (figure of *The Spirit of Eternal Repose*; pl. 29) exhibited 1900; work may have continued until 1907. Not completed, possibly owing to outbreak of First World War.[5]
James M. Whistler	Commissioned 1905. Maquette almost ready 1909. Not completed, probably owing to Rodin's failing health and outbreak of First World War (see text).[6]
Jules-Amédée Barbey d'Aurevilly	Commissioned 1909. Monument consisted of a bust of Barbey d'Aurevilly on a simple base. Inaugurated 1912.
Samuel de Champlain	Inaugurated 1912. A simple monument that used variant cast of a pre-existing sculpture, *La France* (c. 1904–06?, itself derived from a much earlier [c. 1884?] portrait of Camille Claudel; pl. 32).[7]
Eugène Carrière	Proposed 1912. Maquette consisted of a revision of an earlier composition, *The Hero*, exhibited in 1900.[8] Not completed.

The simple nature of the last three monuments, two of which were little more than reused works that had been created many years earlier, shows how Rodin's involvement with public commissions dwindled after the rejection of the *Balzac*. He undertook only two significant commissions afterward, the monuments to Puvis de Chavannes and James McNeill Whistler. The *Whistler* monument he accepted eagerly, in all likelihood because of its international prestige and possibly as a retort to the controversies endured with the *Balzac*. There were several reasons, however, for his diminished interest in public monuments after 1898. The production of smaller marble sculptures for private clients around 1900 brought him increased revenue. By about 1908 he had achieved a comfortable level of financial security and no longer depended on securing public commissions, or on completing them.[9] Furthermore, his advancing age seemed to heighten his impatience with the need for customary refinements (such as the adjustment of proportions and the finishing of surfaces) in completing a work of art. Although in 1910 Rodin insisted that he preferred to work slowly,[10] an urgency might be perceived in his increasing experiments with fragmentary sculptures and the recombination of pre-existing compositions to produce new works of art. His physical condition was declining, and this doubtlessly also affected his productivity. Finally, the distress caused by the circumstances surrounding the *Balzac* crystallized his disillusionment with a salient aspect of commissions for public monuments: the necessity of submitting to a collective judgment in order to obtain approval from the group entity that paid for the monument. This aspect of patronage became especially decisive in France during Rodin's lifetime.

In the second half of the nineteenth century an astonishing array of free-standing public sculptures was erected throughout Europe and the Americas, especially in France, and in particular in Paris. This phenomenon warrants its own name in modern historical literature: *statuomanie* ("craze for statues"). The Paris of the Second Empire (1852–70) was rebuilt and physically reorganized with new boulevards and open squares. The city was redecorated and its new public spaces were accented with statuary. With the establishment of the Third Republic in 1870, the art of sculpture was more

than ever applied to the validation of political subjects, in addition to its traditional purpose of honoring great literary, historic, scientific, and artistic heroes. That function had been enhanced with the spread, internationally, of the Romantic movement, which put a premium on heroic individualism. (Ornamental sculpture was fostered, too: it has been calculated[11] that 335 sculptors worked on the decoration of the Louvre, 131 on the Opéra, and 230 on the Hôtel de Ville, among them Rodin, who created the statue of Jean-Baptiste d'Alembert on its façade in 1880.) From 1870 until 1914, as many as 150 monuments were erected in Paris alone.[12] Their number eventually began to be deemed excessive, to the point that the Municipal Council of Paris decided to prohibit a memorial to anyone who had died within the previous 10 years. This may have been one of the reasons that Rodin's monument to Eugène Carrière was never carried out.[13] In addition, a law passed on April 5, 1884, granted new autonomy to municipalities in the erection of public monuments.[14]

Sculpture is by its very nature suited to the adornment of public spaces. More durable than painting, it can to some extent resist exposure to the elements. Unlike painting, it possesses in its plastic three dimensions a command of its environment: monumental sculpture is a highly public art, and it customarily responds to a civic ideal, no matter if that ideal is determined by an authoritarian ruler (such as Cosimo de' Medici in Renaissance Tuscany) or if it takes the form of an aristocrat's gesture to provide a service to his city (such as the sculptured fountain erected in the sixteenth century by the chancellor René de Birague in his neighborhood of Paris, and those in the early nineteenth century provided by Napoleon Bonaparte). In Rodin's time the democratic ideal responded in its turn to sculpture: public subscriptions were the primary means of financing the majority of monuments in France in the nineteenth century (subscriptions have been estimated to have provided the funds for as many as two-thirds of them), while the creation of only one painting is known to have been supported in the same way.[15]

Rodin competed for several public commissions before he began to obtain them with any regularity.[16] In retrospect it is surprising to find that projects funded by a government or popular subscription continued to be awarded to him despite the unusually innovative character of his sculptures (which were indeed frequently incomprehensible to their patrons), and in spite of the fact that he became notorious for not fulfilling his contracts. Rodin's protracted meandering on *The Gates of Hell*, for example, would come to haunt him in the affair of the *Balzac* (begun a decade later)—despite his intention to finish the *Gates* "at all costs," as he had written in January 1888,[17] when other patrons became alarmed by the slow advancement of *The Burghers of Calais*.

The Burghers of Calais

This was Rodin's first commission for a free-standing public monument (see pl. 37). Unlike *The Gates of Hell*, which depended on a related project (the establishment of a new museum), the *Burghers* was not subsidiary to anything. It was an autonomous, free-standing, civic monument, and thus was particularly significant in Rodin's career. There is small wonder, then, that Rodin advanced his work with what was for him considerable decisiveness, coherence, and speed.

In 1884 the city of Calais revived its long-standing intention to erect a monument to its heroes of 1347, who volunteered to surrender themselves to Edward III, King of England, in exchange for the liberation of their besieged city, which lay strategically on the northern coast of France. This early episode of the Hundred Years' War began with Edward's claim to the French crown. It was recounted in the chronicles of Jean Froissart (*c.* 1333–*c.* 1410), written around 1360–65:

> The king of England greatly desired to conquer Calais and laid siege to it, and said he would starve them, and he waited through summer and all winter. The people of Calais realized when the king of France withdrew, that the help in which they trusted had failed them. Their famine was so great that neither the weak nor the strong could bear it. They met in council and decided that it would be better to surrender to the king of England, if no greater succor could be found, rather than to die one after another from famine. Many were losing their bodies and their souls from madness caused by hunger.
>
> [The king was informed of this and sent an emissary to tell them:] "The only mercy they can have from me is if six of their most notable *bourgeois* (burghers) leave their city, stripped, with ropes around their necks and the keys in their hands; and with them I shall do what I please." [This was reported to the French king's governor of Calais, who had negotiated the surrender with the king.] Jean de Vienne [*sic*], who gathered everyone in the town hall. When he explained, they began to weep and cry. ... Then Eustache de Saint-Pierre, the richest property-owner in the city, rose to his feet, and said: "My Lords, It would be a terrible pity to let such a people as these die by famine or other means when we could find another way [to save them]; and it would be a great kindness and charity before our Lord God to save them from such evil. I myself have such faith that I shall find grace and

forgiveness in our Lord God if I die to save these people, that I want to be the first, and I willingly [strip down to] my undershirt, my head bare, with a noose around my neck, for the will of the king of England."

After Eustache de Saint-Pierre said this, each one went to him and hailed his pity, and many threw themselves at his feet, weeping. Next a very honest man, and successful, rose and said he would join his comrade Eustache de Saint-Pierre. This one was called Jean d'Aire. Next rose a third, named Jacques de Vissant [*sic*], who was wealthy with property and his inheritance, and he said he would join his cousins. His brother Pierre de Vissant [*sic*] did the same; and then the fifth and the sixth; and they stripped down to their undershirts in the city of Calais, and put the yoke around their necks, and took the keys to the city and the fortress; each one held a fistful. When they were thus arrayed, Jean de Vienne took the lead, and went to the gates of the city.

Everyone rose and wrung their hands and wept bitterly ... and they all went to the city gates, sobbing. Jean de Vienne opened the gates and thus confined himself with the six burghers between the walls of the city and the barricades. He came to the king's emissary who was waiting there and said: "As commander of Calais I deliver to you, with the consent of the poor people of that city, these six burghers, and I swear to you that they are the most honored and important in terms of their possessions and ancestry; they bring the keys to the city and the castle. If you could plead with the king of England not to have them put to death." "I do not know what the king wishes to do with them, but I promise you I shall do the most I can," he replied. The barricades were opened, and they went to the king of England; Jean de Vienne returned to Calais.

The king, surrounded by his lords, went out into the square. He stared at the burghers with enormous anger, because he detested the inhabitants of Calais, for the great damage they had done to his ships in the past. The burghers were on their knees before him; they clasped their hands and said: "Kind sir and king. You see us six before you; we are from the old families of Calais and great merchants; and we surrender ourselves before you as you ordered, to save the people of Calais, who have suffered grievously. If you would have pity on us, as you are noble." The king looked at them with fury. He was seized with such anger that he could not speak. And when he did speak, he ordered them to be decapitated.

The king's lords begged him to have pity, but he would hear none of it. His emissary then said: "Noble Sire, rein in your boldness, for you are famed for your kindness and nobility, and you should not do anything by which that will be diminished, nor that anyone could speak ill of you. If you do not have pity on these citizens, everyone will speak of your great cruelty, that you were so merciless that you executed these honest men, who of their own volition surrendered to save the rest." But the king ordered the executioner to come, saying it was right to have them die: "Those of Calais have killed so many of my men, that it is right for them to die too."

Then the queen of England, who was greatly pregnant, humbly appealed to the king, and cried so piteously that she could not remain standing. She threw herself to her knees before him and said: "Since the time that I followed you across the sea, in

34. Rodin, Auguste
Jean d'Aire, 2nd Maquette
1885–86. Musée Rodin cast 1/12 in
1970
Bronze
Susse
27½ × 9½ × 9¾ in.
(69.8 × 24.1 × 24.8 cm)
Iris and B. Gerald Cantor
Foundation

great danger, I have asked nothing of you, but I beg you humbly now, as a gift, and for the Son of the Virgin, and for my love, if you would show these men some pity." The king waited a bit before replying and looked at his wife, who was weeping on her knees. It softened his heart, and he said: "Lady, I would much prefer it if you took another part than this, but you beg me in such a way that I cannot refuse, and no matter how much it grieves me, I give them to you, if that will please you." The queen thanked him, and rose, and bid the burghers to rise, removed the ropes from their necks, dressed them and fed them, and led them to safety.[18]

Since 1845, the city had intermittently attempted to have a monument created in honor of Eustache de Saint-Pierre. Funds began to be raised toward the realization of a statue by Pierre-Jean David d'Angers (1788–1856), but this project was interrupted by the *coup d'état* of Louis-Napoleon, who established an imperial government and named himself Napoleon III in 1851. In 1864 the idea of a monument was again considered. A commission was awarded four years later to Auguste Clésinger (1814–1883), but the Franco-Prussian War terminated it.[19]

When the project for the monument was renewed in 1884, the Medieval fortifications of the old city of Calais were about to be demolished in order to merge the historic center with the industrialized suburb of Saint-Pierre, which had grown up outside the city's walls. The intention of Calais to commemorate its historical identity in these new circumstances (which were politically and economically charged)[20] provided a new impetus to erect the monument as a veritable personification of old Calais, and as noted above,[21] the project's renewal coincided with the law of April 5, 1884, which made the realization of a commission simpler for the municipality to achieve. The faded glory of the city became a point of dispute, however, when the suburb of Saint-Pierre (and others) associated the fourteenth-century burghers' wealth with later interpretations of Froissart's account which viewed the burghers' surrender not as a sacrifice but as treason. (In fact the burghers' very prominence would have led the king of England to choose them, and no others, for execution: by doing so, he would obliterate the city's leadership, its morale, and its hope of insurrection.)[22] Calais, however, having previously defended the burghers' reputation, championed it again successfully,[23] and the subscription was launched with broad advertising. This included a synopsis of Froissart's narrative, and Rodin apparently had a copy of it: he referred to an "extract from Froissart" when he wrote about the project in November 1884 to Omer Dewavrin, the mayor of Calais, who was the head of the committee for the monument.[24]

Five sculptors had submitted maquettes, but there seems to have been no formal competition for the commission.[25] The mayor had been reassured about the choice of Rodin by the painter J.P. Laurens and the mayor's agent in Paris, the journalist P.A. Isaac, whose recommendation cited Rodin's *The Age of Bronze* (pl. 17), *Adam* (pl. 84), and *St. John the Baptist Preaching* (pl. 137) as recognized successes, in addition to the fact that Rodin had the state commission for *The Gates of Hell*. Furthermore, he added, several noteworthy artists (including Albert-Ernst Carrier-Belleuse and Jules Dalou) had agreed to sit for Rodin for their portraits. A bust of Victor Hugo was also mentioned to support the nomination of Rodin (see p. 66 for the unusual circumstances regarding the creation of this portrait).[26]

Rodin submitted his maquette in November 1884, the month after Dewavrin met him for the first time. He had already created something quite novel: instead of providing a statue to commemorate Eustache de Saint-Pierre alone, he modeled all six of the Burghers rushing forward (pl. 33). They were, moreover, in an isocephalic mass. This was a complete departure from traditional heroic monuments, which consisted either of a single figure or of a group arranged in a focused, pyramidal composition. (It is useful to recall in this context that Frédéric Bartholdi's allegorical *Liberty Enlightening the World*, better known as the Statue of Liberty, was erected in New York Harbor that very year.) From this first sketch Rodin quickly invented an intermediate maquette, or rather six separate figures in strikingly different emotional attitudes (pls. 34, 35). This group of six statuettes definitively secured the contract for him over the protests of the other sculptors, who insisted that Rodin could not produce his multi-figured monument within the estimated cost.

35. Rodin, Auguste
Monument to the Burghers of Calais, 2nd maquette
1884
Plaster
Approximate height 24 in. (70 cm)
Width and depth variable
Paris, Musée Rodin

The chronology of the rest of the commission is now well known:[27] the project was officially awarded to Rodin at the end of January 1885. A definitive maquette at one-third of the full scale was requested from him a month later, but it was July before he provided models of the individual figures to the committee in Calais. These sculptures had been well received in Paris, but they were condemned in the Calais press. The sculptor and the mayor persevered in the face of this opposition. By January 1886 Rodin had worked up three of the figures to full size in clay, just when Calais was hit by a banking crisis. A little more than a year later, in May 1887, three life-size sculptures were ready in plaster, three were near completion, and Rodin promised the bronze monument for the spring of 1888.

To respond to the committee's reservations about what the members saw as the unfocused nature of the design, Dewavrin asked the sculptor in January 1888 for a drawing of what the completed monument would look like: "The photograph of the individual figures gives no idea of what the monument will be to people who haven't been initiated into your method," the mayor wrote.[28] Evidently the individual figures were known to the monument's patrons, but not as a unified whole in its definitive arrangement. Rodin replied that his idea could not be adequately revealed in a drawing, which would "only give rise to bad impressions. ... As soon as I have assembled the large figures I shall have them photographed [next he mentions that he must "get rid of the Gates of Hell"]. Only two figures still need any work, and then I shall put them together and harmonize them."[29]

Rodin may have been referring to the committee's doubts in an interview in September 1888 about a monument to Balzac (for which he had not yet been awarded the commission). He said: "When a number of people, no matter how expert and intelligent they might be, come together to judge works of art ... they will be able to agree only on a work that is utterly neutral. A work that is truly superior and very personal, but which manifests some sort of peculiarity or audacity ... won't stand a chance."[30]

By the time the finished plaster model was ready in 1889 (shown prominently in an exhibition in Paris devoted exclusively to the work of Rodin and Monet),[31] no funds remained for casting it in bronze. The project was held in abeyance until 1893. That year Dewavrin, who had ceased to be mayor of Calais in 1885 when his city merged with Saint-Pierre, was re-elected, and a national subscription was launched to complete the

36. Rodin, Auguste
Andrieu d'Andres
c. 1886–87, Musée Rodin cast 11 in
1966
Bronze
Georges Rudier
18½ × 7¾ × 8½ in.
(45.7 × 19.7 × 21.6 cm)
Iris and B. Gerald Cantor
Foundation

OVERLEAF: 37. Rodin, Auguste
The Burghers of Calais
1884–88, Musée Rodin cast 1/11 in
1985
Bronze
Coubertin
82½ × 94 × 75 in.
(209.6 × 238.8 × 190.5 cm)
The Metropolitan Museum of Art,
Gift of Iris and B. Gerald Cantor,
1988

LEFT: 38. Rodin, Auguste
Eustache de Saint-Pierre, Vêtu
1886–87, Musée Rodin cast III/IV in
1987
Bronze
Coubertin
85 × 30 × 48 in.
(215.9 × 76.2 × 121.9 cm)
Iris and B. Gerald Cantor Collection,
promised gift to the Iris and
B. Gerald Cantor Foundation

39. Bodmer, Karl-Henri (Charles)
Rodin's *Pierre de Wiessant, Nude in
Clay*
c. 1885
Gelatin silver print
Paris, Musée Rodin

monument. Somewhat fitfully, the new funds were raised and a decision was reached regarding the choice of foundry. In April 1895 the foundation for the pedestal was set, next the bronze was cast,[32] and the monument was inaugurated in June.

The base of the sculpture as completed preserves in its irregular levels evidence of Rodin's method of assembling the composition from the group of sculptures that won him the commission in January 1885. The small figures were enlarged to mid-scale. With the exception of the figure called *Andrieu d'Andres*, more detailed nudes were then created, enlarged to mid-scale, in the attitudes of the small sketches. (*Andrieu d'Andres* [pl. 36] was the only figure never modeled as a nude. Rodin seems to have determined the attitude of this draped figure virtually at the outset, and thereafter changed it little.) The large nude was then elaborated: two of the stages can be seen together in a photograph taken in Rodin's studio (pl. 39). Finally the full-scale nude was draped, and the figure was completed. The reduced versions of the final, draped, life-sized figures were cast from 1895 to 1910, having become enormously popular, after the monument was inaugurated.[33] Rodin also had *Jean d'Aire* recreated in enameled terracotta (Musée Rodin, Meudon), in addition to six glazed terracotta versions of the bust of the same figure.[34]

Rodin used the same head and hands for different figures, revealing already in the mid-1880s a process of assembling compositions from pre-existing components—a process he would exploit for the next 40 years. (It was reported during his lifetime that several of the *Burghers'* hands had been created by Camille Claudel, with whom he had formed a passionate liaison.)[35] Except for *Eustache de Saint-Pierre* (pl. 38), the figures

40. Rodin, Auguste
Jean de Fiennes, Vêtu
1885–86, Musée Rodin cast 5/8 in
1983
Bronze
Coubertin
82 × 48 × 38 in.
(208.3 × 121.9 × 96.5 cm)
Iris and B. Gerald Cantor
Foundation

42. Rodin, Auguste
Pierre de Wiessant, Vêtu
c. 1886–87. Musée Rodin cast 7/8 in
1983
Bronze
Coubertin
81 × 40 × 48 in.
(205.7 × 101.6 × 121.9 cm)
Iris and B. Gerald Cantor Collection,
promised gift to the Iris and
B. Gerald Cantor Foundation

41. Rodin, Auguste
Jacques de Wiessant, Vêtu
1885–86. Musée Rodin cast 3/8 in
1989
Bronze
Coubertin
83⅞ × 26⅜ × 49⅝ in.
(213 × 67 × 126 cm)
Iris and B. Gerald Cantor Collection,
promised gift to the Iris and
B. Gerald Cantor Foundation

in the monument were not identified as individuals when Rodin exhibited them. The two central heroes, Eustache de Saint-Pierre and Jean d'Aire, and the next two, the brothers Jacques de Vissant (*sic*) and Pierre de Vissant (*sic*)—the latter called *The Walking Burgher* when Rodin exhibited the sculpture separately—were clearly mentioned in all versions of Froissart's narrative, but only a fourth version of the story, preserved in the Vatican Library, named the last two: Jean de Fiennes (pl. 40) and Andrieu d'Andres.[36] The names (and the regularized spellings) assigned today to the figures originated with Georges Grappe, who compiled the first published catalogue of the Musée Rodin. Rodin incorporated the head of *Jean d'Aire* (compare pl. 45) in *Andrieu d'Andres* (called *The Despairing Burgher* when exhibited independently in Rodin's lifetime) and *Jacques de Wiessant* (pl. 41), even though Froissart's account reported that only two burghers were brothers. Rodin re-used several hands, in particular the highly expressive right hand of *Pierre de Wiessant* (pls. 42, 43), which was later transformed into *The Hand of God* (pls. 5, 130, 133). Colossal versions of the heads (pls. 44, 45) were first cast about 1909–10, when Rodin experimented with enlargements of pre-existing models.

As an aggregate composition, the *Burghers* is superbly unified (or, to use Rodin's own description, "harmonized") through the expressive gestures and attitudes of the bodies. In a now-famous letter, Rodin explained his intentions when the realization of the entire monument—including the pedestal and installation—was imminent. On December 8, 1893, he wrote to the mayor:

43. Rodin, Auguste
Right Hand of Pierre and Jacques de Wiessant
c. 1884–89, date of cast unknown
Bronze
Alexis Rudier
12½ × 7 × 3 in.
(31.7 × 17.8 × 7.62 cm)
Iris and B. Gerald Cantor Collection,
promised gift to the Iris and
B. Gerald Cantor Foundation

At the beginning I thought of the Burghers leaving the marketplace, in the confusion of their farewells, only Saint-Pierre … beginning to move ahead to cut short this painful scene; I had thought that placed very low the group would become more *familier* and would make the public enter the character of the episode, its misery and its sacrifice, of the drama, I would say. It might be that I was mistaken, because I never can really judge until I see the work set up; so, being undecided, I yield to the decision of the committee … .

This must refer to the committee's preference for a traditional pedestal. Rodin proceeded to analyze how the silhouette of the monument would be perceived in different orientations (against buildings, open sky, or the park), and remarked that, if it were seen against trees, it would not be set off correctly. Since that was the case, he would return to his "idea of having it very low to let the public penetrate into the heart of the subject, as in the *mises au tombeau* (entombment groups) … where the group is virtually on the ground."[37]

The committee ignored Rodin's advice, installed the monument against the backdrop of the park, elevated it on a boring pedestal, and fenced it off from the public.

The fortunate viewer who now comes upon it in its improved circumstances, or sees casts in other locations (pl. 37), is offered a rich experience. The blocklike form of the whole, pierced by voids at a variety of angles, offers a multitude of changing vignettes. The strong channels and folds in the simple, functional drapery (from which all histori-

44. Rodin, Auguste
Monumental Head of Pierre de Wiessant
c. 1884–85, enlarged about 1909, date of cast unknown
Bronze
Godard
32 × 19 × 20½ in.
(81.3 × 48.3 × 52.1 cm)
Iris and B. Gerald Cantor Foundation

cizing details have been purged) respond to vertical, dominant voids in the whole group, repeatedly marking the ensemble like the ribs of Gothic vaulting so prized by Rodin. In the casts exposed to the elements, the verticality is accentuated by streaks of corrosion caused by rain, like tears that fell from heaven. The forcefulness of its drama is communicated by the heroes' divergent and ambiguous responses to their own fateful decisions. They are trapped in a timeless circle of doubt, fear, hope, desperation, resolve, and heroic confrontation with destiny. Like all truly great civic monuments, *The Burghers of Calais* personifies the highest ideals of the community that erected it: self-sacrifice, courage, and responsibility for the well-being of their fellow man. Filled with compelling meaning and emotion, it justifiably has become one of the great masterpieces of Western sculpture.

The Monument to Victor Hugo

Rodin was awarded the commission for a monument to Victor Hugo in 1889, the same year his final model for *The Burghers of Calais* was exhibited in Paris. No one at the time could have foreseen the disputes and complexity through which the project would be dissipated and eventually collapse.

Today Victor Hugo (1802–1885; pl. 46)[38] is primarily remembered as the author of the quintessentially romantic novel *Notre-Dame de Paris* (1831, translated as *The Hunchback of Notre-Dame*) and the gripping *Les Misérables* (begun in 1845, published in 1862). He was, however, not only one of France's greatest writers but also one of its most riveting political figures, both a fearless critic of totalitarian government and an advocate for social responsibility. His biography reads as dramatically as his novels. Born to an illustrious soldier who was ennobled by Napoleon Bonaparte, and a mother who harbored her lover, a political fugitive, in the chapel of their garden in Paris, the young Victor Hugo traveled to such exotic locales as Corsica, Elba, Italy, and Spain as his parents periodically attempted a reconciliation. The Napoleonic Wars nourished his imagination and admiration for the emperor, whom he saw as France's savior after the terrifying anarchy of the French Revolution of 1789.

One of his brothers and one of his daughters went mad, and another daughter drowned with her husband on their honeymoon. Hugo was fluent in Latin, studied philosophy and mathematics, and was a gifted draughtsman. His first book of poems, published when he was only 20 years old, went through five editions and was the harbinger of a stupefying productivity that stretched across almost all of the nineteenth century. *Notre-Dame* and *Les Misérables* became his most enduring creations, despite the cold reserve of other writers that greeted their publication: the Realist Honoré de Balzac condemned *Notre-Dame* as "an impossible tale ... full of architectural pretensions."[39] Hugo's style, twinkling with strange images, flowing with streams of adjectives, metaphors and similes, and communicated in a classical French scattered with popular expressions, is marked by phrases and sentences so long that the reader is left gasping for air. Improbable turns of events and extremes of incandescent ecstasy, irony, and bitter tragedy are hallmarks of his fiction, in which he condemned the wretched conditions in which the destitute were suffering.

46. Unknown photographer.
Victor Hugo on the Rock of Guernsey
1853–55
Gum bichromate print
Paris, Musée Rodin

45. Rodin, Auguste
Monumental Head of Jean d'Aire
c. 1884–86, enlarged 1909–10, date of
cast unknown
Bronze
Georges Rudier
26¾ × 19⅞ × 22½ in.
(67.9 × 50.3 × 57.2 cm)
Iris and B. Gerald Cantor
Foundation

Although Hugo was an aristocrat, the series of revolts that swept through Europe in 1848 altered his opinions. In 1849 he was elected to the legislative assembly, where he delivered fiery harangues against the government's lack of assistance for the poor, voted to abolish the death penalty, and defended a free press, universal suffrage, the right of private inheritance, and the provision of public, non-sectarian education to everyone. When Napoleon's nephew Louis-Napoleon imposed a regime of censorship and repression in 1851, proclaiming himself Napoleon III the following year, Hugo's loyalty was betrayed. He fled to Belgium at the end of 1851 and eventually settled on the island of Guernsey, where he produced virulent denunciations of "Napoleon the Little," as he called the new emperor (in contrast with Napoleon the Great). From the island he continued to rail against the stifling of the press, capital punishment and the inflexible penal code, the sordid conditions of prisons, slavery in the United States, and the misery of child labor. He wrote some of his most brilliant satires, romances, and poems in a creative flood that has rarely been matched, in addition to producing hundreds of fantastic drawings and watercolors.

47. Rodin, Auguste
Monument to Victor Hugo
Large model incomplete 1897, definitive model completed shortly after 1900, Musée Rodin cast 1/8 in 1996
Bronze
Coubertin
72¾ × 112⅛ × 63¾ in.
(184.8 × 310 × 162.6 cm)
Iris and B. Gerald Cantor Foundation

49. Rodin, Auguste
Victor Hugo (Frontal View)
1886
Drypoint
8¾ × 6½ in.
(22.2 × 16.5 cm)
Iris and B. Gerald Cantor
Foundation

48. Freuler, E.?
Bust of Victor Hugo with Rodin
behind it
1883
Albumin print
Paris, Musée Rodin

Hugo ended his exile as the Franco-Prussian War reached its climax with the siege of Paris in 1870, and he returned in glory as a hero who had unflinchingly maintained his integrity and his commitment to humanitarian ideals and individual liberty. Napoleon III had capitulated, and democracy would be restored in France. With political conditions in constant flux, however, Hugo was as much marginalized as he was celebrated. A cerebral hemorrhage in 1879 reduced his activity, but earlier works were published and he continued to be elected to the government. In 1881, when he entered his eightieth year, an enormous popular celebration was held in his honor. Four years later he passed away. A million mourners lined the route that took his body across the city from a vigil beneath the Arc de Triomphe to the Panthéon. Nothing like it had ever been seen before in Paris.[40] His was the first state funeral for a private citizen in France.

Rodin had been introduced to Victor Hugo in circumstances that arose from the aftermath of the scandal surrounding *The Age of Bronze* (pl. 17), in which the sculptor had been accused of submitting a life-cast to the Salon as though he had created it with his own hands. In addition to demonstrating in the small figures of *The Gates of Hell* that he had no need for recourse to life-casts, Rodin was advised by his friend the journalist Edmond Bazire to create portraits of well-known figures, among them Victor Hugo. Such was Hugo's probity that he would never have allowed a life-cast made from his face to be called an original sculpture.[41] Bazire was one of the organizers of the celebration of 1881, and he convinced Hugo to allow Rodin to meet him in 1883.

Although Rodin was admitted to Hugo's residence, he was forbidden to sketch him because Hugo had just endured long sittings before another sculptor, with disappointing results. In fact Hugo categorically preferred the bust that David d'Angers had created of him in 1838, when he was in his prime as a leader of the Romantic movement. (Coincidentally, a portrait by David d'Angers confronted Rodin again when the commission for the monument to Balzac was awarded to him.) Rodin therefore surreptitiously made tiny drawings of Hugo on cigarette paper while at the dining table (pl. 49), and, positioning himself out of the way on a balcony, he modeled the clay portrait (pl. 48).

This remarkably vibrant, lifelike portrait displeased Hugo's family because it was not idealized, but at the Salon of 1884 it was praised in tandem with Rodin's bust of the sculptor Jules Dalou (1883). Dalou (1838–1902) and Rodin were friends, and Rodin introduced him to Hugo barely three months before the old poet died in May 1885. To Rodin's great annoyance, Dalou was chosen by Hugo's family to do the death-mask and on his own proceeded to design a grandiose tomb in the poet's memory.[42] It is widely believed that Dalou's intention was to see his monument installed in the Panthéon, which for the interment of Victor Hugo had just been reconverted a third time from its original religious purpose (as the church of Ste-Geneviève, erected 1757–89) to a non-sectarian, purely commemorative use as a mausoleum for France's great men.[43]

In 1889 a relative of Victor Hugo, Edward Lockroy, who had just been appointed Minister of Fine Arts, announced that a series of nearly 100 commemorative sculptures would be commissioned for the Panthéon.[44] He assigned responsibility for the program's concept and commissions to an autonomous committee set up specifically for the purpose, since the political climate in France at that time was as changeable as the weather. There was no guarantee that a government minister would remain in office long enough to see the completion of the project. Indeed, Lockroy resigned two days after the program was declared, and the man he had appointed as Director of Fine Arts—Gustave Larroumet, one of Rodin's admirers—took his place.[45] Dalou and two other sculptors, Henri Chapu (1833–1891) and Eugène Guillaume (1822–1905), were included on the committee. Dalou, however, was not chosen for the monument to Victor Hugo, which was instead awarded to Rodin. It was one of the first two monuments mandated for the Panthéon; the other was to commemorate the charismatic revolutionary Honoré-Gabriel Mirabeau (1749–1791), whose body had been the first to be interred in the Panthéon during the building's earliest transformation from church to mausoleum in 1791. This sculpture was to be carried out by Jean-Antonin Injalbert (1845–1933). Dalou, Alexandre Falguière (1831–1900) and Antonin Mercié (1845–1916), along with others, were each awarded further commissions, with several being assigned to Dalou.

In order to maintain some sense of harmony throughout the whole series of monuments in the Panthéon,[46] the committee logically made general recommendations about their scale and format. With regard to the sculptures of Mirabeau and Hugo, it was advised that their silhouettes should be low enough to prevent their blocking the view of other works of art at either end of the transept.[47] (These first two significant monuments were intended to be free-standing in the arms of the transept, not backed up against the piers of the crossing. Therefore Dalou's wall monument could not have been

50. Rodin, Auguste
Heroic Bust of Victor Hugo
1890–97 or 1901–02, Musée Rodin
cast 7/12 in 1981
Bronze
Coubertin
29¼ × 23½ × 21¼ in.
(74.3 × 59.7 × 54 cm)
Iris and B. Gerald Cantor Collection,
promised gift to the Iris and
B. Gerald Cantor Foundation

51. Rodin, Auguste
Iris, Messenger of the Gods
1895. Musée Rodin cast 1969
Bronze
Georges Rudier
38 × 32½ × 15½ in.
(96.5 × 82.5 × 39.37 cm)
Iris and B. Gerald Cantor Collection,
promised gift to the Iris and B.
Gerald Cantor Foundation

selected.)[48] Rodin consequently first created a model showing Hugo seated. The report dated September 10, 1889 describes Rodin's idea—"seated on the rocks of Guernsey, behind him in the curve of a wave, the three muses of Youth, Maturity, and Old Age, breathing inspiration into him"[49]—but the report does not state that his maquette existed by that time. It is quite possible that Rodin had, like Dalou, understood that a monument to Victor Hugo would one day be commissioned for the Panthéon, and, intending to secure the commission for himself, had already formulated a general idea for it. The sculptures that are believed to be early sketches for his monument (a small bronze in the Musée Rodin, inv. no. 1073; slightly later, a larger plaster in the same collection, inv. no. S.54; and, again slightly later, a large terracotta in the Österreichische Galerie, Vienna)[50] lack the curling wave. In March 1890 Rodin instead described a maquette with Hugo on the wave-swept rock surrounded not by the Three Ages of Man (or the stages of his career), but by muses symbolizing two of his most significant works, and a third as "an ideal."[51]

52. Rodin, Auguste
Meditation With Arms
Originally conceived for *The Gates of Hell*, 1880s; enlarged about 1896.
Musée Rodin cast 8/12 in 1979
Bronze
Coubertin
61 × 25 × 25 in.
(154.9 × 63.5 × 63.5 cm)
Iris and B. Gerald Cantor Collection,
promised gift to the Iris and
B. Gerald Cantor Foundation

After the maquette was viewed, the committee decided to have a painted facsimile fabricated so that the design's effect in the Panthéon could be judged. It was unanimously condemned in July 1890 for "lack of clarity and [for] its confused silhouette," and Rodin was directed to conceive another more in keeping with the architecture of the

53. Rodin, Auguste
Meditation Without Arms
(*The Inner Voice*)
Originally conceived for *The Gates of Hell*, 1880s; enlarged about 1896.
Musée Rodin cast 6/8 in 1983
Bronze
Coubertin
57½ × 28 × 22⅛ in.
(146 × 59 × 46 cm)
Iris and B. Gerald Cantor Collection,
promised gift to the Iris and
B. Gerald Cantor Foundation

building.[52] in other words to create a sculpture with a vertical orientation. Although Rodin resisted this affront and was vehemently defended by his partisans in the press, there was no choice but to comply with the wishes of the committee. A compromise was suggested by Larroumet, who proposed commissioning a marble version of the horizontal example for the Jardin du Luxembourg; Rodin was to agree to create a new composition for the Panthéon. He would call this *The Apotheosis of Victor Hugo* (pl. 54).

Hugo was now (1891) represented standing among the rocks of his exile; a mass of sirens emerged from the waves at his feet, and the muses flew overhead. By enveloping the figure in allegories, Rodin seems to have merged into one sculpture the two salient features of his *Monument to Claude Lorrain*, which had been commissioned almost simultaneously with the *Monument to Victor Hugo*: a symbolic base and a realistic statue above it. The base of *Claude Lorrain* represents the sun-god Apollo in his chariot bursting from the clouds; with *Victor Hugo* the human being was no longer supported by a mythological image but was instead united with the personifications of his inspiration. Rodin soon modified the maquette to eliminate Hugo's dated costume. The venerated poet was portrayed in heroic nudity with the figure adapted from the nude *Iris, Messenger of the Gods* (pl. 51)[53] flying overhead, like Rodin's early idea of the "curling wave" coming up behind him.

This composition was never carved in marble. The changing governments' attitudes toward Victor Hugo's own political views, waning interest in the project, Rodin's slow progress and finally his death caused the commission for the Panthéon to be abandoned in 1921. A simplified marble version (pl. 57) of the rejected horizontal composition, the one salvaged by Larroumet, was achieved instead, possibly because its completion, vouchsafed by Larroumet, did not depend on a collective judgment. It was neither as ambitious a composition as the *Apotheosis* nor dependent upon variable government administrations.

For Larroumet's commission Rodin awkwardly incorporated an adaptation of his first portrait of Victor Hugo in new plaster elaborations of the horizontal composition. The *Heroic Bust of Victor Hugo* (pl. 50) was derived from the upper part of the new reclining figure.[54] A beautiful standing nude, enlarged from an element in *The Gates of Hell*, was installed behind the reclining poet. It referred to one of Hugo's anthologies and was called *The Inner Voice* (pl. 53).[55] An alternative title, *Meditation* (pl. 52), was also used for it. Rodin seems to have had a marked preference for this figure and experimented with several versions of it, varying the arms' positions or breaking them off entirely. Sections of the legs, which were understood to be concealed when the figure was attached to that of Victor Hugo, instead seemed hacked away when *The Inner Voice* was exhibited separately. This sculpture is thus a prime example of Rodin's complete satisfaction with what, to the public's eye, were incomplete figures.[56]

In 1897 Rodin exhibited a plaster model for the *Monument to Victor Hugo* as it would be intended, with slight adjustments, for the Jardin du Luxembourg. (It had been finished two years before.) Either the plaster or the marble can be seen reversed in a famous photograph of Rodin, from 1902, by Edward Steichen (pl. 55). Two other photographs of the partial maquette omit *The Inner Voice* and emphasize the complexity of the composition by clearly showing the makeshift chassis that supported the individual members of the ensemble (pl. 57).[57] The one figure that remained of the three originally

56. Braun, Adolphe
Rodin's *Monument to Victor Hugo*
No date
Carbon print
Paris. Musée Rodin

imagined above the poet's head, the *Tragic Muse* (pl. 59), is precariously held up on its own small scaffold. It was small wonder that Rodin's chief marble-carver was horrified by the prospect of having to transform this assemblage into a coherent self-supporting whole.[58] However, Rodin stated that while his composition could be executed either in marble or in bronze (the tensile strength of the latter was perhaps better suited to a composition of this intricacy), marble would be better. In 1890 he had written to Larroumet: "To do it in marble will cost 45,000 francs, the bronze will be a little less but the sculpture will lose something."[59] Rodin was presumably referring to the atmospheric effects that he wanted his executants to achieve when carving his compositions in marble, as though the sculptures were veiled in fog.

The reclining figure and the separate *Tragic Muse* were eventually carved in marble, but only *Victor Hugo* (by Rodin's choice) was installed as a monument, and not in the Jardin du Luxembourg. Instead it was set up in the Jardin du Palais Royal in 1909 on a pile of marble slabs fitted together. This other "assemblage," a pedestal much praised for what is perceived as its modernity, is shown in early photographs (pl. 56) before the sculpture was transferred to the Musée Rodin in 1933.[60] The idea for the unusual base may have come to Rodin from the casually superimposed blocks of marble that temporarily served as makeshift pedestals at the Dépôt des Marbres in Paris (pl. 58).

A bronze cast of the adjusted 1897 maquette was made in 1964 for installation on the avenue Victor-Hugo in Paris. A lost-wax cast in bronze was commissioned in 1995 by the Iris and B. Gerald Cantor Foundation (pl. 47). The examples in bronze offer an

57. Unknown photographer
Rodin's *Monument to Victor Hugo*,
with three unidentified men
No date
Aristotype
Paris. Musée Rodin

interesting study in the contrast between Rodin's ideas about the atmospheric treatment of his forms in marble and the practicality of bronze. For the Jardin du Palais Royal, Rodin continued with Larroumet's commission for marble, a medium for which the sculptor showed a marked preference around 1900, despite the fact that in marble Victor Hugo's majestic gesture of calming the waves, which echoed that of traditional representations of the Classical sea-god Neptune,[61] required an unsightly strut to sustain it. Rodin's attitude toward the choice of medium for a sculpture was equally equivocal and yet more pragmatic for the realization of the *Monument to Whistler* (commissioned in 1903). In 1907 he wrote about its delay: "For the execution in stone or in marble, one year will be necessary; or in bronze, which would be more rapid."[62] Nevertheless, Rodin eventually did reveal that he was sensitive to the appropriateness of material for a particular design, at least when it was obvious. Late in his life, he condemned a monument in Florence that had recently been erected in honor of Michelangelo. It consisted of bronze casts of Michelangelo's *David* and the *Times of Day* from the Medici tombs, arranged in an ungainly way around a free-standing support in the form of a Classical candelabrum. Designed to rest on massive sarcophagi with their backs concealed from view, the allegorical figures were now frighteningly cantilevered out into the open air. Rodin said the sculptures "were made for marble," so they should not have been reproduced in bronze.[63]

In any case the origin of Rodin's other monument to Victor Hugo, the *Apotheosis*, lay with the need to fulfill a very specific function, a marble commemorative sculpture destined for a mausoleum. The governing committee for the sculptural program in the Panthéon had determined that the monuments were to be carved from marble. There was therefore no possibility for the use of bronze or of glazed terracotta, another material that Rodin appre-

58. Unknown photographer
Dépôt des Marbres
From *Le Magasin pittoresque*, 1901

ciated.[64] In the taste of the time, terracotta might have been viewed as inappropriate for the vast interior of the Panthéon, which is as icy and rigid as death itself, having been altered in 1793, when its lantern and 38 of its 47 original windows were filled in.

A different monument to Victor Hugo, commissioned from Rodin's collaborator Henry Cros (1840–1907) at the end of 1902 for the Maison de Victor Hugo in Paris (pl. 60), was completed in *pâte-de-verre*,[65] another polychrome medium that entranced the sculptor, and at which Cros excelled. Like a picture by Puvis de Chavannes in relief, it offers a lyrical postscript to the memory of the epic commission for the Panthéon, a building that had been in part decorated with frescoes by that very painter—one most admired by Rodin.

The Monument to Balzac

Rodin's misadventure with the commission (1891) for a monument to Balzac (pl. 30) nonetheless produced the sculpture he would describe in 1908 as "the result of my whole life, in fact the pivot of my esthetic,"[66] a full decade after his patrons rejected the plaster model he provided to them. The story of its public failure combines literary pretentiousness and intellectual factionalism with anti-Semitism and rigid nationalistic obtuseness. The fundamental question of the sculpture's artistic validity was confounded and obscured by these things when the commission was canceled in 1898.

Honoré de Balzac (1799–1850; the honorific "de" was apparently his own invention) was one of France's most prolific novelists and is seen as the progenitor of the Realist movement (and, by extension, of Naturalism) in French literature. Defying his father's insistence that he become a lawyer, Balzac endured a few years bordering on poverty to begin a career in literature even after he had obtained his license and worked with a notary. His early stories, fully couched in Romanticism, went to press under pseudonyms; the first novel published under his own name was *Le Dernier Chouan*, which appeared in 1827 (reprinted as *Les Chouans* in 1829). Balzac's financial mishaps as a publisher and printer, which had begun just a few years earlier, would plague him with debts for much of his brief career. It was in 1842, after the publication of *Physiologie du mariage* and *La Peau de chagrin* that he determined to cement a series of novels and stories into a vast tableau called *La Comédie humaine* (*The Human Comedy*). In these he invented, dissected, and described with astounding clarity and detail the multitude of images and qualities that made up his characters' appearance, their inner lives and motives, their foibles and their activities from the most petty to the noble. With deft perception, he offered his readers minute descriptions of almost clinical exactitude. They are like literary parallels to the classic exercise in elementary chemistry of listing 60 observations about a lighted candle. Balzac, however, would have further conveyed a sense of how the candle's light filled a room that he had invented and meticulously described, and, as though prefiguring the mobile cinematic lens, would move the reader's imagination through his eyes beyond the window to reveal the world outside. His trenchant criticisms of pretensions and banal behavior flowed out, not all of them lacking a touch of piquant, ironic maliciousness, despite the fact that Balzac was himself almost universally regarded as one of the truly jovial figures in France's literary firmament. It has been estimated that he conceived a population of no fewer than 2000 people in his narratives.[67]

Balzac's own physical appearance was just as objectively and humanely analyzed by his own pen. He had no illusions about the lack of fundamental structure in his pudgy countenance. When David d'Angers completed his portrait (pl. 61), Balzac was in ecstasy about the way the great Romantic sculptor had transformed his "great bulldog face" into that of an idealized god, as he described it to Countess Evelina Hanska, the Polish-Russian widow to whom he was devoted and who finally married him about six months before he died.[68] David d'Angers's sculpture squares the head, focuses Balzac's regard to achieve an air of decisive insight, and, by exaggerating the long hair thrown back to the shoulders, emphasizes the prodigious creativity that sprang from the writer's imagination. A cast of this sculpture was installed over his grave about 1854, apparently

60. Cros, Henry
The Apotheosis of Victor Hugo
1902–05
Pâte-de-verre
66 × 96 in.
(168 × 242 cm)
Paris, Musée Victor Hugo

77

the choice of Balzac's widow, who assiduously resisted the idea of any other monument to him.[69] Attempts to create another monument were made by the sculptor Antoine Etex in 1850 and by the writer Alexandre Dumas in 1853–54, but came to nothing, and it is assumed that Etex's colleagues Auguste Clésinger and Auguste Préault entertained similar ambitions.[70]

The Naturalist author Emile Zola became interested in the memorial in 1880. Balzac's widow died in 1882, and the city of Tours, Balzac's birthplace, launched a subscription to finance a monument to the writer in 1885. It was the success of Tours' intention that provided the real impetus to achieve a monument to Balzac in the capital.[71] The project was undertaken in 1888 by the Société des Gens de Lettres, the literary society founded on Balzac's idea and of which he had been the first president. Of several candidates, including Rodin, Dalou, Antonin Mercié, and Count Anatole Marquet de Vasselot (1840–1904), it was Henri Chapu (1833–1891) who was given the responsibility for realizing the monument, but his death prevented him from completing it.[72]

Zola's election as president of the society (1891) decisively altered the project: he preferred Rodin by far, and ensured not only that the commission would be transferred to him, but also that the site of the monument itself would be transferred from the colonnaded gallery surrounding the Jardin du Palais Royal to the open square in front of the palace.[73] Rodin's name had already been put forward in 1888 by the architect Frantz Jourdain, who encouraged him to pursue the commission by confirming to Zola that he could produce a monument 4 meters (13 feet) high, with a pedestal, within the cost and time (18 months) required by the society. Rodin complied, furnishing, however, a proposal for a monument only 3 meters (10 feet) high. A vote was taken among the members of the society. Rodin won the commission at the expense of the only other remaining competitor, Marquet de Vasselot, whose intrigues to secure the project for himself continued for as long as it took for Rodin's model to be created and rejected.[74]

At the beginning Rodin was determined to come to grips with Balzac's true appearance. In contrast to his experience with the sculpture of Victor Hugo, whose face he knew well, Rodin was now confronted with the challenge of executing a posthumous portrait. There was no death-mask to use as a model. By analyzing David d'Angers's sculpture, studying photographs, prints, and paintings of the writer, reading his works and descriptions of him, and traveling to Tours in 1891 (just when his monument to Claude Lorrain was due to be finished) to observe the physiognomies of the inhabitants of the region, Rodin hoped to obtain a sense of the vitality of the man whose image he was now charged with recreating. At Tours he immersed himself in a kind of anthropological project to find a living model who resembled Balzac, and thus risked drowning his objectivity in his method. Balzac's family was not originally from that region on the Loire River. Rodin was warned about this by, among others, a colleague of the greatest expert on Balzac at the time, the Belgian viscount Charles de Spoelberch de Lovenjoul (1836–1907), whom Rodin visited in 1892 so that he could consult Lovenjoul's collection of documents relating to the writer.[75]

These exhaustive, initial efforts likely resulted in the realistic model called *Balzac in a Frockcoat*, datable to about 1891, but the maquette that was apparently first approved was described in 1892 as a nude with folded arms. This model, customarily referred to

62. Rodin, Auguste
Nude Study of Balzac
(*Reduction, Type "C"*)
Probably 1892. Musée Rodin cast
11/12 in 1972
Bronze
Georges Rudier
30 × 16¾ × 13½ in.
(76.2 × 42.5 × 34.3 cm)
Iris and B. Gerald Cantor
Foundation

by an alphabetic classification as the "C" nude, *Nude Study of Balzac (Type "C";* pl. 62),[76] was then to be draped. Although from the first study it retained the arms folded across the chest, it had a new, heroic, and aggressive stance that significantly changed the relaxed attitude of the earlier, realistic sculpture. Rodin by then must have already dispensed with the idea of using the dandy's frockcoat in favor of the white robe Balzac was known to have preferred to wear while writing furiously at home in the middle of the night. The robe offered a timeless alternative to contemporary costume, just as the long shirts of *The Burghers of Calais* did. They were neutral enough to lack any historicizing details. Writing to Zola about the nude figure in February 1892, Rodin proposed using a process to judge its effect—oddly enough, a process that had already produced significantly unpleasant results for him with the *Monument to Victor Hugo*—that is, setting up a two-dimensional facsimile to obtain an idea of how the finished monument would be perceived when erected on its pedestal:

> When the figure is ready, and maybe even has its robe I shall contact Jourdain [for the pedestal] but that will only be in about six or seven months at the earliest ... . Once my figure is done, or very advanced, it will be photographed and we shall have a canvas maquette of it prepared so that you can judge its size [or proportion] in relation to its site, even though this décor does not give the effect of the real thing.[77]

The length of time mentioned in this letter did not bode well, because it meant that Rodin would already be significantly behind the schedule he had promised his patrons.

In 1893 progress was stymied by Rodin's need to complete *The Burghers of Calais* and the dual monuments to Victor Hugo. Rodin complained of anemia and the departure of the model who was posing for him. In 1894 the obesity of his nude sketch was criticized, and although Rodin seemed determined to pursue its elaboration at that time, the criticism may have led him simultaneously to create another, more graceful type, *Balzac in a Dominican Robe* (pl. 63), which has previously been considered an earlier work (c. 1892) from the time when Rodin was more preoccupied with achieving a realistic recreation of Balzac's appearance.[78] The boldly expressionistic modeling of the head further suggests that this sculpture is more to be associated with the later studies for the *Monument to Balzac* than with the initial phase, when realism was of greater concern to the sculptor. At about the same time he may have applied an earlier study of a more realistic head to a bust related to this model.

Late in 1893 Rodin warned Zola that the final cast of an enlarged maquette could not be made before 1895. The real urgency now came from his champion, Zola, whose presidency of the society would end in 1894. Zola begged Rodin to advance the sculpture. Even while recognizing that as a fellow artist he ought to show empathy with the creative process unfolding at its own pace, Zola had every reason to want to see the sculpture completed by the artist he himself had chosen, and the monument unveiled while he was still president of the society that organized its financing. Be that as it may, Rodin apparently reached his own decisive moment in the commission at about that time (1894). Having draped the obese nude, he seems to have become dissatisfied with it. Recollecting the strength of his nude *Jean d'Aire*, the enlargement of which he would soon have had cast in bronze, he created a new model in its place: the composition custom-

63. Rodin, Auguste
Balzac in a Dominican Robe
1893–94, Musée Rodin cast 9 in 1981
Bronze
Georges Rudier
41¾ × 20⅛ × 20 in.
(106 × 51.2 × 50.8 cm)
Iris and B. Gerald Cantor Collection,
promised gift to the Iris and
B. Gerald Cantor Foundation

arily called *The Athlete* under the alphabetic designation "B," which was elaborated during 1896 (*Athlete "F"*: pl. 64) toward the definitive monument.[79]

The society's consternation at the delay came to a head in 1894. Some members, fearing that Rodin would never realize the monument, called for a cancellation of his contract and the reimbursement of the funds that had been paid to him. They had a fiduciary responsibility toward the subscription's contributors to provide a finished monument. Rodin, despite having other projects to complete at the same time, insisted that he intended to fulfill his contract for the *Monument to Balzac*. Amazingly he also agreed that year to take on the *Monument to Labor* and the monument to the Argentine education reformer Domingo Faustino Sarmiento, and to have the *Burghers* cast. The new president of the society, the poet Jean Aicard, sympathized with Rodin's artistic requirements. To avoid an ugly and ultimately useless lawsuit a compromise was proposed in which the funds would be put in escrow until the sculptor produced a monument that satisfied his patrons. Aicard, however, trumped by other members of the society who demanded that a deadline be imposed on the sculptor, resigned in protest over protocol in the negotiations. Some of these disputes were caused by an envy of Zola and the fact that he had unilaterally advanced funds to Rodin without having first obtained the society's permission. Much was reported in the press. The different factions in the society—Realist, Naturalist, Symbolist—had specific opinions about Rodin's behavior and his sculpture. These would ultimately be overshadowed by a national dispute related to the Dreyfus Affair in 1898.

The society elected a new president at the end of 1894, just when the Romantics' idea of the supreme position of the artist as a superhuman creator was climbing toward its zenith. Rodin was now not only defended in the controversy but also lionized in a variety of publications. In overripe language beside which even Rilke's most florid scribblings paled, the humanitarian journalist Séverine (Caroline Rémy), who should have known better, went so far as to imply that Rodin was a kind of obstetrician who delivered Beauty from Nature.[80] Not to be outdone, the Belgian Symbolist Georges Rodenbach, in a remarkable panegyric about Rodin's genius, repeated the same ridiculous metaphor two years later.[81]

In 1895, not without controversy, Zola was re-elected president of the society. Rodin apparently made little significant progress on the monument until very late that year, and Zola's disillusionment is easy to discern in their correspondence.[82] However, Rodin was now arriving at the massive form he would adapt for Balzac's head (pl. 65) as it was finally realized, and in April 1896 the maquette for the nude was said to be close to completion. This report would be more correct a year later. At that time a nude figure more closely corresponding to *The Athlete* was being draped. The head was being modified and the pose was given more of its now-characteristic sweep. An enlargement was probably undertaken in the summer of 1897 and completed in October, but it was not until March 1898 that Rodin was finally satisfied with what he had created.[83]

The existing studies suggest that Rodin had almost systematically closed the drapery around the figure, unified the contour of its silhouette, and achieved a sense of movement within the composition by manipulating only the planes of the drapery and the lapels, and by adjusting its plastic density. In contrast, Balzac's originally benevolent face had been transformed into a violently modeled, haughty mass that seemed to be

64. Rodin, Auguste
Nude Study of Balzac as an Athlete (Type "F")
c. 1896, Musée Rodin cast 5 in 1974
Bronze
Georges Rudier
37 × 16 × 15½ in.
(94.0 × 40.6 × 39.4 cm)
Iris and B. Gerald Cantor Foundation

65. Rodin, Auguste
Monumental Head of Balzac (Enlargement)
1897, Musée Rodin cast 9/12 in 1980
Bronze
Georges Rudier
20 × 17½ × 16 in.
(50.8 × 44.5 × 40.6 cm)
Iris and B. Gerald Cantor Foundation

marked by an almost frightening hostility. Viewed in the round, the head offered arresting profiles and turned away from the prime viewing point of the whole sculpture. Jourdain's pedestal responded to this ambiguity with its beveled corners. The whole form of the statue was drawn up and backward, so that Balzac seemed ready to regard with disdain the swarm of humanity that would circulate around the pedestal in the Place du Palais Royal. No allegorical figure (although one was originally contemplated) was to be applied to Jourdain's pedestal[84] as an intermediary between this strangely austere, quite narrow, and shocking figure, and the living people below its feet. The sculpture's form could ultimately be interpreted more as a marker than a statue, and thus Rodin, probably unwittingly but very appropriately, inserted his monument into the long tradition of funerary and commemorative monuments that for centuries had been described as pyramids.[85]

The Italian sculptor Medardo Rosso asserted that his influence on Rodin, as shown by the *Balzac*, was decisive. His claims, analyzed afresh by Antoinette Le Normand-Romain, stated that Rodin had used not only his sense of pyramidal composition and understanding of form in its environment but also his sculptures' relation to light and the way they approximate to painting.[86] Rosso's sculptures are perhaps well described by a word normally used for photographic media: photosensitive. The title of the yellow wax head *Child in Sunlight* (Rome, Museo nazionale dell'arte moderna) makes sense only if its features are understood as having been violently flattened optically by the effect of intense sunlight. His *Street Scene at Night* (location unknown) similarly requires prolonged intellectual reconstruction in the viewer's imagination, both of the reverse effects of lamplight in the evening and of the scene itself, whereas Rodin did ultimately design his monument with an environment in mind—a real one, the square in front of the Palais Royal, which was just as real as the square in which he preferred *The Burghers of Calais* to be witnessed. The pyramidal composition that Rosso claimed to be visible in Rodin's *Balzac*, as derived from his own *Bookmaker* (Museo nazionale dell'arte moderna), had in fact been recognized by Gabriele d'Annunzio in 1892 in the work of another of their colleagues, Prince Paul Troubetzkoy: "[He] guides the eye of the viewer ... right to the head of the hero ... . He chooses the pyramid for his basic form; it is, in the abstract geometric sense, the symbol of greatness; having broken it off at the top, he uses the head of the hero to mark off that ideal apex. Nothing distracts the viewer's eye, trained on that apex."[87] It is likely that Troubetzkoy was influenced by Rosso.

On April 30, 1898, the final enlarged plaster of *Balzac* was exhibited in Paris. Some critics admired it, but mostly the statue was vilified, provoking an outburst from the public, unusually vehement comments from many journalists, and an insulting response from its patrons in the literary society. Dozens of articles about the sculpture's slow progress had already been published, tracing Rodin's every effort. Now there was even more in the press, and the facts were bitterly exaggerated in tandem with the debate over the innocence of Alfred Dreyfus, the army captain who had been falsely accused in 1894 of spying for Germany. In January 1898, when efforts to reopen the case had brought the real traitor to trial and exonerated Dreyfus, Zola launched his famous call for justice and was condemned to a year in prison for it. Zola's sentence was soon overturned. Riots and assassination attempts against his and Dreyfus's supporters followed.

The fact that Dreyfus was Jewish brought forth a horrifying wave of anti-Semitism in France.

Stupidly, many critics confounded artistic novelty with political radicalism, and they condemned Rodin's sculpture as though it represented an affront to France's honor.[88] The committee of the literary society announced that it did not "recognize" (*reconnaître*) Balzac, and therefore enjoined Rodin from having the sculpture cast in bronze. This decision on its own also produced a torrent of debate, primarily around the interpretation of the word "recognize." It seems logical to believe that the patrons of the monument had chosen this word for its very vagueness in order to dissolve the contract with Rodin.

In response, Rodin's partisans decided to launch their own subscription to buy the sculpture, but much to his displeasure, a number of signatories to this subscription had also supported Dreyfus's innocence. Rodin remained convinced that Dreyfus was guilty. Zola's role in Dreyfus's defense and in *The Monument to Balzac* embittered Rodin's view of the controversy over his sculpture and of the man who had, in fact, been one of his most enlightened patrons.[89] In the end he decided not only against having the sculpture cast,[90] but also against selling it to private collectors who could have realized it in bronze. Nevertheless, *Balzac* remained one of his preferred creations.

It is unique in his œuvre. Its odd silhouette and its equally particular completeness remain without compare in his work. From this sculpture, simultaneously expressionistic and abstract, he would not only revert to a previous formula that combined an allegorical pedestal with a standing realistic figure, but also concurrently demonstrate his facility in realizing a vivid portrait of a deceased person, as in the bust of Barbey d'Aurevilly. The former is illustrated by the Sarmiento monument, which was supported on a pedestal carved to represent a striding Apollo, whose figure was derived from one that was called "Mercury" when treated as an independent figure, but which had originally been created a decade earlier for *The Gates of Hell*. It is widely recognized that late in life Rodin achieved a kind of classicizing tranquillity in his sculpture. This can be seen in the Whistler memorial and in the serene maquette for the *Monument to Puvis de Chavannes* (pl. 66). They may have been inspired by Classical prototypes: respectively the *Victory Writing on a Shield*[91] and *Pothos* attributed to Skopas (Rome, Capitoline Museum). Taken together, these very different compositions that were created after the *Balzac* reveal how remarkably versatile, truly creative, and expressive Rodin was. This is why his career and his sculptures are endlessly fascinating.

ACKNOWLEDGMENTS

A sincere expression of gratitude is here offered to Iris Cantor, Chairman and President of the Iris and B. Gerald Cantor Foundation, and to Rachael Blackburn, former Executive Director, for having included this essay in the catalog of the Foundation's collection. Recognition is also due to Anne Diederick and the staff of the Balch Research Library of the Los Angeles County Museum of Art, and to the staff of the library of the Research Institute of the Getty Trust for facilitating research in its preparation. Rina Brill and Danna Freedy Kay, both of the Cantor Foundation, kindly assisted in obtaining photographs to illustrate it. Sophie Grossiord of the Maison de Victor Hugo in Paris graciously provided information about, and bibliographic material for, Henry Cros's *Apotheosis of Victor Hugo*, in addition to other information about Rodin's *Heroic*

66. Limet. Jean-François
Monument to Puris de Charannes
No date
Aristotype
Paris. Musée Rodin

Bust of Victor Hugo. Professor A.A. Donohue of Bryn Mawr College generously recommended bibliographic material for Classical sculptures referred to in this essay. Finally. the extraordinary contribution made by Antoinette Le Normand-Romain of the Musée Rodin to a better. well-documented understanding of Rodin's work cannot be underestimated.

Notes

1 Most dates (unless otherwise noted) are derived from John Tancock. *The Sculpture of Auguste Rodin*. Philadelphia Museum of Art/Boston: David R. Godine. 1976. Compare the list provided by Elisabeth Lebon. "Rodin et le socle." in *Le Serment des Horaces. Revue d'art international*. no. 5. Autumn 1990–Winter 1991. pp. 166–68. which includes some portrait busts reused in funerary monuments.

2 These dates are proposed by J.A. Schmoll gen. Eisenwerth. "Rodin und Lothringen." in *Rodin-Studien*. Munich: Prestel-Verlag. 1983. p. 33 (agreeing with Thérèse Charpentier. "Notes sur le Claude Gellée de Rodin. à Nancy." in *Bulletin de la Société de l'Histoire de l'art français*. 1968. pp. 149–58).

3 For the competition see Véronique Wiesinger. "Le concours pour le monument à Claude Gellée …." in

86

Anne Pingeot *et al.*, *La Sculpture française au XIXe siècle*, exhib. cat., Paris: Grand Palais, 1986, pp. 218–23. For an alternate date (1884) for the commission, see Monique Laurent, "Le monument des Bourgeois de Calais ...," in Claudie Judrin, Monique Laurent, and Dominique Viéville, *Auguste Rodin. Le monument des Bourgeois de Calais (1884–1895)* ..., exhib. cat., Paris: Musée Rodin and Calais: Musée des Beaux-Arts de Calais, 1977 (hereafter referred to as *Calais*-1977). Most sources give 1889 as the date of the commission.

4   Véronique Wiesinger, "Les Collaborations," in Pingeot, *op. cit.* note 3, pp. 111–14. Wiesinger p. 114 notes that Rodin's practitioners Jules Desbois, Victor Peter, and Jean Escoula were occupied with the sculpture while Rodin was traveling in Tours; Rodin was already away investigating the appearance of Balzac for the monument whose commission he received that year.

5   The logical reason suggested by Nicole Barbier, *Marbres de Rodin*, Paris: Musée Rodin, 1987, p. 236.

6   See Antoinette Le Normand-Romain, *Rodin, Whistler, et la Muse*, Paris: Musée Rodin, 1995 (hereafter referred to as ALNR-*Whistler*).

7   Tancock, *op. cit.* note 1, p. 602; illustrated p. 604.

8   *Ibid.*, p. 340.

9   ALNR-*Whistler*, *op. cit.* note 6, p. 60.

10   *Ibid.*, pp. 60–61, quoting an interview with Rodin: "I am unfortunately a slow worker ... the conception of [a] work slowly takes shape and slowly comes to maturity." Later, in 1912, he remarked: "I cannot work quickly ... . It often happens that I must turn from the work I have been engaged on to another ... till I feel myself called back to the first."

11   Catherine Chevillot, *La République et ses grands hommes*, Paris: Hachette/Réunion des Musées Nationaux, 1990, p. 2.

12   *Ibid.*, p. 3. See also Julius von Schlosser, "Von modernen Denkmalkultus," in *Vorträge der Bibliothek Warburg* (1926–27), pp. 1–21.

13   Jacques de Caso and Patricia B. Sanders, *Rodin's Sculpture. A Critical Study of the Spreckels Collection*, San Francisco and Rutland, Vermont: Fine Arts Museums of San Francisco and Charles E. Tuttle Co., Inc., 1977, p. 243 and note 5, p. 247: the monument was proposed for the Champs-Elysées, a site from which monuments were now (1912) to be banned.

14   See *Calais*-1977, *op. cit.* note 3, pp. 29–30.

15   Chantal Martinet, "La Souscription," in Pingeot *et al.*, *op. cit.* note 3, pp. 231–32; note 3, p. 417 for the cautious estimate of two-thirds of the sculptures. Subscriptions included municipal, regional, national, and international commissions, in addition to those undertaken by private groups. See *ibid.*, pp. 235–38 for the democratic nature of public subscriptions.

16   A summary is given by Monique Laurent, "Le monument des Bourgeois de Calais ...," in *Calais*-1977, *op. cit.* note 3, p. 14.

17   Viéville, in *Calais*-1977, *op. cit.* note 3, p. 64: Rodin's undated letter to the mayor of Calais, a response to the mayor's letter of January 11, 1888? (Archives municipales de la ville de Calais): "Je suis très bousculé en ce moment pour me débarasser de ma porte qu'il faut que je finisse coûte que coûte." Viéville notes Albert Elsen's reference (Albert Elsen, *Rodin's Gates of Hell*, Minneapolis: University of Minnesota Press, 1960, note p. 149) to the fact that 1888 marked the government's abandonment of the commission for *The Gates of Hell*.

18   Quoted in Annette Haudiquet, ed., *Les Bourgeois de Calais, fortunes d'un mythe*, exhib. cat., Calais: Musée des Beaux-Arts et de la Dentelle, 1995, p. 7.

19   Viéville, in *Calais*-1977, *op. cit.* note 3, pp. 26–27. Mary Jo McNamara, *Rodin's "Burghers of Calais"* (Ph.D. dissertation, Stanford University, 1983), Ann Arbor, 1987, pp. 6–7, recognizing the importance of Hermann Bünemann's *Auguste Rodin, Die Bürgher von Calais*, revised edn, Stuttgart, 1957 for research about the earlier projects. In about 1764 an idea for a monument to Eustache de Saint-Pierre had also been proposed: J.A. Schmoll gen. Eisenwerth, "Les Bourgeois de Calais," in *Auguste Rodin: Les Bourgeois de Calais—Postérité et filiations*, exhib. cat., Marl: Skulpturenmuseum Glaskasten Marl and Mariemont: Musée Royal de Mariemont, 1997, pp. 22–23 (hereafter referred to as *Schmoll-Mariemont*). Schmoll also notes that 1845 was two years before the five-hundredth anniversary of the events of 1347.

20   McNamara, *ibid.*, pp. 21–27, emphasizes the social, economic, and political hostility between Calais and Saint-Pierre: Calais had earlier been a wealthy city but declined while Saint-Pierre's fortunes grew. Furthermore, Calais was more nationalistic and patriotic, while Saint-Pierre was primarily socialist. Viéville, in *Calais*-1977, *op. cit.* note 3, p. 30, quotes the mayor's speech to his municipal council on

September 26, 1884, in which he says "our city is going to cease to be herself."

21 See Viéville, in *Calais-1977*, *op. cit.* note 3, pp. 29–30.

22 See McNamara, *op. cit.* note 19, pp. 29, 45–47, for the charges of treason; the intelligent interpretation of Edward III's strategy is offered by *Schmoll-Mariemont*, *op. cit.* note 19, p. 18. Schmoll points out also that Edward III had already put the inhabitants of Caen to the sword for having resisted him.

23 See Christian Borde, "Romantisme ou vérité historique …." in *Les Bourgeois de Calais …*, *op. cit.* note 18, especially pp. 24–28; and McNamara, *op. cit.* note 19, pp. 41–42. Although Froissart's veracity had been challenged, the fact that he was secretary to Philippa, the queen of England who saved the Burghers, would in any event give credence to his narrative. He was her secretary in 1361–65, at the time when he wrote his chronicles. Philippa was Flemish and of French descent, so she may also have been sympathetic to the inhabitants of the city close to her country of origin. Froissart, a native of nearby Valenciennes, was honored in a monument (1855–56) there by Henri Lemaire: see Annie Scottez, "Jehan Froissart," in Dominique Viéville, *De Carpeaux à Matisse, La Sculpture française de 1850 à 1914 dans les musées … du Nord de la France*, exhib. cat., Calais, Lille, Arras, *et al.* 1982–83, pp. 244–45.

24 Viéville points this out in *Calais-1977*, *op. cit.* note 3, pp. 44, 113. For the remarkable breadth of the advertising of the subscription, see *ibid.*, p. 105.

25 *Ibid.*

26 *Ibid.*, pp. 31–33.

27 See *Calais-1977*, *op. cit.* note 3, and McNamara and *Schmoll-Mariemont*, both *op. cit.* note 19.

28 "La photographie des personnages isolés ne dit absolument rien pour ceux qui ne sont pas initiés à votre idée." letter of January 11, 1888. *Calais-1977*, *op. cit.* note 3, p. 64.

29 *Ibid.*: "et ferait naître de mauvaises impressions. Mais sitôt que j'aurai rassemblé les grandes figures je les ferai photographier … puis les mettre ensemble et les harmoniser." *Schmoll-Mariemont*, *op. cit.* note 19, p. 29 emphasizes how much this interchange reveals about Rodin's working method. Rodin's repositioning of elements in an ensemble was happening simultaneously in *The Gates of Hell*. Given the complexity of the silhouettes' overlapping in the final monument, it is unlikely that a drawing could have done the ensemble justice, whereas a series of photographs could illustrate all the figures—even the one that is ordinarily concealed from the standard front view of the *Burghers*.

30 Quoted by Frederic Grunfeld, *Auguste Rodin: a Biography*, New York: Henry Holt, 1987, p. 309, from an unsigned interview, "Au jour le jour. La Statue de Balzac," in *Le Temps*, Paris, September 12, 1888.

31 See Alain Beausire, Jacques Vilain, *et al.*, *Claude Monet–Auguste Rodin: Centenaire de l'exposition de 1889*, exhib. cat., Paris: Musée Rodin, 1989.

32 In addition to the first cast in Calais, other casts are at the Ny Carlsberg Glyptotek (Copenhagen), the Houses of Parliament of Great Britain (London), the park of Mariemont (Brussels), the Kunsthaus (Basle), the Musée Rodin (Paris), the Norton Simon Museum (Pasadena, California), the Rodin Museum (Philadelphia), the National Museum of Western Art (Tokyo), the Hirshhorn Museum and Sculpture Garden (Washington, D.C.) and the Metropolitan Museum of Art (New York).

33 Laurent, in *Calais-1977*, *op. cit.* note 3, p. 222.

34 *Ibid.*, pp. 230–33, dating from 1900 to 1904. See also Anne Lajoix, "Auguste Rodin et les arts du feu." in *Revue de l'Art*, no. 116, 1997:2, pp. 83–84, kindly brought to the author's attention by Constance and David Yates.

35 She might also have created some of the tiny sketches for heads of the figures, for example one called *Head of a Slave*, which closely resembles the head of Jean de Fiennes: see Mary Levkoff, *Rodin in His Time: the Cantor Gifts to the Los Angeles County Museum of Art*, Los Angeles/New York: LACMA/Rizzoli, 2000, p. 117.

36 *Schmoll-Mariemont*, *op. cit.* note 19, p. 18.

37 *Calais-1977*, *op. cit.* note 3, p. 76. These sculptured groups of the entombment of Christ are now generally called *tableaux vivants*; well-known examples from the fifteenth and early sixteenth centuries can be found in France in Solesmes, Tonnerre, and Chaource, in addition to examples in northern Italy. A famous painting by Ary Scheffer (1819; see *Les Bourgeois de Calais, Fortunes d'un mythe*, *op. cit.* note 18, cat. 45) may also have inspired Rodin: see *Schmoll-Mariemont*, *op. cit.* note 19, pp. 20–21, citing Christian Beutler, "Les Bourgeois de Calais de Rodin et d'Ary Scheffer," in *Gazette des Beaux-Arts*, LXXIX, January 1972, pp. 39–50.

38 See Graham Robb, *Victor Hugo*, London/New York, 1997, as well as the remarkably well condensed and illustrated introduction by Sophie Grossiord, *Victor Hugo, "Et s'il n'en reste qu'un …"* in the series

"Découvertes Gallimard," no. 341, Paris, 1998. For Hugo's imagery, see Pierre Georgel *et al.*, *La Gloire de Victor Hugo*, exhib. cat., Paris: Grand Palais, 1985. Much of the text included in the present essay is derived from the author's didactic material written for the exhibition *Rodin's Monument to Victor Hugo*, Los Angeles: LACMA 1998–99, organized by the Iris and B. Gerald Cantor Foundation.

39 Hugo was among the first to defend the merit of Gothic architecture, which had been roundly condemned (literally and figuratively) by the advocates of Neo-classicism (see, for example, Patrice Béghain, ed., *Guerre aux démolisseurs!: Hugo, Proust, Barrès …*, Vénissieux: Paroles d'aube, 1997). Rodin credited Hugo with having awakened his own appreciation of Gothic architecture: see Ruth Butler, *Rodin: the Shape of Genius*, New Haven: Yale University Press, 1993, p. 434.

40 Compare Jeanine Parisier Plottel, "Rodin's Victor Hugo," in *Rodin's Monument to Victor Hugo*, exhib. cat., Los Angeles, Portland, Oregon, New York, and Jacksonville, Florida, 1998, pp. 23–26 (hereafter referred to as *Rodin's Monument*).

41 Butler, *op. cit.* note 39, p. 172 and p. 529, note 7. Rodin's continued sensitivity about the accusation of having used a life-cast can be judged from a letter he wrote in October 1888 about the *Burghers of Calais*, in which he pointed out to the mayor of Calais that he needed time to model the figures because he did not work from life-casts, which to him were simply the equivalent of photographs, not artistic creations (quoted in *Schmoll-Mariemont, op. cit.* note 19, p. 29).

42 See Butler, *op. cit.* note 39, pp. 172–76 for Rodin's portrait. For Dalou's monument, see Jane Mayo Roos, "Steichen's Choice," *Rodin's Monument, op. cit.* note 40, fig. 35.

43 Jane Mayo Roos, "Steichen's Choice," in *Rodin's Monument, op. cit.* note 40, pp. 62–67. The church had been deconsecrated for use as a mausoleum in 1791–93; it was partially returned to religious use in 1806, and then completely in 1816. In 1830 it was again reinstituted as a pantheon.

44 Jane Mayo Roos, "Rodin's *Monument to Victor Hugo*," in *The Art Bulletin*, LXVIII, no. 4, December 1986, p. 640 (hereafter referred to as Roos 1986).

45 Roos, in *Rodin's Monument, op. cit.* note 40, pp. 65–66; Roos's essay in *Rodin's Monument* and her article give much information about the commission, particularly the political aspects of its later episodes. Further significant details are provided by Cécile Goldscheider, "Rodin et le monument de Victor Hugo," in *La Revue des Arts*, no. 3, October 1956, pp. 179–84.

46 "Pour maintenir … l'unité de la conception *générale*," as quoted by Goldscheider, *op. cit.* note 45, p. 179.

47 Roos, *Rodin's Monument, op. cit.* note 40, p. 68.

48 Tancock, *op. cit.* note 1, p. 423, note 26, quotes a report of 1891 referring to the second idea (the *Apotheosis*), the back of which was criticized for being uninteresting: "it will offer little of interest to the public, which will move around the group and see it from all sides, like the *Mirabeau* that will be erected in the opposite arm of the transept." ("dénuée d'intérêt … au Public qui doit tourner autour du groupe … comme … le *Mirabeau* qui s'élève dans le bras de la croix opposé".) One wonders if the free-standing sculptures were intended to diminish the effect of the church's cruciform plan by partly filling the arms of the transept.

49 Quoted in Goldscheider, *op. cit.* note 45, p. 179: "assis sur le rocher de Guernesey, derrière lui dans la volute d'une vague, les trois muses de la Jeunesse, de l'Age mûr et de la Vieillesse, lui soufflent l'inspiration."

50 The bronze is illustrated in Roos, *Rodin's Monument, op. cit.* note 40, fig. 36. Antoinette Le Normand-Romain advised (in a letter to Danna Freedy Kay of the Iris and B. Gerald Cantor Foundation) that the bronze (15 in./38.2 cm high) could not be datable much before the end of 1889, and is more likely to date from 1890; the plaster, which is considerably larger (32 in./80.7 cm) may be a further advanced version of the bronze; it is possibly the maquette seen by the committee on March 22, 1890 and refused in July of that year. Both Roos 1986, *op. cit.* note 44, p. 643, note 60, and Goldscheider, *op. cit.* note 45, p. 181 and p. 180, fig. 3, believe that a plaster nude of Hugo with his right hand to his lips (Paris, Musée Rodin) must be either the first or a very early sketch. It might, however, be one of Rodin's later ideas for modifying his horizontal composition when preparing a final maquette for the nude, marble version eventually installed in the Jardin du Palais Royal.

51 Roos 1986, *op. cit.* note 44, pp. 644–45.

52 *Ibid.*, p. 645: "La commission *à l'unanimité* se prononce contre le projet … qui manque de clarté et dont la silhouette est confuse. L'artiste sera donc prié de présenter une autre esquisse en se préoccupant du milieu architectural … ."

53 The *Mask of Iris* appears to be derived from a small head that was attached to the pre-existing headless

stretching figure. The vertical format of a smaller marble sculpture—*Orpheus and Eurydice*, dated 1893 (New York, Metropolitan Museum of Art, inv. no. 10.63.2)—offers a useful comparison to *The Apotheosis of Victor Hugo*. See Clare Vincent, "Rodin at the Metropolitan Museum of Art," in *The Metropolitan Museum of Art Bulletin*, XXXVIII, no. 4, Spring 1981, p. 12.

54 See Levkoff, *op. cit.* note 35, pp. 133–34. Sophie Grossiord, chief curator of the Maison de Victor Hugo, kindly informed the author (letter of September 16, 1998) that the example of the *Heroic Bust* in that museum was commissioned from Rodin by Paul Meurice, founder of the museum in Victor Hugo's house on the place des Vosges, for the inauguration of the museum. A plaster cast was supplied in 1903 (this furnishes a *terminus* for the date of the sculpture); Rodin had it retrieved the next year in order to produce the bronze, which was not delivered until 1908. As for the so-called "silencing" maquette for the monument, the awkwardness of the assemblage of different pieces (arms, head, muses) suggests that it may date from this time and not from an early stage, as suggested by Roos and Goldscheider (see note 50).

55 Antoinette Le Normand-Romain, "La Voix Intérieure," in *Rodin: La Voix Intérieure*, exhib. cat., Marseilles: Musée des Beaux-Arts de Marseille, 1997, pp. 11–36 provides a well-illustrated, fine synopsis of the later stages of development of the horizontal version. See also Anne Pingeot, "Fragments tirés d'un ensemble, I: Rodin: Le monument à Victor Hugo," in Anne Pingeot, ed., *Le Corps en morceaux*, exhib. cat., Paris: Grand Palais and Frankfurt: Schirn Kunsthalle, 1990, pp. 203–15.

56 Le Normand-Romain, *op. cit.* note 55, pp. 26–27, emphasizes the importance of this fragmentary figure: when the plaster maquette of *Victor Hugo* was exhibited in 1897, Rodin insisted that it was complete.

57 In 1901 a plaster cast of the 1897 plaster maquette was commissioned by Carl Jacobsen for his Ny Carlsberg Glyptotek; this was delivered in 1905. It also included supporting scaffolds. See Anne-Birgitte Fonsmark, *Rodin: La collection du Brasseur Carl Jacobsen à la Glyptothèque*, Copenhagen: Ny Carlsberg Glyptotek, 1988, p. 131.

58 This was Jean-Alexandre Pézieux: see Grunfeld, *op. cit.* note 30, pp. 364–65: "The joining is impossible … it will be a terrible lot of trouble … he thinks it will all arrange itself in the marble." Pézieux noticed the admirable beauty of *The Interior Voice*. His critique of the awkward passages in the rest of the assemblage was full of insight: he remarked that such things could be expected from an artist who wasn't capable of doing better, "but Rodin? He's so skilled it wouldn't have cost him any effort."

59 Quoted by Goldscheider, *op. cit.* note 45, p. 182. Tancock, *op. cit.* note 1, p. 422 note 21, referring to Rodin's own condemnation of the monument to Michelangelo erected in the Piazzale Michelangelo in Florence, criticized the eventual casting in bronze of Rodin's horizontal composition. Rodin's attitude may have changed by 1912 when he visited Italy again.

60 See Nicole Barbier, *Marbres de Rodin*, Paris: Editions du musée Rodin, 1987, pp. 224–29.

61 For example, Giambologna's bronze fountain figure in Bologna, 1563–66.

62 ALNR-*Whistler*, *op. cit.* note 6, p. 50.

63 Tancock, *op. cit.* note 1, p. 422, note 21, uses this passage to condemn the casting of *Victor Hugo* in bronze, but Rodin's negative statement must have been made after the Italian journeys in 1912 or 1915, and his opinions then, 25 years after Larroumet rescued the horizontal *Victor Hugo*, may reflect Rodin's late recognition of the validity of the concept of "truth to material."

64 See note 34.

65 *The Apotheosis of Victor Hugo* (1.68 × 2.42 m/5½ × 8 ft), 1903–05, inv. no. MVH473/177. With admirable efficacy, Sophie Grossiord, curator-in-chief of the Maison de Victor Hugo, very generously provided photographs and articles about this relief: Jean-Luc Olivié, "Un atelier et des recherches subventionnés par l'État: Henry Cros à Sèvres," in *La Sculpture du XIXe siècle, une mémoire retrouvée* …, Paris: La Documentation française, Rencontres de L'Ecole du Louvre, 1986, p. 197; Martine Bailly, Béatrice Beillard, and Jean-Luc Olivié, "*L'Apothéose de Victor Hugo*, pâte de verre monumentale de Henry Cros (1840–1907)," in *Revue de l'Association des restaurateurs d'art et d'archéologie de formation universitaire*, December 1990, pp. 37–40.

66 *Le Matin*, July 13, 1908, quoted by Antoinette Le Normand-Romain, "1898: La postérité appartient aux sifflés," in Antoinette Le Normand-Romain *et al.*, *1898: le Balzac de Rodin*, exhib. cat., Paris: Musée Rodin, 1998, p. 93. The present essay is based substantially on this exhaustive study of the *Monument to Balzac* (hereafter referred to as ALNR-*1898*).

67 See Graham Robb, *Balzac: a Biography*, New York: Norton, 1994.

68 Françoise Pitt-Rivers, *Balzac et l'Art*, Paris: Chêne, 1993, p. 133.

69 ALNR-*1898*, *op. cit.* note 66, p. 20, on the fact that no sculpture marked his grave for at least four years after he died.

70 *Ibid.*, pp. 19–21.

71 *Ibid.*, pp. 19–20. See also a fine analysis of the history of the commission by Jacques de Caso, "Rodin and the Cult of Balzac," in *The Burlington Magazine*, CVI, no. 735, June 1964, pp. 279–84, specifically p. 280 on the monument in Tours, which was unveiled in 1889. An excellent summary is provided by Tancock, *op. cit.* note 1, pp. 425–59.

72 ALNR-*1898*, *op. cit.* note 66, p. 26.

73 *Ibid.*, pp. 26–27.

74 *Ibid.*, pp. 29–30; p. 89: on June 6, 1898, Marquet officially withdrew.

75 *Ibid.*, pp. 36, 128–29.

76 *Ibid.*, pp. 41–44.

77 *Ibid.*, pp. 44–45. Letter in Fondation Custodia (Paris), no. 1994-A: "quand [*sic*] au piédestal quand ma figure aura sa valeur et peut-être sa robe j'avertirai Jourdain mais ce n'est qu'en dernier lieu dans six ou 7 mois … Quand [*sic*] à la dimension, ma figure faite, ou très avancée, on la photographiera et on fera une maquette en toile et vous verrez sur la place la dimension. Quoique ces décors embrouillent, parce qu'ils ne donnent pas l'effet véritable."

78 *Ibid.*, p. 46, for Le Normand-Romain's suggestion of redating this figure. For the traditional date compare, for example, Levkoff, *op. cit.* note 35, p. 104.

79 ALNR-*1898*, *op. cit.* note 66, pp. 47, 59, and cat. nos. 76–87 for Le Normand-Romain's remarkable observation about the relationship between *Jean d'Aire* and *Balzac as an Athlete* ("F").

80 Quoted in Grunfeld, *op. cit.* note 30, p. 337.

81 Quoted in ALNR-*1898*, *op. cit.* note 66, p. 64.

82 *Ibid.*, pp. 57–59.

83 *Ibid.*, pp. 64–67.

84 *Ibid.*, pp. 83–84: he had considered putting a gilt bronze allegory of Fame on the pedestal but decided against it.

85 For example, the sixteenth-century monuments to the hearts of Henri II (by Germain Pilon, 1563) and Anne de Montmorency (by Barthélémy Prieur, c. 1570–80) (both in the Louvre) were described in sixteenth- and seventeenth-century sources as pyramids. Andrea Riccio's Paschal Candelabrum in the Santo in Padua (1507–15) was also referred to as a pyramid at the end of the sixteenth century, presumably because it was associated with the symbolism of Christ's death.

86 ALNR-*1898*, *op. cit.* note 66, pp. 84–87.

87 Quoted in Gianna Piantoni and Paolo Venturoli, ed., *Paolo Troubetzkoy 1866–1938*, exhib. cat., Verbania Pallanza: Museo del Paesaggio, 1990, p. 19.

88 See the fine summary by Frédérique Leseur, "Affaire *Balzac*, affaire Dreyfus: une campagne de presse," in ALNR-*1898*, *op. cit.* note 66, pp. 171–86, and in Grunfeld, *op. cit.* note 30, pp. 370–84.

89 The well-known names are given by Grunfeld, *op. cit.* note 30, p. 379.

90 It was cast finally in 1939 and installed at the intersection of the boulevards Raspail and Montparnasse in Paris. Other casts are in the Middelheim Museum (Antwerp, on loan from the Koninklijk Museum voor Schone Kunsten), the Museum of Modern Art (New York), the Los Angeles County Museum of Art, Norton Simon Museum of Art (Pasadena, California), the Shell Offices (Hemel Hempstead, UK), Eindhoven (Netherlands), the Fort Worth Art Center (Fort Worth, Texas), the Houston Museum of Fine Arts (Texas), and the Hirshhorn Museum and Sculpture Gardens, Smithsonian Institution (Washington, D.C.). This list is taken from Tancock, *op. cit.* note 1, p. 459.

91 For *Victory writing on a Shield* attributed to Skopas, see Tonio Hölscher, "Die Victoria von Brescia," in *Antike Plastik*, X, 1970, in particular pp. 72–73, and by the same author, *Victoria Romana*, Mainz am Rhein: Zabern, 1967. The bronze in Brescia (excavated in 1826) is assumed to have been derived from the *Venus of Capua* in Naples; the *Venus de Milo* is considered a variant. Whether or not Rodin was aware of this relationship is unknown, but his first drawings for the monument to Whistler are clearly dependent on the composition of *Victory writing on a Shield*. Compare ALNR-*Whistler*, *op. cit.* note 6, pp. 64–65; the drawing is reproduced as cat. 1 and 2, pp. 82–83.

Rodin's *Gates of Hell*: Sculptural Illustration of Dante's *Divine Comedy*

Aida Audeh

On August 16, 1880, Auguste Rodin received a commission from the French government to create a monumental bronze door composed of relief sculpture panels representing Dante Alighieri's (1265–1321) *Divine Comedy* (*Divina Commedia*), an epic poem about the redemption of the author's soul, comprised of three books: *Inferno, Purgatorio,* and *Paradiso*.[1] *The Gates of Hell* (pl. 67), as they came to be called, were to be placed at a planned, but not realized, French national museum of the decorative arts. Rodin took his task seriously, working on his project for some 20 years before finally exhibiting a partially complete plaster version of the *Gates* in 1900—its casting in bronze would not occur until after his death in 1917.

The Gates of Hell served as a fount for many of Rodin's best-known individual sculptures, including *The Thinker* (frontispiece; pl. 73), *The Kiss* (pl. 83), and several other works in the Cantor Foundation's collection. While scholars of Rodin's work understand that the initial commission called for an illustration of Dante's *Divine Comedy*, the actual meaning of Rodin's *The Gates of Hell* with direct reference to Dante's text has never been fully established in the literature of the history of art.[2] This, the final great work of this extremely influential sculptor's career and the crucible of the ultimate expression of his art, has neither been effectively explored in relation to its source in Dante nor to other nineteenth-century French interpretations of his epic poem.[3]

The Romantic traditions in art and literature of the early nineteenth century had rehabilitated Dante as a poet of genius, and his works continued to enjoy great popularity in France throughout the century. The effect of Dante's work on artists in France was far from limited to its best-known interpretations such as those by Eugène Delacroix (*The Barque of Dante*, 1822) and Jean-Baptiste Carpeaux (*Ugolino*, 1865). The great proliferation of imagery in the nineteenth century related to Dante's life and work should be considered as the context for Rodin's interpretation of Dante's text.

Rodin's *Gates of Hell* must also be seen in the broader literary context, which was extremely influential upon nineteenth-century French imagery and the critical literature surrounding its reception and interpretation. This necessarily involves literary figures such as Chateaubriand, Stendhal, Balzac, and Hugo, each of whom found in Dante's *Inferno* inspiration for their own works of poetry or prose. These authors, finding both deep spiritual significance in Dante's journey and descriptions of torment in his Hell that evoked parallels in the "human comedy" of modern life, often evoked the Italian poet's image and epic in their own literary expressions. The literary identity of Dante constructed by French Romantic authors establishes certain tropes that are repeated consistently throughout the century. These tropes generated within Romantic literature—for example, the association of Dante with Michelangelo as the greatest

68. Rodin, Auguste
Women Damned
c. 1885, Musée Rodin cast 2/12 about
1978
Bronze
Coubertin
8 × 10¾ × 5 in.
(20.3 × 27.3 × 12.7 cm)
Iris and B. Gerald Cantor
Foundation

embodiments of the Romantic ideal of creative genius, the identification of Dante with ideas of revolutionary political liberty and forced exile, the concept of Dante as the Artist/Philosopher who judges mankind from his exalted position, and so on—frame and inform the discourse surrounding visual production in terms of both the subject of works of art and the persona of their creators.

Rodin's thorough knowledge of Dante's text brings his *Gates* much closer to its original source than was previously believed. During the 20 years Rodin worked on the sculpted form of *The Gates of Hell*, he produced hundreds of preparatory drawings that relate to nearly every canto in the *Inferno* and venture occasionally into *Purgatorio* and *Paradiso*. Most important, these drawings often feature Rodin's notations taken directly from Dante's text in French translation alongside the sketched image. Proving Rodin's close reliance on the actual text requires tracing these notations back to the specific translation the sculptor consulted in the process of creating *The Gates of Hell*. In several instances identification of the figures or the specific scene and canto within the *Inferno* portrayed in these sketches depends wholly upon determination of the particular translation used. The tenor of each translation differs and may have affected Rodin's perception of Dante's text, in addition to providing important evidence as to the intended identity of the figures in Rodin's sketches. For this reason I have retained the French titles of Rodin's sketches in this essay.

These sketches not only indicate that Rodin meditated deeply upon the meaning of Dante's text, but also bear a remarkable similarity to Medieval and Renaissance illustrations of the *Divine Comedy* that had come to constitute its particular iconographic tradition in France and Italy. This iconographic concordance reveals Rodin's method of textual interpretation as he absorbs Dante's words and attempts to develop a gestural language particular to the sin or torment described in each canto, with a legibility characteristic of the illustrations of the Middle Ages. By digesting each episode in this way, Rodin arrives at much the same solution for its representation as its earliest interpreters, which, through a series of sketched variations of gestural expression and figure grouping, he then gradually transforms into a sculpted form on the *Gates*. *The Gates of Hell* is heir to Medieval and Renaissance depictions of the *Divine Comedy* expressed within the context of the nineteenth century's artistic and literary vision of the poet.

Rodin's initial ideas for the visual narrative structure of *The Gates of Hell* follow the tradition of Ghiberti's *Gates of Paradise* (commissioned 1425), with various episodes of the *Inferno* illustrated within separate panels (pls. 69, 70). However, his ultimate design for the *Gates* eliminates the separate panels in favor of the dispersion of the individual characters and figural groups on the barren and rocky landscape of Hell, and is thus more closely allied with Medieval and Renaissance traditions of illustration for Dante's poem. Rodin's placement of this multitude of characters within an architectural framework is, in fact, particularly associated with the attempts by Renaissance illustrators to represent the whole of the *Inferno*, or a particular canto within it (pl. 71), or the entrance to Hell itself as described in *Inferno* Canto III (pl. 72).

What Rodin accomplishes in sculpture with *The Gates of Hell* is something that is usually confined to the domain of painting or book illustration—a comprehensive representation of an epic text.[4] In this sense Rodin is indeed a very "literary" sculptor. something of which he was accused by unfavorable critics during his own lifetime. but which should no longer be considered a detriment to his art.[5] The most effective way to demonstrate this intimate relation between sculpture and text is to examine Rodin's *Gates of Hell.* in light of Dante's *Divine Comedy.* and marked by several works derived from the *Gates* held in the Cantor Foundation's collection. While some of the individual works derived from the *Gates* (such as the *Ugolino* group [pl. 108] and *The Kiss*) are based on subjects from Dante's *Inferno* that enjoyed great popularity in French art of the nineteenth century, many others originate in lesser-known episodes that demonstrate Rodin's familiarity with Dante's text. Rodin chose to include episodes and characters drawn not only from Dante's *Inferno.* but also from *Purgatorio* and *Paradiso* as prominent features of *The Gates of Hell.*

71. Unknown artist
Inferno VI
No date
Manuscript illustration
Turin. Biblioteca Nazionale

Rodin's *Gates of Hell* and Dante's *Inferno*

The Thinker—Dante, Inferno 1

Dante begins his journey from Hell to Purgatory and finally to Paradise with the following immortal lines:

> In the middle of the journey of our life. I came to myself within a dark wood where the straight way was lost ... . I cannot rightly tell how I entered there. I was so full of sleep at that moment when I left the true way ... . After I had rested my wearied frame for a little I took my way again over the desert slope ... [and encountered three beasts. a leopard representing lust, a lion representing pride, and a wolf representing covetousness]. This last put such heaviness on me ... that I lost hope of the ascent; and like one who rejoices in his gains and when the time comes that makes him a loser has all his thoughts turned to sadness and lamentation, such did the restless beast make me. coming against me and driving me back step by step to where the sun is silent.
>
> *Inferno* I. 1–60[6]

72. Zuccaro. Federico
Inferno III
1587
Text illustration

The Thinker (pl. 73) represents Dante at the moment when he realizes what is before him—the inevitability of his descent to Hell as a result of his loss of faith. He must experience its nine descending circles of sin and punishment, from Lust to Treachery, and finally see Satan himself before beginning his long ascent up the mountain of Purgatory to the Heavens of Paradise and finally to God. Dante's journey through Hell is guided by the ancient Roman poet Virgil. Dante's first and only true love, Beatrice, guides him through the Heavens to God.[7]

Rodin's *Thinker* recalls the oldest traditions of illustrating Dante in the dark wood of Canto I of the *Inferno*. In Medieval and Renaissance illustrations. Dante is consistently represented in an attitude of sleep (in reference to his description of being "so full of

73. Rodin. Auguste
The Thinker
1880. reduced in 1903. date of cast
unknown
Bronze
Alexis Rudier
14¾ × 7⅞ × 11⅜ in.
(37.5 × 20 × 28.9 cm)
Iris and B. Gerald Cantor
Foundation

75. Unknown artist
Inferno I
Siena. *c.* 1345
Illuminated manuscript
Florence. Biblioteca Laurenziana

76. Rodin. Auguste
Dante et Virgile méditant
c. 1880
Drawing
Paris. Musée Rodin

74. Rodin. Auguste
Fallen Caryatid with Stone
1880–81. enlarged 1911–17. Musée
Rodin cast II/IV in 1988
Bronze
Coubertin
52½ × 33 × 39 in.
(132 × 83.3 × 99.1 cm)
Iris and B. Gerald Cantor
Foundation

sleep" when he lost the straight path of God) or of melancholia (pl. 75: in reference to his momentary rest and his "sadness and lamentation" after his encounter with the three beasts). Rodin provides us with one drawing that represents his nude Dante seated on a rock. with Virgil behind him. both meditating (pl. 76).

This traditional image of Dante's melancholic nature survived within nineteenth-century French artistic production. occurring even as late as the early twentieth century.[8] It is also a consistent presence in biographies of the poet. first appearing in Boccaccio's *Life of Dante* in the fourteenth century. Boccaccio described Dante as a man "of moderate height [who] after reaching maturity. was accustomed to walk somewhat bowed ... his expression ever melancholy and thoughtful."[9] Boccaccio's text was the source for many later biographies. including those published in nineteenth-century France to which Rodin could have had access.[10] Legendary incidents in Dante's life and aspects of his behavior included in Boccaccio's biography were also repeated in later texts. becoming part of the generally known mythology of the poet's experiences and character.[11]

Importantly. French scholars of the legends and incidents of Dante's life recounted by his earliest Italian biographers knew of the "Sasso di Dante." the rock in Florence upon which the poet was said to have sat and pondered the creation of his *Divine Comedy*. This anecdote was repeated in nineteenth-century French travel literature of the genre *"voyages en Italie"* and in texts on the life of Dante such as Sebastien Rhéal's introduction to his translation of the *Divine Comedy* of 1854:

> At one side of Santa Maria del Fiore there is a small block of white marble ... carrying this inscription: "Sasso di Dante." There. before his exile. it is said that he often went to sit. Neither Santa Maria nor the Campanile existed then. From there. which was his usual seat. he could contemplate the Baptistery. his "bel San Giovano." the most important monument of the piazza.[12]

The legend of the Sasso di Dante was the subject of at least one painting. *Dante observant la construction de la cathédrale de Florence* (Dante Observing the Construction of the Cathedral of Florence: pl. 77) by Alphaeus Cole. exhibited at the Paris Salon of 1900.[13] The city of Florence itself referred to the traditional image of Dante as a melancholic seated thinker when it commissioned its *Memorial to Dante* (pl. 78) for the interior of the church of Santa Croce in 1829—the work that perhaps sheds the most direct light on Rodin's conception of Dante in *The Gates of Hell*. Rodin lived in Italy for several months in order to learn for himself the secrets of its great sculptors Michelangelo and Donatello. and visited Florence in 1876. The *Memorial to Dante* in Santa Croce is placed immediately next to the tomb of Michelangelo within the nave of the church. Rodin. in view of his strong interest in both Michelangelo and Dante. very likely saw both funerary monuments during his stay in Florence.

The *Memorial to Dante* includes two large allegorical figures on either side of the poet—an arrangement echoed in Rodin's original conception of *The Gates of Hell*. As early as 1881 Rodin planned to add "two colossal figures" on either side of his monumental *porte*.[14] These figures. as seen in the Stanford University bronze of *The Gates of Hell*. are Adam and Eve. discussed below within the context of Dante's *Paradiso*.

However, what is quite striking regarding *The Thinker*, whose identity has been obscured over time, is the consistent response of viewers of the work in the late nineteenth century, who recognized the figure for who he was: Dante. Gustave Geffroy, for example, writing in 1889, describes his encounter with Rodin's work:

> The *Gates of Hell* is an assemblage, in animated actions, of the instincts, the fates, the desires, the hopelessness, of all that cries and moans in man … . In front, before the writhing crowds which constitute Hell, Dante, or rather the Poet, nude, having no signs which make recognizable an epoch or nationality, meditates, but in the fashion of a man of action in repose.[15]

As Rodin himself said regarding the identity of *The Thinker* on *The Gates of Hell*:

> The Thinker has a story. In the days long gone by, I conceived the idea of the Gates of Hell. Before the door, seated on a rock, Dante, thinking of the plan of his poem. Behind him, Ugolino, Francesca, Paolo, all the characters of the *Divine Comedy*. This project was not realized. Thin, ascetic, in his narrow robe, Dante separated from the whole would have been without meaning. Guided by my first inspiration I conceived another thinker, a naked man, seated upon a rock, his feet drawn under him, his fist against his teeth, he dreams. The fertile thought slowly elaborates itself within his brain. He is no longer dreamer, he is creator.[16]

77. Cole, Alphaeus
Dante observant la construction de la cathédrale de Florence
1900
Oil on canvas
Dimensions and location unknown

Fugitive Love, I am Beautiful, The Kiss—Paolo and Francesca, Inferno V

Canto V of the *Inferno* finds Dante in the circle where the Lustful are punished. Here he meets the tragic lovers of Medieval Italy, Paolo Malatesta and Francesca da Rimini, the subject of innumerable works of art throughout the nineteenth century. Rodin, like many artists and writers of nineteenth-century France, was extremely moved by Dante's dramatic meeting with the lovers, and devoted at least three sculpture groups and nearly the entire right pilaster panel of *The Gates of Hell* to this moment of the *Inferno*.

In Dante's Hell, Paolo and Francesca and all the Lustful are swept by an incessant whirlwind, representative of the uncontrolled nature of their passions in life (pl. 79). Dante asks the dolorous couple to approach and tell him of their love:

78. Ricci, Stefano
Memorial to Dante, Florence, Church of Santa Croce
1829
Marble
Engraving reproduced in E. Rod, *Dante* (Paris, 1891)

> As doves, summoned by desire, come with wings poised and motionless to the sweet nest, borne by their will through the air … [Paolo and Francesca came] … to us through the malignant air.
>
> *Inferno* V, 82–87

Rodin represents the couple in the whirlwind in two additional works in the Cantor Collection: *Fugitive Love* and *I am Beautiful* (pls. 80, 81). As they hover in the air before Dante, Francesca tells the tragic tale of their adulterous love while Paolo weeps, recounting her sad marriage to Paolo's brother and their murder at his hands upon his discovering them in an embrace. Rodin's *Fugitive Love* is well within the tradition of

interpretation of the two lovers seen in painting and book illustration of the nineteenth century, such as that by Eugène Deully of 1897 (pl. 82). The scene is not commonly found in sculpture owing to the technical difficulties inherent in representing two figures floating in space.[17] Rodin's *I am Beautiful* is unprecedented in artistic representations of the whirlwind scene of Canto V, but surely represents the ecstacy of their passion for one another, as present in death as it was in life.

Rodin's well-known work *The Kiss* (pl. 83), derived from embracing figures on the right pilaster of the *Gates*, represents the moment when the illicit love and sad fate of Paolo and Francesca are sealed—the moment of their first kiss as they read a chivalric tale of romance. Francesca describes for Dante the moment just before their murder:

> We read one day for pastime of Lancelot ... . Many times that reading drew our eyes together and changed the colour in our faces, but one point alone it was that mastered us: when we read that the longed-for smile was kissed by so great a lover, he who never shall be parted from me, all trembling, kissed my mouth ... . That day we read in it no farther.
>
> *Inferno* V, 127–38

As in many interpretations of their fatal moment, Rodin presents the couple embracing, and in Paolo's left hand we see the book that enticed them to their first kiss. Gustave Doré's illustration for a French edition of the *Inferno* published in 1861 is representative

81. Rodin, Auguste
I am Beautiful
Before 1886, date of cast unknown
Bronze
Alexis Rudier
27¾ × 12 × 12½ in.
(70.5 × 30.5 × 31.7 cm)
Iris and B. Gerald Cantor
Foundation

83. Rodin, Auguste
The Kiss
c. 1881–82, date of cast unknown
Bronze
Alexis Rudier
34 × 17 × 22 in.
(86.4 × 43.2 × 55.9 cm)
Iris and B. Gerald Cantor
Foundation

of nineteenth-century interpretations, including the kiss, the book dropping from the hand of Francesca, and the enraged husband preparing to strike the couple at once with his dagger. Doré's interpretation is also typical in that it presents the characters with Medieval trappings of costume and architecture, following very much the Troubadour traditions of painting, where this scene originated as an artistic subject in the early nineteenth century.[18] Freeing the figures of Paolo and Francesca from these trappings, Rodin departs from tradition to reveal the essence of a passion that survives the grave.

82. Deully, Eugène
Françoise de Rimini (Paolo et Francesca aux enfer)
1897
Oil on canvas
Lille, Musée des Beaux-Arts

Despairing Adolescent, Fallen Caryatid with Stone—The Prodigal, Inferno VII

In Canto VII Dante encounters souls guilty of Avarice (excessive hoarding) and those guilty of excessive spending, the Prodigal. The Avaricious and the Prodigal are punished by "rolling weights by main force of chest," clashing together when they meet at the half-circle, turning and clashing again on the opposite side. Rodin represents these sinners with figures known independently as *Despairing Adolescent* (pl. 85) and *Fallen Caryatid with Stone* (pls. 74, 142). Traditionally this episode of the *Inferno* is illustrated literally, with the souls straining to push their boulders in an eternal and pointless joust (pl. 86). Rodin's *Fallen Caryatid with Stone* is the most direct translation of this scene.

However, in the less traditional representation of the Prodigal in Rodin's *Despairing Adolescent*, he omits the weight—the physical manifestation of the burden of excessive

LEFT: 85. Rodin, Auguste
Despairing Adolescent
1882. Musée Rodin cast 3/12 in 1975
Bronze
Godard
16¼ × 5½ × 5¾ in.
(41.3 × 14 × 14.6 cm)
Iris and B. Gerald Cantor Collection,
promised gift to the Iris and
B. Gerald Cantor Foundation

RIGHT: 84. Rodin, Auguste
Adam
1880–81. Musée Rodin cast 7/8 in
1984
Bronze
Coubertin
75½ × 29½ × 29½ in.
(191.8 × 74.9 × 74.9 cm)
Iris and B. Gerald Cantor Collection,
promised gift to the Iris and
B. Gerald Cantor Foundation

concern for earthly possessions. Rodin instead develops in gestural form the essence of the sin. In Rodin's study for the *Prodigal Son* (pl. 87), the artist makes direct reference to the Biblical account of the Prodigal Son: he who spends his wealth recklessly in the world, then returns home to the welcoming arms of his father who celebrates his return with the killing of the "fatted calf." In a further study for this episode (pl. 88) we see the son, the Prodigal, standing alone with his arms outstretched and empty, waiting for them to be filled again, expressing the irresponsibility of his loss of material possessions and the need to return to safety. This is the figure who appears in *The Gates of Hell*.

The similarity of the gesture of the Prodigal to that of the desperate lover Paolo in *Fugitive Love* and *I am Beautiful* is telling. Both types of sin involve a reckless abandonment of rationality to sensual or material excess. Both episodes are contained within the first circles of Hell, in which the Incontinent, those who suffer a weakness of flesh and, more seriously, of spirit, are punished.

Another sculptural group on the *Gates*, known as *Avarice and Lust*, is located near the *Prodigal Son* on the lower right panel. Rodin takes the gesture of the Prodigal—the outstretched arms reaching endlessly into space—and fills it with the material body of a woman, representing the hoarding spirit of the Avaricious. Appropriately the expression and gesture of the Hoarder are those of anguished grasping, not of secure possession.

86. Unknown artist
Inferno VII
Pisa, c. 1345
Drawing
Chantilly, Musée Condé

87. Rodin, Auguste
L'Enfant prodigue
c. 1880
Drawing
10¾ × 7½ in.
(27.5 × 19.3 cm)
Paris, Musée Rodin

The Sirens—The Three Furies, Inferno IX

Rodin's *Sirens* (pl. 89) as they are on the *Gates*, three voluptuous kneeling figures, represent the three Furies whom Dante encounters in Canto IX of the *Inferno*. Dante and Virgil have just crossed the River Styx with the boatman Phlegyas (the subject of Delacroix's *Barque of Dante*) and are approaching the infernal city of Dis, the entrance to the lower regions of Hell. As Dante draws nearer to the walled city, he sees the three Furies. Dante writes:

> My sight had drawn me wholly to the lofty tower with the glowing summit, where all at once were risen erect three hellish, blood-stained Furies that had the parts and the bearing of women and were girt with hydras of bright green, and for hair ... had little serpents and horned snakes twined about the savage temples.
>
> *Inferno IX, 34–42*

The Furies threaten to summon Medusa, one of the Gorgon sisters of Greek mythology, who is able to turn men to stone with one glance. Virgil warns Dante not to continue looking at the Furies for fear that Medusa join them, and covers Dante's face with his own hands to shield him.

That Rodin studied this scene closely for his *Gates of Hell* is demonstrated by a drawing with the inscription "*si Méduse te voyait, tu aurais cessé de vivre*" ("if Medusa sees you, you will cease to live"; pl. 90), nearly a direct quotation of Dante's words in French translation. Rodin's drawing recalls the traditional iconographic means of representing Virgil's protective gesture towards Dante at the sight of the Furies, found in some of the earliest illustrated editions of the *Divine Comedy* (pl. 91). His sculpted

88. Rodin, Auguste
Ombre
c. 1880
Drawing
Paris, Musée des Arts Décoratifs

RIGHT: 89. Rodin, Auguste
The Sirens
1880s, Musée Rodin cast 5/12 in 1967
Bronze
17 × 17¼ × 12⅝ in.
(43.2 × 43.8 × 32.1 cm)
Brooklyn Museum of Art, Gift of the
Iris and B. Gerald Cantor
Foundation

Furies are innovative in that they are presented as dangerously sensual beauties, without the serpents and snakes but all the while as alluring and threatening to Dante's senses.

Rodin's interest in Canto IX continues: near the top right corner of the left panel of *The Gates of Hell* he includes the Angel in Dante's text who swiftly arrives to open effortlessly the locked Gates of Dis for the poet and his guide. The arriving Angel is visible at the left of Dante and Virgil in the fifteenth-century illustration in plate 91. Further on, beyond the gates of the city of Dis, Dante encounters the open tombs of the Heretics, heated from below by incessant flames. As Dante leaves the circle of the Heretics he stops to contemplate the last of them in Canto XI, the apparently closed tomb of Pope Anastasius (pl. 92), who, according to Medieval belief, had denied the divine birth of Christ. At the base of the right and left panels of *The Gates of Hell* Rodin has placed two closed tombs, much like that of Anastasius represented in the fifteenth-century illustration in plate 92.[19]

The Three Shades—The Sodomites, Inferno XVI

The Three Shades (pl. 95) derive from an episode described in Canto XVI of the Inferno, in which Dante meets the condemned souls of three Florentines punished for

109

sodomy—or, in Dante's terms, for committing Violence Against Nature.[20] The Sodomites are burned by an incessant rain of fire and are continually in motion for fear of being unable to shield themselves from the scorching rain if they were to rest. The three Florentines recognize Dante as a countryman and approach him. Dante describes their motion:

> When they reached us all three made a wheel of themselves as champions are used to do, naked and oiled, watching their advantage for a grip before the exchange of thrusts and blows; and thus wheeling each kept directing his face towards me, so that they had both their neck and their feet in continual movement.
>
> *Inferno* XVI, 19–27

90. Rodin, Auguste
Si Méduse te voyait, tu aurais cessé de vivre
c. 1880
Drawing
6 × 4½ in.
(15.2 × 11.6 cm)
Paris, Musée Rodin

In Rodin's many drawings for this episode we see at first static representations of three figures and sometimes of single figures. In further studies (pl. 93) Rodin experiments with the means for portraying the wheeling, circling and continual motion of the three Florentines as they speak to Dante, recalling Medieval representations of this scene (pl. 94). These drawings relate as well to an engraving in the Cantor Foundation's collection, *La Ronde* (The Round), an allegorical Dance of Death signifying that each in his turn will die. In further drawings, very close to the final appearance of *The Three Shades* on *The Gates of Hell*, the three figures are intertwined, connecting at various parts of the body, twisting from head to foot to represent their continual and perverse guard, as Dante describes.

The Three Shades crown *The Gates of Hell*, mirror images of each other, embodying the interminable motion of the Sodomists, the barren love of the homosexuals in Dante's *Inferno* who turn continually in unproductive association.

91. Vitae Imperatorum Master
Inferno IX
Lombard, c. 1440
Manuscript illustration
Paris, Bibliothèque Nationale

She Who Was the Helmet-maker's Beautiful Wife—Thaïs, Inferno XVIII

In Canto XVIII Dante meets those who have ended in Hell for practicing in life the fraudulence of flattery. Dante's description of this round is particularly vivid, comparing the stench of its moat to "a filth which seemed to have come from human privies" (*Inferno* XVIII, 112–14). In this moat are the Flatterers, including the legendary prostitute Thaïs: "that foul and dishevelled drab who is scratching herself there with her filthy nails and is now squatting, now standing up" (*Inferno* XVIII, 127–36).

Rodin's figure of Thaïs, related to the free-standing work known independently by various titles including *The Old Courtesan* and *She Who Was the Helmet-maker's Beautiful Wife* (pl. 98), is found on the lower left pilaster of *The Gates of Hell*. Old and withered, she resembles Medieval and Early Renaissance representations of the aged prostitute enduring her punishment in Hell. Nineteenth- and early twentieth-century images, such as that by Antoine Auguste Thivet (pl. 96),[21] tend to present a voluptuous Thaïs, reminiscent of her youthful heyday of power and betrayal. Rodin's placement of his withered Thaïs immediately adjacent to the figure of a nude young woman is an effective means of communicating the truth of the deceitful courtesan's wanton past on earth and her wretched existence in Hell.

92. Vitae Imperatorum Master
Inferno XI
Lombard, c. 1440
Manuscript illustration
Paris, Bibliothèque Nationale

93. Rodin, Auguste
Danse
c. 1880
Drawing
3⅞ × 5¼ in.
(9.8 × 13.4 cm)
Paris, Musée Rodin

94. Fruosino, Bartolomeo di
Inferno XVI
Italy, c. 1420
Manuscript illustration
Paris, Bibliothèque Nationale

Danaïd, Falling Man—The Barrators, Inferno XXII

A very interesting and complex situation is presented in Rodin's studies for Cantos XXI and XXII. These cantos describe the fifth round of the eighth circle of Hell, in which the Barrators, or Swindlers in Public Office, are punished. These sinners are among the Fraudulent, the worst of souls who use their God-given mental agility for sinful ends. The Barrators represent those who commit sin under the surface, such as simony in the Church, this being betrayal of public trust in state office.

The Barrators find themselves immersed in boiling pitch, continually taunted by horned and winged black devils who lift them from the tar with their taloned forks, flay their skin, carry them, and throw them again into the pitch. Dante describes the sinners in the pitch as raising their backs occasionally like "dolphins," and then quickly drawing themselves back under the boiling tar to avoid the taunts of the demons. Rodin's *Danaïd* (pl. 99), as she appears on the *Gates*, represents one of these miserable souls rising momentarily from the pitch. A more complex situation is presented by the *Falling Man* (pl. 102), who is also likely to be a "climbing man" in the context of Dante's text. Rodin's drawings of this episode are nearly sequential in nature, falling very much into the tradition of Late Medieval and Early Renaissance representations of this scene, such as the drawing by Botticelli (pl. 97). Rodin's sequence of drawings, *Démon retirant une ombre du feu* (Demon taking a shade from the fire; pl. 100), *Démon emportant une ombre* (Demon carrying a shade; pl. 101), and *Démon montrant une ombre tombée dans la poix* (Demon showing a shade fallen in the pitch; pl. 103), seems to combine Dante's description of the sequence of events:

> I saw behind us a black devil come running up the ridge ... with open wings and light on his feet! His shoulder, which was sharp and high, was laden with both thighs of a sinner and he held him clutched by the tendons of his feet ... . He flung him [the sinner] down and turned back on the flinty ridge ... . The sinner plunged in and rose again, doubled up, but the demons that were covered by the bridge cried: 'The Holy Face is not here for thee ... .' Then they caught at him with more than a hundred gaffs.
>
> *Inferno* XXI, 25–57

It seems as if Rodin has taken the sequences of imagery developed in these drawings and placed them in the *Gates*, using the entire right panel as a backdrop. We see at the summit of the *Gates* in the tympanum, the figure of the only horned demon who appears in this sculpture, his grimace and outstretched arm as menacing as Dante describes. A little below this figure, near the trumeau of the doors, on the right panel, a male figure appears to fall toward the *Gates'* lower level, his arms stretched out in a cruciform position. And near the bottom of the right panel, nearly hidden, we find a male figure plunging head first into the black abyss in a position similar to that of the shade held by his ankles in Rodin's drawing. On the upper left panel we see the *Falling Man*, or perhaps "Climbing Man," trying to escape the pitch below. The position and gesture of the *Falling Man* are remarkably like those in Josef Anton Koch's representation of the *Inferno* (pl. 104) at the Casino Massimo in Rome. Koch indicates clearly that

96. Thivet, Antoine Auguste
Le Huitième Cercle
1903
Oil on canvas

97. Botticelli, Sandro
Inferno XXI
c. 1495
Manuscript illustration
Berlin Kupferstichkabinett

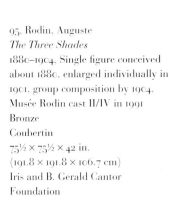

95. Rodin, Auguste
The Three Shades
1880–1904. Single figure conceived
about 1880, enlarged individually in
1901, group composition by 1904.
Musée Rodin cast II/IV in 1991
Bronze
Coubertin
75½ × 75½ × 42 in.
(191.8 × 191.8 × 106.7 cm)
Iris and B. Gerald Cantor
Foundation

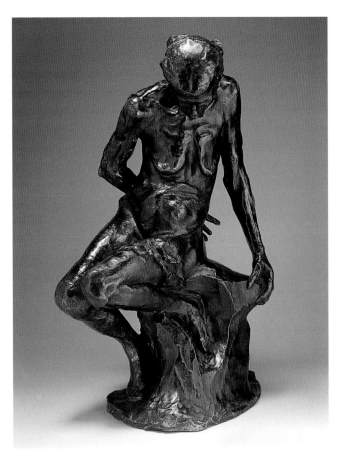

98. Rodin, Auguste
*She Who Was the Helmet-maker's
Beautiful Wife*
1880–90, date of cast unknown
Bronze
Perzinka
19¾ × 11½ × 10¼ in.
(50.1 × 29.2 × 26 cm)
Iris and B. Gerald Cantor Collection,
promised gift to the Iris and
B. Gerald Cantor Foundation

this figure is one of the Barrators tormented by the demons of Canto XXI and XXII. However, further research is needed to determine Rodin's familiarity with Koch's version of this episode.

Mask of the Man with the Broken Nose, Ugolino—The Treacherous, Canto XXXIII

Rodin's *Mask of the Man with the Broken Nose* (pl. 107) and all the faces bordering the tympanum represent the multitude of anonymous sinners in the lowest circle of Hell, nearest to Satan. Unlike most conceptions of Hell, Dante's lowest depth is all of ice, analogous to the absolute coldness of heart and soul of those furthest from God. As they walk on the ice, Virgil warns Dante to watch his step, so as not to "tread on the heads of the wretched." Dante sees under his feet "a lake which through frost had the appearance of glass and not of water" in which the sinners guilty of Treachery (betrayal of trust) are confined. In Cocytus, as Dante calls his Ice Hell, sinners are frozen in a lake of ice up to their faces, some looking down, and the worst of them looking up. Dante's poignant description of these last sinners recalls Rodin's drawing (pl. 105):

The very weeping there does not let them weep and the pain which finds a barrier in the eyes turns inward to increase the anguish: for the first tears form a cluster and, like a crystal visor, fill up all the hollow under the brows.

Inferno XXXIII, 94–99

99. Rodin. Auguste
Danaïd
1885–89. Musée Rodin cast 8 in 1979
Bronze
Godard
12¾ × 28¾ × 22½ in.
(32.4 × 73 × 57.2 cm)
Iris and B. Gerald Cantor
Foundation

100. Rodin, Auguste
Démon retirant une ombre du feu
c. 1880
Drawing
4½ × 3¾ in.
(11.6 × 9.6 cm)
Paris, Musée Rodin

101. After Rodin, Auguste
Démon emportant une ombre
c. 1880
Colour photogravure by Jean
Boussard, Manzi, Joyant & Cie
6½ × 3¾ in.
(16.5 × 9.7 cm)
Bordeaux, Musée Goupil: Direction
des Musées de Bordeaux

102. Rodin, Auguste
Falling Man
1882, Musée Rodin cast 8 in 1979
Bronze
Godard
23¼ × 17 × 10 in.
(59 × 43.2 × 25.4 cm)
Iris and B. Gerald Cantor
Foundation

Rodin's drawing is bathed in a blue wash of watercolor, which implies the glacial lake of Cocytus—the only circle in the *Inferno* in ice rather than flames.

Dante's encounter with Ugolino in Canto XXXIII is, along with the story of Paolo and Francesca, one of most popular scenes of the *Inferno*, and was the first of its episodes to form the subject of a Salon painting in nineteenth-century France.[22] Rodin's sculptural group of *Ugolino and Sons* (pl. 108) is based on a moment in Ugolino's story that is less common as a subject. Rodin's many drawings reveal that he did indeed study the episode closely, from Dante's initial encounter with Ugolino in Cocytus to the recounting of the events on earth that lead to Ugolino's tragic end.

Dante first encounters Ugolino in the ice hell of Cocytus, gnawing "like a dog on a bone" on the neck of his arch-enemy Ruggieri, who is there with him for eternity. Ugolino looks up from his "cruel repast" to tell Dante his story (pl. 106). As a result of a political coup, Ugolino had been locked in a tower by Ruggieri and left there with his three sons to die of starvation. Ugolino tells Dante of his realization of their fate when he heard the doors to the tower being nailed shut. As Ugolino faced the inevitability of their starvation he put his hands to his teeth in horror; this particular moment is the subject of most nineteenth-century representations of the Ugolino story, such as that by Carpeaux. His children, misunderstanding their father's gesture as one of hunger, offer to give him their own bodies to eat to ease his pain. This scene is the subject of a drawing by Rodin in the collection of the Musée Rodin in Paris. Then the inevitable happens as the children, weaker than their father, die first, leaving Ugolino in his grief as the last

103. Rodin, Auguste
*Démon montrant une ombre tombée
dans la poix*
c. 1880
Drawing
6⅓ × 5¼ in.
(16.1 × 13.3 cm)
Paris, Musée Rodin

LEFT: 104. Koch, Josef Anton
Inferno
c. 1825
Rome, Casino Massimo

105. After Rodin, Auguste
Masque d'homme
c. 1880
Colour photogravure by Jean
Boussard, Manzi, Joyant & Cie
4¾ × 3¾ in.
(12.4 × 9.7 cm)
Bordeaux, Musée Goupil: Direction
des Musées de Bordeaux

to succumb. This is the moment, one of utter desperation and helplessness, that Rodin chooses to illustrate sculpturally on *The Gates of Hell*:

> I saw the three drop one by one during the fifth day and the sixth; therefore I gave myself, now blind, to groping over each and for two days called on them after they were dead. Then fasting had more power than grief.

Inferno XXXIII, 70–75

106. Rodin, Auguste
*Ugolin interrompt son cruel repas et
raconte au Dante son histoire*
c. 1880
Drawing
7½ × 2¾ in.
(18.9 × 7 cm)
Paris, Musée Rodin

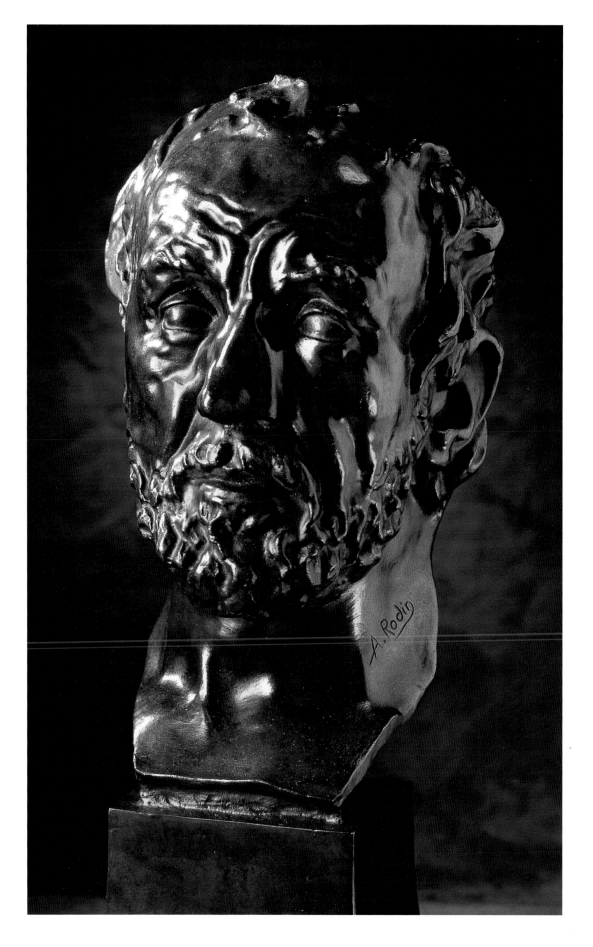

107. Rodin, Auguste
*Mask of the Man with the Broken
Nose*
1863–64. Musée Rodin cast 3/12,
probably in the 1970s
Bronze
Coubertin
12½ × 7¼ × 6 in.
(31.8 × 18.4 × 15.2 cm)
Iris and B. Gerald Cantor
Foundation

This represents the lowest level of Hell—the last significant episode before Dante's sight of Satan in Canto XXXIV and his subsequent ascent to Purgatory and then Paradise.

108. Rodin, Auguste
Ugolino and Sons
c. 1881–82, date of cast unknown
Bronze
No foundry mark
16⅛ × 16⅞ × 19⅞ in.
(41 × 42.9 × 50.5 cm)
Iris and B. Gerald Cantor
Foundation

Rodin's *Gates of Hell* and Dante's *Purgatorio*

The Prayer—Purgatorio

Although Rodin's personal interest seems to have been centered on the *Inferno*, it should be recalled that he was commissioned originally to represent the entire *Divine Comedy* in his *Gates of Hell*. However, the specific subjects of innumerable drawings Rodin composed in preparing the commission remain to be identified and very probably will reveal their source to be in *Purgatorio* and *Paradiso*.

A case in point is the figure of *The Prayer* (pl. 110), which on *The Gates of Hell* includes arms, head, and feet, based on a drawing Rodin called *Purgatoire* (Purgatory:

109. After Rodin, Auguste
Purgatoire
c. 1880
Colour photogravure by Jean
Boussard, Manzi, Joyant & Cie
5¾ × 3¼ in.
(14.9 × 8.1 cm)
Bordeaux, Musée Goupil: Direction
des Musées de Bordeaux

110. Rodin, Auguste
The Prayer
1910, Musée Rodin cast 3/12 in 1977
Bronze
Georges Rudier
49½ × 21⅝ × 19⅝ in.
(125.7 × 54.9 × 49.8 cm)
Iris and B. Gerald Cantor Collection,
promised gift to the Iris and
B. Gerald Cantor Foundation

112. Rodin, Auguste
Dante et Béatrice
c. 1880
Drawing
7¾ × 5 in.
(12.8 × 19.5 cm)
Paris, Musée Rodin

RIGHT: 113. Botticelli, Sandro
Paradiso V (Dante and Beatrice)
c. 1495
Manuscript illustration
Berlin Kupferstichkabinett

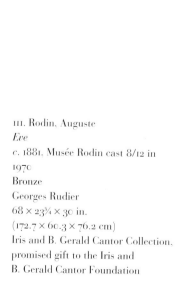

111. Rodin, Auguste
Eve
c. 1881, Musée Rodin cast 8/12 in
1970
Bronze
Georges Rudier
68 × 23¾ × 30 in.
(172.7 × 60.3 × 76.2 cm)
Iris and B. Gerald Cantor Collection,
promised gift to the Iris and
B. Gerald Cantor Foundation

pl. 109). This type of praying figure is common in illustrations of *Paradiso*, indicating the Heavenly Spheres in which live a multitude of angels. However, for Rodin this gesture seems to indicate more generally the hope of salvation, which is the subject of Dante's *Purgatorio*, and the ascent toward the ultimate paradise of the presence of God that is attained momentarily in the last canto of *Paradiso*.

Rodin's *Gates of Hell* and Dante's *Paradiso*

Adam and Eve, St. John the Baptist — The Empyrean, Paradiso XXXII

Rodin's drawing of Dante meeting Beatrice (pl. 112) could be a reference to their first meeting in Purgatory, but the iconography is like that common to representations of the couple's journey through Paradise, such as in Botticelli's illustration (pl. 113). This demonstrates Rodin's familiarity with *Paradiso* and perhaps his intent to include it at least peripherally in his *Gates of Hell*.

Adam and Eve (pls. 84, 111) in Dante's text are found in the the highest circle of Heaven. During the Harrowing of Hell, just after the Crucifixion and before the Resurrection, Christ had rescued the first sinners from Limbo and brought them to Heaven to rest at the feet of Mary. Rodin, as indicated in the Stanford University bronze of *The Gates of Hell* (pl. 67), placed Adam and Eve outside the portal itself in an attitude of shame, in reference to the Expulsion from Eden and to the general human condition of sinner approaching Hell. The presence of Adam and Eve, for Dante and for

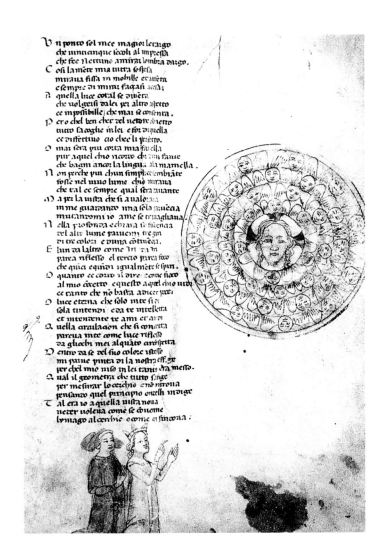

114. Anonymous
Paradiso XXXIII
Italy, mid-14th century
Manuscript illustration
Paris, Bibliothèque de l'Arsenal

Rodin, serves as a reminder of original sin, but also as an assurance of the possibility of ultimate salvation through Christ.

Rodin's *Monumental Head of St. John the Baptist* (pl. 115) is included in *The Gates of Hell*, but appropriately sequestered from the population of Hell. Similarly, Dante includes John the Baptist in the highest circle of Heaven. However, in iconographic traditions of illustration for Dante's *Divine Comedy*, a face alone, such as Rodin's *St. John* in the *Gates*, usually represents the Trinitarian Godhead as described in Canto XXXIII of *Paradiso* (pl. 114). From the position of *The Thinker* witnessing Hell, the face of St. John the Baptist/God/Christ in Heaven is hidden, but present, awaiting discovery. In this way, ever so subtly, Rodin has given us indications not only of the punishments of the *Inferno*, but also of the hope of salvation presented in *Purgatorio*, and the ultimate joy of God's presence in *Paradiso*.

Notes

1   Archives Nationales, inv. no. F/21/2109, série artistes, dossier Rodin. The document reads: "M. Rodin, artiste sculpteur, est chargé d'exécuter moyennant la somme de Huit mille francs le modèle d'une porte décorative destinée au Musée des Arts décoratifs: *Bas reliefs représentant la Divine Comédie du Dante.*" The initial sum of 8000 francs was augmented several times and by 1888 had been increased to 30,000 francs in response to Rodin's requests for more funding to complete his work. By the end of

115. Rodin, Auguste
Monumental Head of St. John the Baptist
c. 1879, Musée Rodin cast 4/8 in 1986
Bronze
Godard
21½ × 20¾ × 15¼ in.
(54.6 × 52.7 × 38.6 cm)
Iris and B. Gerald Cantor Collection,
promised gift to the Iris and
B. Gerald Cantor Foundation

his life, in November 1917, Rodin had actually expended 25,700 francs of the 30,000 allocated to him.

2 Within the field of art history two major works on Rodin's *Gates of Hell* have been written, both by the late Albert Elsen (1960 and 1985). Elsen only mentions briefly in one of these texts the rich context of French nineteenth-century art and literature inspired by Dante and does not investigate the issue of French translations of Dante possibly used by Rodin. While some work has been carried out on Rodin's drawings done in preparation for *The Gates of Hell*, notably by Claudie Judrin, Jacques de Caso, and Kirk Varnedoe, a comprehensive treatment of them in relation to both Dante's text in French transla-tion and to the finished work of sculpture has not been attempted. In the field of literature two major works of relatively recent scholarship exploring Dante's relationship to French literature of the nine-teenth century are available, by Werner P. Friederich (1950) and Michael Pitwood (1985). While these texts are invaluable as basic sources, they are essentially limited in their treatment of the vital interac-tion of literature and the visual arts that took place in the nineteenth century with Dante at its center. The most substantial works on illustrations of the *Divine Comedy* have been produced by Peter Brieger and Millard Meiss, and Eugene Nassar. Brieger and Meiss (1968) confine their studies to illuminated manuscript illustrations (and thus to Medieval and Early Renaissance depictions). Nassar's text (1994) surveys illustrations from the fourteenth century to the late twentieth century. These studies do not contextualize illustrations of the *Inferno* within the French cultural developments of the nineteenth century that concern my research.

3 The author's doctoral dissertation seeks to establish the filiation between Rodin's *Gates of Hell* and its textual source, Dante's *Divine Comedy*, and to explore the relationship of Rodin's work to the art and literature of nineteenth-century France also inspired by Dante. See, for example, the author's articles in the journal *Dante Studies*, 1999, and the *Journal of the Iris and B. Gerald Cantor Center for Visual Arts at Stanford University*, 1998–99.

4 In painting, for example, Paul Chenavard used three separate panels of round format to represent each of the three canticles of the *Divine Comedy*. Louis Janmot produced over 20 paintings and drawings for his own Dantesque literary epic, the *Poem of the Soul*. Both artists were members of the Lyon school of ultramontane artists and writers who showed particular interest in Dante and his works. This interest is explored in the author's dissertation.

5 The view of Rodin as a "literary" sculptor was largely forgotten in twentieth-century critique, which came to realize and focus upon the profound influence Rodin exercised on developments of modern sculpture. Scholarship should now consider Rodin's relationship to artistic traditions to provide a more comprehensive understanding of his work.

6 All quotations from Dante's *Divine Comedy* are from the translation by John D. Sinclair, New York: Oxford University Press, 1961.

7 Most generally, *The Thinker*, in his position before Hell, as such recalls immediately the figure of Christ in the Last Judgment common to Medieval tympana sculpture and featured in the Renaissance work with which it is most often compared, Michelangelo's painting of the *Last Judgment* in the Sistine Chapel in Rome. This tradition was certainly well known not only to Rodin, a student of the Italian Renaissance as well as of the Romanesque and Gothic traditions of French sculpture, but to the French public as well. In giving *The Thinker* this placement, Rodin begins to aggrandize Dante's presence, likening the Poet/Artist in a larger sense to Christ.

8 Seated figures appear in early Christian manuscripts as the traditional means to represent a scribe or sometimes a prophet or saint as he records his wisdom. In Medieval illustrations to the text, Dante is sometimes portrayed sitting at his writing desk in the middle of the dark wood of Canto I. More specifi-cally, the seated figure in art with hand to chin traditionally represents philosophy, thought, or contemplation—an iconographic tradition traceable as far back as antiquity, and in the Middle Ages associated with representations of Melancholia, one of the Four Temperaments and associated specifi-cally with creativity.

9 *The Earliest Lives of Dante: Boccaccio and Aretino*, New York: Ungar, 1963, p. 42.

10 Melancholy in fact became the trait most frequently associated with French artists of the Romantic era, and was idealized in its more furious form in their image of Michelangelo, seen in direct opposition to the calm hero of the classicists, Raphael. Dante, too, was idealized by the Romantics in the same spirit as Michelangelo. Thus the French scholar and author of the very influential *Dante and Catholic Philosophy* (New York 1913), Frederic Ozanam, wrote in 1839 this Romanticized literary portrait of Dante that emphasizes his melancholic nature:

In the year 1265, under sinister auspices ... a child was born—Dante Alighieri ... In the person of

Dante were found the three faculties which ... constitute genius, namely, intellect to perceive, imagination to idealize, and will to execute. The task still remains to tell by what mysterious bonds these faculties were interwoven into a perfect unity: how three destinies weighed upon a single head which they might bow, but could not crush [pp. 104–15].

11   One of these legends repeated in nineteenth-century French biographies of Dante stated that the poet had spent some time in Paris during his years of exile from Italy. It was often declared that Dante had passed some time in 1302 debating theology at the Sorbonne, slept at the church of St-Julien-le-Pauvre, and prayed at the church of St-Severin, all in the Latin Quarter of Left-Bank Paris. It is also claimed that Dante went as far as England during his travels, studying at Oxford. None of these legends of Dante's travels in France and England has been substantiated, however. I explore the origin of *The Thinker* as Dante in my article "Rodin's *Gates of Hell* and Aubé's *Monument to Dante*: Romantic Tribute to the Image of the Poet in Nineteenth-century France," in *Journal of the Iris and B. Gerald Cantor Center for Visual Arts at Stanford University*, vol. I, 1998–99, pp. 33–46.

12   Dante Alighieri, *La Divine Comédie*, trans. by Sebastien Rhéal, illus. by Antoine Etex, Paris: J. Bry Aîné, 1854, p. 12. Rhéal wrote: "Les habitants du bourg de Tolmino, situé dans les montagnes, montreut aux étrangers la grotte et la pierre appelées 'la Sedia di Dante'. Il y a pareillement à Florence, vers le côté méridional de Sainte-Marie del Fiore, un petit carré de marbre blanc enchâssé dans un trottoir, portant cette inscription: 'Sasso di Dante'. Là aussi, avant son exil, on dit qu'il venait souvent s'asseoir. Ni Sante-Marie, ni la Campanille n'existaient alors. Du banc, qui était son siège accoutumé, il pouvait contempler le Baptistère, son 'bel San Giovano', le monument le plus important de la place."

13   Alphaeus Cole, an American artist born in New Jersey, exhibited his painting as *Dante observant la construction de la cathédrale de Florence* at the Salon of 1900 (no. 318). Cole listed himself in the Salon exhibition catalog as living in Paris (3 rue Dutot) as the student of French artists Jean-Paul Laurens and Benjamin-Constant.

14   Letter from Rodin to Edmond Turquet, October 20, 1881. Paris: Archives Nationales, inv. no. F/21/2109, série artistes, dossier Rodin.

15   Gustave Geffroy, *Auguste Rodin*, exhib. cat., Paris: Galerie Georges Petit, 1889, pp. 56–60; reprinted in *Claude Monet–Auguste Rodin: Centenaire de l'exposition de 1889*, Paris: Musée Rodin, 1989, pp. 61–62.

16   Letter from Rodin to Marcel Adam, published in *Gil Blas*, July 7, 1904; quoted by Albert Elsen, *The Gates of Hell by Auguste Rodin*, Stanford, California: Stanford University Press, 1985, p. 73.

17   Dominique-Jean-Baptise Hugues exhibited his sculpted version of Paolo and Francesca in the whirlwind at the Salon of 1879 (no. 5105) as *Ombres de Françoise de Rimini et de Paolo Malatesta*. The Musée d'Orsay in Paris has a small plaster version of this work.

18   The earliest known representation of the embrace of Paolo and Francesca in French art is that by Coupin de la Coupérie exhibited at the Salon of 1812 (no. 227). Ingres's famous version of this scene, certainly influenced by Coupin's, first appeared in 1814.

19   The closed tombs on *The Gates of Hell* also suggest the moment in the Last Judgment when all time stops and all the graves of those in Hell are sealed.

20   Rodin's drawings and sculpture of *The Three Shades* in relation to Dante's *Inferno* are the subject of my full-length essay, "I Tre Fiorentini: Rodin's Three Shades and their Origin in Medieval Illustrations of Dante's *Inferno* 15 and 16," *Dante Studies*, CXVII, 1999, pp. 133–69.

21   Antoine Auguste Thivet, a student of Gérôme, exhibited his painting featuring Thaïs at the Paris Salon of 1903 (no. 1672) with the title *Le Huitième Cercle*, in reference to the eighth circle of Hell, where the Flatterers are punished. The subject of Thaïs was common in the early twentieth century, owing to the presentation of a theater piece based on her legend at that time.

22   The first work with Ugolino as subject was that of Fortuné Dufau, a student of Jacques-Louis David, exhibited at the Salon of 1800. It is interesting that many of the first works in French art based on Dante come from students or associates of David. That Dante as subject seems to transcend all genres and movements throughout nineteenth-century French art is the subject of longer study within my doctoral dissertation.

Rodin's Partial Figures

Daniel Rosenfeld

Et les cathédrales, est-ce qu'elles sont finies?[1]

In 1969 the late Rodin scholar Albert E. Elsen mounted an exhibition on the "partial figure" in modern sculpture, in which he focused on this signature aspect of Rodin's art and its legacy.[2] The phrase "partial figure," which appears to have been coined by Elsen, was what he used to describe Rodin's polymorphous fragmentations of the human figure. Critics and scholars who were contemporaries of Rodin had variously observed his use of the fragment, the novelty of his working methods, and the influence of Michelangelo and of antique sculpture.[3] Elsen's exploration of this subject, however, was the first to take a systematic look at some of the historical antecedents for Rodin's partial figures, his multi-faceted approach to this aspect of his work, and its influence on sculptors up to the time in which this exhibition was mounted. By treating in isolation this feature of Rodin's sculptural achievement, Elsen provided the most important assessment to date of Rodin's modernity and influence. As he wrote in the introduction to the exhibition catalog:

> Until Rodin, the partial figure and figural part were found as symbols and mementos, decorative objects and museum relics. It is doubtful that the partial figure, such as the torso, was either the central preoccupation of any sculptor or was the focus of the most important art. That the torsos and smaller parts of the body should play an important role in the evolution of a sculptor's work, be widespread in serious art, and as a motif have a rich secular as well as spiritual implication is a phenomenon in art history reserved for the last ninety years of western sculpture.[4]

This essay will revisit this aspect of Rodin's sculptural development as it has been illuminated by the abundance of scholarship on Rodin and the art of the nineteenth century generally, which has emerged in the intervening years.[5] We tend to look at artists from the past through the lens of our own time. A generation ago, for writers such as Professor Elsen, who came to Rodin in the wake of the Second World War and the rise of Modernism in the United States, Rodin's fundamental reinvention of the language of the figure was valued for its far-reaching impact on a branch of the visual arts that seemed moribund by comparison to its sister arts of painting, poetry, and literature. From our current perspective, owing in no small part to Professor Elsen's contributions, the scope of Rodin's modernity has been well established. There has been a corollary impulse, sustained by the enlightened administration over the last 30 years of the resources available at the Musée Rodin in Paris, to understand with some precision the historical circumstances from which his modernity emerged. The Musée Rodin

116. Rodin. Auguste
The Cathedral
Original stone version executed in 1908, Musée Rodin cast in 1955
Bronze
Georges Rudier
25¼ × 12¾ × 13½ in.
(64.1 × 32.3 × 34.3 cm)
Iris and B. Gerald Cantor
Foundation

continues steadily to publish valuable research from its collections, to bring new information to light, and to make its resources available to scholars, resulting in the publication of such singularly important studies as the biography by Ruth Butler—the first of consequence to appear since Judith Cladel's account of 1936.[6]

From this perspective, it may be useful to begin by taking a fresh look at the historical circumstances of French sculpture and theory in Rodin's time, and at the dominating presence of the art of antiquity, which provided the most immediate example of the sculptural fragment in the visual sphere.[7] Rodin's relationship to the French Academy, from which he was excluded, remains a complex issue, but it seems nonetheless that his treatment of the partial figure and his evolving notions of sculptural finish were the result of a triangular relationship between Rodin, the prejudices of the Ecole des Beaux-Arts, and the ubiquitous presence of ancient art in his time. In addition, we must understand that the partial figure was one among a variety of devices that Rodin deployed in order to achieve what he perceived to be a greater degree of directness and integrity in his work. From his earliest submissions to the Salon, he presented an evolving re-evaluation of the normative standards of "finish," of the hierarchies of the sketch, and of materials. He deployed for this purpose an arsenal of techniques that included not only fragmentation but also recombination, replication, and a broad range of *non-finito* surface treatments that were expressions of this purpose.[8] His explorations of sculpture's relationship to its support and to the surrounding environment are also a reflection of this broader impulse. It is relevant to our interpretation of these devices to understand when and in what degree they became part of the public identity of his work, as distinguished from what in the jargon of the period would have been called "secrets of the atelier." Therefore we will look with particular emphasis at Rodin's exhibition history. Not least of all, we must try to understand the significance of these developments as they pertained not only to the formal evolution of his work, but also to its meaning and cultural significance.

In his 1969 study, Elsen referenced a variety of precedents for the fragmentation of the human figure in the history of art, ranging from prehistoric cult objects, to the Greek herm, to the Medieval reliquary.[9] These were, it seems, ancillary to the overwhelming presence and singular importance for Rodin—no less than for his contemporaries from the Ecole—of the sculptural fragments handed down from ancient Greece and Rome (pl. 117). As often known through pristine plaster casts as through their originals, these were characteristically assembled, classified, and offered to the art student and the general public as an authoritative compendium of the Classical tradition.[10] The modern knowledge of the sculpture of antiquity derives principally from such deracinated "ruins."

Their identity as the surviving vestiges of time's rapacious assault provided a trope for many artists and poets of the late eighteenth and nineteenth centuries, who alternately found in the fragment a symbol of art's longevity (*"ars longa, vita brevis"*), or of the inexorable crush of time, which lays waste to all things.[11] The prevailing taste among European antiquarians before the nineteenth century had been, whenever possible, to restore antique fragments, replacing missing limbs or patching over unsightly surface breaks. This preference diminished gradually in the nineteenth century, whether because of a more cautious and refined approach to conservation generally, or because

117. Unknown photographer
Ecole des Beaux-Arts. Vestibule du Palais (from a postcard postmarked 1904)

118. *The Winged Victory of Samothrace*
Greece, beginning of the 3rd century BC
Marble
Height 129 in. (328 cm)
Paris, Musée du Louvre

119. Rodin, Auguste
Large Clenched Left Hand
c. 1885. Musée Rodin cast 3/12 in 1966
Bronze
Georges Rudier
18¼ × 10⅜ × 7⅝ in.
(46.4 × 26.4 × 19.3 cm)
Iris and B. Gerald Cantor Foundation

120. *Venus de Milo*
Greece, 2nd century BC
Parian marble
Height 79½ in. (202 cm)
Paris, Musée du Louvre

121. Rodin, Auguste
Clenched Left Hand with Figure
1906 or 1907, Musée Rodin cast 1/12
in 1970
Bronze
Godard
17½ × 11½ × 10⅜ in.
(44.5 × 29.2 × 26.4 cm)
Iris and B. Gerald Cantor Collection,
promised gift to the Iris and
B. Gerald Cantor Foundation

in individual cases antiquarians could not agree on the proper form these restorations should assume.[12]

Of singular importance to the evolution of modern tastes for the antique was the expatriation of the marble sculptures from the Parthenon to London between 1802 and 1812, through the single-minded efforts of Robert Bruce, the Earl of Elgin (at the time the British ambassador to the Ottoman government in Constantinople). The Elgin Marbles influenced a re-evaluation of the principles of Classical art that had been advanced by Johann Winckelmann (1717–1768) (who, ironically, had never seen the Parthenon sculptures).[13] Whereas Winckelmann had based his most prescient observations on works that often turned out to be later and inferior copies of lost originals, the Parthenon marbles transported to London by Lord Elgin, in Jonah Siegel's apt phrase, were "warranted," possessing an authority that derived from their identity as originals.[14] Lord Elgin had hoped to restore the sculptures once they arrived in London, but John Flaxman and Antonio Canova dissuaded him from pursuing that path. Their advice—coming from two of the most distinguished Neo-classical sculptors of the period—reflects an increasing reticence to reconstitute originals with potentially inferior or inaccurate modern embellishments. There was nevertheless strong resistance at first to the harsh lessons presented by the Parthenon fragments. Ozias Humphrey, a painter, described the marbles in 1808 as "a Mass of ruins"; and the collector, dilettante, and amateur Sir George Beaumont wrote with evident agitation to Benjamin Robert Haydon, a strong advocate for Lord Elgin's marbles, that "the mutilated fragments should be restored, as at present they excite rather disgust than pleasure ... to see parts of limbs, of bodys [*sic*], stumps of arms &c."[15]

A generation later, when Rodin came of age, attitudes regarding the antique had evolved considerably under the coinciding influences of Romanticism, Positivism, and Naturalism. Neo-classicism of the eighteenth century—the Neo-classicism of Winckelmann—had looked to ancient Greek art as the expression of a higher order of human achievement and possibility, and hence there was a moral imperative, reflected in the urgency of Beaumont's comments to Haydon, to reconstitute that lost perfection, rather than to look upon the remains as evidence of decay. Although these views continued to hold sway in the more conservative reaches of the Ecole, by the mid-nineteenth century the antique fragment, now characteristically framed within a museological setting, might be seen by the Romantic as a metaphor of the collapse and disintegration of great cultures from the past; by the Positivist as an artifact revealing evidence of periodicity or style; and by the Naturalist as a reflection of the strong organic impulse that was revealed by Greek art and perceived as the true basis (by their standards) for its durability and completeness, even in fragmentary form.[16]

Among the profusion of antique fragments (or their casts) that found their way into the museums of Europe in the nineteenth century, it may be useful to take brief note of three works that stand out as touchstones for the prominence of the fragment in Rodin's purview: the *Winged Victory of Samothrace* (pl. 118), the *Venus de Milo* (pl. 120), and the Belvedere *Torso* (pl. 122). These works have become such icons in the lexicon of Hellenistic art that we may lose sight of their importance little more than a century ago, when the first two of these, in particular, still emanated an aura of recent discovery and revelation. The *Winged Victory of Samothrace* in the Louvre, regarded by Proust's Mme.

Verdurin as no less than a supreme "masterpiece of the Universe,"[17] had special currency in Rodin's time, owing to its discovery by a team of French archaeologists in 1863 and its installation in the Salle des Caryatides of the Louvre three years later (Rodin was 26 at the time), followed by its prominent resituation in 1884 at the top of the Escalier Darou, where it has stood ever since.[18] The iconicity of this sculpture is suggested by its appearance in Rodin's conversations with Paul Gsell and F.T. Marinetti's incendiary "Founding and Manifesto of Futurism" (1909), in which he famously asserted that "a roaring car that seems to ride on grapeshot is more beautiful ... ."[19]

The *Venus de Milo* was discovered in 1820 and acquired by the Louvre the following year. In spite of its missing limbs and its problematic identity, this figure came to personify a Western ideal of feminine beauty, and in many cultures it still does.[20] As with the *Winged Victory of Samothrace*, the modern viewer tends to ignore its dismembered condition, and the absence of its arms has the unintentional effect of accentuating the sculpture's contours and de-emphasizing iconographic traits, while adding to its appeal as an aestheticized object. It seems hard to imagine, but it is important to understand, the values and expectations that caused Sir George Beaumont, with absolute sincerity, to look upon the Parthenon marbles as "mutilations." By the middle of the nineteenth century, conditioned by exposure to this and many other fragments from antiquity, the standards for biological wholeness so important to Beaumont had largely been eclipsed by standards of aesthetic legitimacy that were an important precondition for Rodin's development of the fragment in his own work.

Third but not last in this triumvirate is the Belvedere *Torso* in the Vatican Museum, sometimes referred to as the *Torso of Michelangelo*. Of these three fragments, this robust torso may have been the most resonant for Rodin, especially in his formative years, by virtue of its linkage to Michelangelo, as well as by its familiarity as a symbol of the art of sculpture.[21] Following this tradition, in 1874 Rodin created a copy of the Belvedere *Torso* for an *Allegory of Art* that had been commissioned for the Palais des Académies in Brussels. This was his first real use of the partial figure, although in this case the fragment is "readymade," a pastiche of an extant work as it appears, symbolizing itself.

The Brussels torso was obviously copied from a plaster cast of the original. It was only in the following year, during his trip to Rome at the time of the celebration of the 400th anniversary of Michelangelo's birth, that Rodin would have seen the original. It is very likely that he would have been aware of this torso's importance to Michelangelo, of the legends regarding the Renaissance sculptor's reverence for it, and of the influence he was said to have exerted to leave the fragment unrestored. Rodin might also have been aware of Michelangelo's discovery in it of "a certain principle ... which gave his works a grandeur of gusto equal to the best antiques."[22] It is striking how much this characterization of discovery for Michelangelo resembles Rodin's description in his letters to Rose Beuret from Italy of his efforts to unlock the "secrets" of Michelangelo: "I have drawn thumbnail sketches [*croquis*] evenings in my room, not from his works, but from all the structures, the systems that I have invented in order to understand him; and well, I have succeeded in my opinion to give them the attraction, that something without name that he alone knew how to create."[23]

122. Belvedere *Torso*
Greece, mid-2nd century BC (?)
Marble
Height 62 in. (157.5 cm)
Rome, Vatican Museum

123. Rodin, Auguste
Large Left Hand of a Pianist
1885. Musée Rodin cast 9/12 in 1969
Bronze
Georges Rudier
7¼ × 10 × 4⅞ in.
(18.4 × 25.4 × 12.4 cm)
Iris and B. Gerald Cantor
Foundation

The antique fragment was of value to Rodin for aesthetic as well as symbolic reasons. From a purely aesthetic point of view, the fragment diverts the viewer's attention away from the subject and toward the object, encouraging the admiration of the finely rendered *morceau*, which could be valued independent of narrative or precise iconographic identity. Rodin's later panegyrics on ancient Greek sculpture resonate with language that reflects a highly aestheticized appreciation. Of the *Venus de Milo*, for example, he wrote: "For poets, seekers, modest artists, amid the tumult of the city, you offer long moments of refuge. *Although mutilated, you remain complete in their eyes.* If the injuries of time have allowed [this], it is so that a trace remains of [time's] impious efforts, and of its impotence."[24] Rodin communicates concisely in this phrase his belief in the aesthetic self-sufficiency of the fragment: implicitly, and by association, he links his fragmentation of the figure to the art of ancient Greece, not as it was conceived but as it has been handed down through the vagaries of time; and by extension, symbolically,

he correlates the "mutilated" fragment with the complex symbolism of time and decay. The metamorphosis of the partial figure in Rodin's work can be seen as a synthesis of these intermingling beliefs, which respectively encompass core aspects of the artist's patrimony, his aesthetic, and symbolic intentions.

Elsen's term "partial figure" in fact describes more than a few variations on this theme in Rodin's œuvre. The most conspicuous varieties of the partial figure include the torso-fragment, in which the core of the human torso is represented without the head and/or limbs (pls. 139, 140), or, alternatively, works in which the limbs are treated separately from the core of the body (pls. 119, 121). Works of the latter category may have originated from or have been designated for a known sculpture (in these examples the hands may have been intended for one of *The Burghers of Calais*, but ultimately were not used).[25] There are as well scores of independent "partial figures" that were not conceived for or drawn from an identifiable work, but which reveal what has the

124. Rodin, Auguste
Hand of Rodin Holding Torso
1917. Musée Rodin cast in 1968
Bronze
Georges Rudier
6⅛ × 8¾ × 4⅛ in.
(15.8 × 22.2 × 10.7 cm)
Iris and B. Gerald Cantor Collection,
promised gift to the Iris and
B. Gerald Cantor Foundation

appearance of a veritable arsenal of prostheses in waiting (pl. 127). Rodin also created a small but significant number of symbolic hands (pl. 116), most importantly *The Hand of God* (pls. 5, 130, 133), which are not easily classified as "fragments." Such works may have been derived from a previous sculpture (in this case the right hand of *Pierre de Wiessant*; pl. 43),[26] but Rodin treats them both formally and iconographically as complete and whole unto themselves, giving them the kind of self-sufficiency that is normally reserved for figural groupings.

The term "partial figure" is by design more specific and less subjective or pejorative than the description of Rodin's work as "unfinished," although the sculptor's uses of the partial figure, among other devices, challenged head-on the standards of finish that prevailed in the nineteenth century. The term "unfinished" suggests a state of incompleteness and the possibility that in other circumstances the "unfinished" may have been brought to a condition of greater resolution, either by virtue of a work's material of execution (bronze or marble traditionally being more "finished" than plaster or clay), or through its size or clarity of detail. There are in Rodin's œuvre many examples of "unfinished" works, but the use of this term to describe an unfulfilled intention is not always easy to ascertain. Rodin often applied an elastic understanding of what was "finished" and what was not, and freely exhibited work that was transitional in one way or another. As Elsen has noted elsewhere, conventional "finish" was an anathema to Rodin, who always reflexively saw ways of extending his own art and never saw a work as unalterable (regardless of its medium of execution), retaining a notion of its potential for perpetual evolution.[27]

125. Rodin, Auguste
Severed Head of St. John the Baptist
c. 1887–1907
Marble
8 × 15¾ × 13½ in.
(20.3 × 40 × 34.3 cm)
Los Angeles County Museum of Art,
Museum purchase made possible by
the Cantor Foundation in memory of
B. Gerald Cantor

OVERLEAF: 126. Unknown photographer
The Salon of the Société Nationale
des Beaux-Arts, Paris (Galerie des
Machines, Champs-de-Mars), showing the placement of Rodin's *The Kiss* and the *Monument to Balzac*
1898
Photograph

128. Druet, Eugène
Rodin's *The Kiss* in the Salon of 1898
Gelatin silver print
Paris, Musée Rodin

LEFT: 127.Unknown photographer
Drawer from Rodin's studio contain-
ing twenty-seven pieces in plaster
No date
Photograph
Paris, Musée Rodin

Before turning to specific instances of partial figures in Rodin's sculpture and its evolution, it will be useful to focus briefly on a salient issue of aesthetics germane to their place in his work, expressed at the peak of his maturity, when the *Monument to Balzac* (in plaster) and *The Kiss* (in marble) were exhibited together in the Salon of 1898 (pl. 126). The events of this moment in Rodin's career played out with the consequence and finality of the climax in a Greek tragedy. And though neither of these works is remotely "partial" in any way, their juxtaposition at this pivotal moment in Rodin's career was intended to demonstrate principles that may be seen in hindsight as essential to Rodin's development of the partial figure. It is no coincidence, by extension, that while there were many prior appearances of the partial figure in Rodin's public display of his sculpture (notably in the Salon of the preceding year), it is really in the wake of this climactic moment that the partial figure sees its fullest efflorescence.

The marble *Kiss* (pl. 128), an offspring of *The Gates of Hell*, had been commissioned by the French state and was destined for the Musée du Luxembourg, where it would join the company of a number of Rodin's most important sculptures from the preceding decades: *The Age of Bronze* (pl. 136; installed in the Jardin du Luxembourg), *St. John the Baptist Preaching* (pl. 137), the marble *Danaïd*, and the vibrant marble bust of Mme. Morla Vicuña (pl. 147). By any standard, *The Kiss* represented the fulfillment of the norms of finish that Rodin in many of his other works had done so much to undermine. The compositional resolution of this complex figural grouping, its monumental size, its material, and the relative polish of its execution all conformed to the highest

129. Rodin, Auguste
Head of a Shade with Two Hands
c. 1910, date of cast unknown
Bronze
Alexis Rudier
7⅝ × 10¾ × 8⅛ in.
(19.4 × 27.3 × 20.9 cm)
Iris and B. Gerald Cantor
Foundation

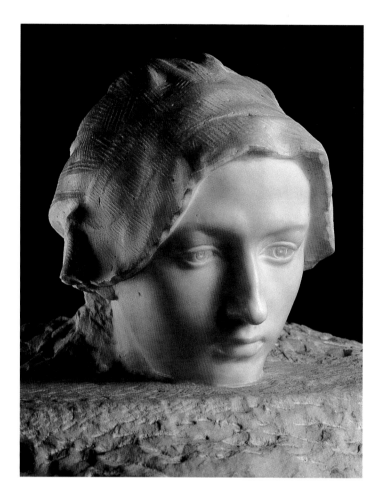

131. Rodin, Auguste
Thought
1895
Marble
29¼ × 17⅛ × 18⅛ in.
(74.2 × 43.5 × 46.1 cm)
Paris, Musée Rodin

standards of finish valued by the Ecole. Inspired by Dante's account in the *Inferno* of the tragic love of Paolo and Francesca, *The Kiss* symbolized the human, carnal, and spiritual tragedy that was the focus of the *Gates*. The commission for the *Gates* had played a singular role in Rodin's emerging reputation during the 1880s. However, as of 1898, it saw no immediate prospect of ever being cast into bronze and situated in public, and had long been surpassed in the public's memory by the many offspring from the portal that Rodin developed into self-sufficient works. In the milieu of the 1898 Salon, this life-sized marble, destined for the Luxembourg, stood in for Rodin's achievement in the *Gates*, revealing within the hierarchies of finish at that time a kind of valedictory of that achievement.

The Monument to Balzac (pl. 132), commissioned by the Société des Gens des Lettres, had been plagued by controversy from the time of its commission in 1891, when Emile Zola, the new president of this society, secured the commission for Rodin through maneuvers that many viewed as heavy-handed. The climate in which Rodin developed this figure was poisonous. The society had already rejected one maquette for the monument submitted by Rodin in 1893. The figure exhibited in 1898 was the product of his intensive and protracted labor that was fueled partly by an identification with his subject, as well as by the conviction that in this work he had discovered something new and portentous for the future of sculpture. Notwithstanding this, the Société rejected the monument, and Rodin bitterly removed it from the Salon, where it had been subjected to more than its share of critical abuse.

130. Rodin, Auguste
The Hand of God
1898, Musée Rodin cast 11/12 in 1966
Bronze
Georges Rudier
12¾ × 11¼ × 11¾ in.
(32.4 × 26 × 29.8 cm)
Iris and B. Gerald Cantor Collection,
promised gift to the Iris and
B. Gerald Cantor Foundation

The juxtaposition of these two sculptures—the one backward-looking, the other prophetic of a future direction in Rodin's work—effectively bracketed the artist's career, as if to suggest, "this is where I have come from, and this is where I am going."[28] It is fair to observe that even if the Société des Gens des Lettres had not been roiling in the internecine literary politics of the *fin de siècle*, they (and their public) may not have been prepared for the degree of abstraction revealed by this forward-looking monument. With the benefit of hindsight, looking back through Rodin's career and the development of his work, one can understand the logic of its evolution and its pivotal importance in his sculptural development. Yet from the floor of the Salon in 1898, this work was challenging even for some of Rodin's staunchest supporters, especially when gauged by the delimiting demands of the public monument.

Rodin was embittered by this failure and motivated subsequently to defend the achievement of the *Balzac* at the expense of his marble *Kiss*. He commented to Camille Mauclair at the time of this reversal that the marble seemed "soft" (*mou*) when compared to the *Balzac*, and he continued:

> The essential modeling is there [in the *Balzac*] and would be diminished if I "finished" it any further. As for polishing and repolishing the toes, or the locks of hair, that has absolutely no interest in my opinion, and would compromise the central idea, the broad lines, the spirit of that which I had intended, and I have nothing further to say on this subject to the public.[29]

Elaborating on this perspective a few years later with greater equanimity and the benefit of time, Rodin once again drew a distinction between *The Kiss* and the *Balzac*, arguing for the superiority of the latter:

> Without a doubt the arrangement of the Kiss is appealing. But I discovered nothing in this group. It is a theme treated in conformity with the scholarly tradition: a subject complete in itself and artificially isolated from the surrounding world—a large "bibelot" sculpted according to the habitual formula, directing the viewer's attention narrowly upon the two figures, instead of opening broad horizons to the imagination.
>
> My Balzac by contrast, by its pose and its expression, enables [the viewer] to imagine surrounding it the milieu in which he walked, where he lived, [and] where he thought. He is not isolated from the surrounding environment. He is a veritable living being.

In this interview, Rodin extends the same interpretation to the *Walking Man* (pl. 134), and continues:

> An art that ... bypasses by means of suggestion the sculpted figure and renders it bound up with an ensemble that the imagination recomposes by degrees is, I think, a fertile innovation.[30]

Rodin's comments provide a passionate and articulate defense of his monument against criticism that it was "unfinished," summary, and unresolved in its detail, accusations

132. Druet, Eugène
Rodin's *Monument to Balzac* in the
Salon of 1898
Gelatin silver print
Paris, Musée Rodin

133. Rodin, Auguste
The Hand of God
1898, date of cast unknown
Bronze
Alexis Rudier
5¼ × 3½ × 3⅝ in.
(13.3 × 8.9 × 9.1 cm)
Iris and B. Gerald Cantor Collection,
promised gift to the Iris and
B. Gerald Cantor Foundation

134. Rodin. Auguste
Walking Man
c. 1889, date of cast unknown
Bronze
No foundry mark
33 × 20¼ × 20 in.
(83.8 × 51.4 × 50.8 cm)
Iris and B. Gerald Cantor
Foundation

that, as Francis Haskell observed, are often a refuge of first resort for critics unable to comprehend—let alone embrace—the innovations of modernity.[31]

This notion of a sculpture bound up with an ensemble that transcends its physical limits was indeed a fertile innovation, and a major component of Rodin's modernity, finding expression in many different forms of his work. The *Balzac* was the most resolved expression of this aesthetic until then, or perhaps thereafter. However, one can look back to earlier examples in Rodin's work and identify this as the guiding impulse that conditioned his development of the partial figure, his *non-finito* treatment of surfaces in every material, his prevailing disregard for academic standards of finish, and even his open-ended approach to subject-matter. Gustave Geffroy, one of the artist's most knowledgeable observers, had earlier praised this feature, writing "he does not separate the beings he represents from the atmosphere in which they live."[32] The most immediate artistic connection may be drawn to the Impressionists, but by the late 1890s this impulse may also be related to important aspects of Symbolist art, with demonstrable connections to such contemporaries as Eugène Carrière.

It also comes as no surprise to observe that Rodin would equate this impulse in his work with expressive aspects of the antique fragment. Writing of the *Three Fates* from the Parthenon, which are among the most impressive of the Elgin Marbles, he commented offhandedly that the actual identity of these headless figures was of little importance: "They are just three seated women, but their pose is so serene, so majestic, that they seem to participate in some aspect of enormity that cannot be seen. Great mystery reigns above them: immaterial Reason, eternal, which all Nature obeys, and of which they themselves are its celestial servants."[33] It would be shortsighted to dismiss such grandiose allusions, drawn at the end of his career and so blatantly inimical to the spirit of Modernism, merely as retroactive embellishments designed to legitimize his work by linking it with the ancients (though they were that, too). More broadly, in his seniority, Rodin seems to be searching for the origins of his own modernity, and finding it in his subjective response to these antique fragments. Paraphrasing Oscar Wilde's observation that we tend to see nature through art, it may also be said of Rodin, ever the sensitive observer, that he also saw art through art, in particular his own.

Rodin's attitudes toward finish may be associated respectively with his efforts to bring "life" to sculpture, to expose the sterility of his nemesis—the Academy—and to claim for himself its mantle as the rightful successor to the ancient Greeks. This was not solely a manifestation of his late years. He complained to his first biographer, Truman Bartlett, in 1889 that his contemporaries from the Ecole "study nature to make it Greek, and copy the latter because they think it ideal," whereas, he asserts, "Greek sculpture" (like his own work) "... is warm, strong, firm, simple, true to nature and full of power. It is life itself."[34] "*Le style académique*," on the other hand, presenting a noteworthy antithesis to Rodin's ambitions and achievement, was defined by the *Dictionnaire de l'Académie des Beaux-Arts*, with characteristic rhetorical excess, as:

the protest of the regulated imagination against imagination without rules, an art inspired, but also [an art] of conviction and scrupulousness, [an art] which stands in opposition to carelessness and negligence; a return to antiquity, which finds moral beauty in physical beauty; a means of transporting [our] spirit through the aid of art into superior spheres of grandeur, purity and the ideal.[35]

Rodin's persistent refusal, with a few notable exceptions, to conform even remotely to these accepted standards was a fundamental cause for complaint among conservative critics, leveled against his œuvre well into the twentieth century. Progressive-minded critics, on the other hand, identified Rodin's departures from these standards—whether revealed in his exploitation of the fragment, the *non-finito* details of his execution, or the consideration of almost any version of his sculpture as the potential component of a new and separate work—as the basis for its unprecedented modernity and social relevance.

It may be difficult, more than a century later, to appreciate the importance this issue held for Rodin's most passionate supporters, and for his equally acerbic detractors; it may likewise be difficult to understand the fervor that made this issue such a fault-line between rear- and avant-garde taste regarding sculpture in the second half of the nineteenth century. In the parallel history of late nineteenth-century painting, in which the label "Impressionist" originated as an epithet, the perception of radicalism associated with this movement's looseness of facture seems no longer quite so alarming as it may have in 1874. When looking at the paintings of Monet, Renoir, or even the socialist Pissarro, we may understandably be impressed foremost by their sensual attraction, undisturbed by their non-declamatory subjects, which accounts for their widespread and undiminished popularity following the initial shocks of the 1870s.

Sculpture, on the other hand, continued to bear the burden of its public and didactic functions far longer than its sister art of painting, even while critics of every persuasion saw it as an art in decline.[36] The sculptor Falconet (1716–1791), who was an important theorist of his time (he contributed the article on sculpture to Diderot's *Encyclopédie*), articulated a point of view that became the common denominator of French academic theory of the nineteenth century: that "Sculpture, along with history, is the most durable repository of human virtues." "The most dignified purpose of sculpture," he continued, "in visualizing the moral side [of life] is ... to perpetuate the memory of famous men, and to provide models of virtue ... ."[37] Throughout the nineteenth century, which in France was marked by fairly constant political upheaval, there was a complementary impulse, in the famous phrase of Charles Blanc, to provide the man on the street, absorbed by his mundane affairs, with "the shock of great ideas."[38] This purpose was broadly understood as an article of faith. "The Art of Statuary," the conservative Eméric-David concluded in an influential tract, is foremost "... the art of governments and kings." Prophetically, in advance of the proliferation of public monuments that was catalyzed by the Franco-Prussian War, he argued that the government should oversee the erection "in every village" of public monuments "glorifying France and its heroes." And in a phrase especially relevant to an important aspect of Rodin's alternative development, he continued: "The Art of Statuary is corrupted in the boudoir, and achieves perfection in the public square."[39]

There were, in short, political and economic as well as aesthetic factors that contributed to a conservative view of sculpture in Rodin's time. In this environment, experimentation was disproportionately restricted in the art of sculpture, which more so than easel painting was tied to the receipt of public commissions, and by extension to the leveling impact of selection by committee. The perception of sculpture's "durability," although material in origin, invested it with an aesthetic of gravity that was equally inhibiting. Charles Blanc, whose *Grammaire* is an important, systematic expression of the aesthetics of the academic style, spelled out these delimiting conditions in an instructive passage on *"le caractère"*:

> Before they are altered by the emotions of the spirit, human forms have an apparent expression that is their "character." That which is ephemeral in the sentiments that are expressed by the face or countenance of a man, that which is transitory in his affections, or fugitive in his look or his smile, can be rendered in [the art of] painting; the art of sculpture here will be powerless; but this powerlessness is a condition of its greatness. Accident evades [sculpture]; the eternal remains.[40]

This distinction between the purview of painting and sculpture brings us closer to an understanding of Rodin's departure from the academic canon, and his disdain for the austere conditions for sculpture iterated by Blanc. From his earliest major independent work, *The Man With the Broken Nose*, Rodin demonstrated a predilection for exploring the picturesque qualities in sculpture through what he referred to as the "science of modeling."[41] Significantly, this was also the first instance of a true fragment in his own work, the result of a studio accident in which the clay froze, and the back of the bust fell off, leaving Rodin to treat this portrait as a mask (pl. 107).[42] This was Rodin's most sustained effort up to this time. He told Truman Bartlett that he had spent 18 months working on the sculpture, which he modeled from the features of a workman named Bibi who swept the studios in the Faubourg Saint-Marcel.[43] In his eagerness to submit this work to the Salon of 1865, he cast what survived of the clay portrait in plaster and sent it off, whereupon it was promptly rejected by the Salon jury.[44]

It is no surprise that the work was rejected: it probably seemed to the jurors to be little more than a fragmentary study by an artist who was at the time only 25 years old, who had no formal training at the Ecole des Beaux-Arts, and was entirely unknown in official circles. It also featured a subject with a physical deformity, which may have struck the jurors as ignoble, and which probably prompted Rodin to comment to Bartlett at a later date: "He had a fine head; belonged to a fine race—*in form*—no matter if he was brutalized. *It was made as a piece of sculpture, solely, and without reference to the character of the model.*"[45] This disclaimer is important for a number of reasons. Rodin seems at pains to emphasize to Bartlett that his ambitions were not directly linked to the social politics of Realism; that is, that this is not the portrait of a modern proletarian that threatened the decorum of subject-matter, and to this end he represented a fillet in his subject's hair, which was no doubt designed to designate this sculpture's debt to Classical portraits.[46] This is the first expression of Rodin's lifelong desire to convey his links to the ancient Greeks, and by extension to argue his legitimacy as their rightful heir (as always, at the expense of the Ecole). Finally, and not least of all, it is his first deliberate expression of an interest in "pure sculpture," which became, as his work matured, a persistent rationale for his development of the partial figure, along with other related forms of the *non-finito* in his sculpture.[47]

135. Rodin, Auguste
The Man with the Broken Nose
1875
Marble
17½ × 16¼ × 9⅓ in.
(44.5 × 41.3 × 23.7 cm)
Paris, Musée Rodin

The rejection of *Mask of the Man with the Broken Nose* by the Salon jury would be the first of many reversals Rodin suffered in the official Salon. It is also evident that Rodin understood that this rejection was related at least in part to the bust's fragmentation, for when he took it up again, in 1872, he reworked the mask into a more finished bust that was successfully submitted in plaster to the Brussels Salon of that year, and in marble to the Paris Salon of 1875 (pl. 135). It is also probable that Rodin had little regard for this "fleshing-out" of his fragment, for it was uniquely as a mask that he executed numerous bronze casts during his lifetime. He commented to Truman Bartlett: "That mask [*sic*] determined all my future work. It was the first good piece of modeling I ever did … . I have kept that mask before my mind in everything I have done … . In fact, I have never succeeded in making a figure as good as 'The Broken Nose.'"[48]

The marble *Man with the Broken Nose* was Rodin's first successful submission to the Paris Salon. Coming a full decade after its rejection the first time around, it may have seemed more of a denouement than a debut, even while it may also have underscored the importance of finish and the standards of "grandeur, purity, and the ideal" that were enforced by the Salon jury. Rodin's next major effort, *The Age of Bronze* (pl. 136), exhibited in plaster first at the Cercle Artistique et Littéraire in Brussels during the winter of 1877, and that spring at the Salon in Paris, was a coming-out of a whole different order, with important consequences for Rodin's future artistic directions. This was Rodin's first foray into the public sphere as a *statuaire*. Although this was the first and the most completely developed full figure that Rodin brought into the public

136. Marconi, Guglielmo
Rodin's *The Age of Bronze*
Albumin print
Paris, Musée Rodin

sphere, it was, as we shall see, a work whose indeterminacy of meaning bears upon the later development of the partial figure. Rodin had been living and working in Brussels since 1870, scraping by as an assistant to other sculptors, and he was eager to make a name for himself in Paris as an artist of monumental statues, considered to be the highest ambition for a sculptor. Like *The Man with the Broken Nose*, *The Age of Bronze* too was a protracted effort carried out over 18 months, interrupted by a sojourn in Italy where Rodin "discovered" Michelangelo, seeking a basis in the art of his predecessor for his own development of the life-size human figure.

From the time of its display in Brussels, Rodin was nagged by accusations or indirect insinuations that this sculpture was cast from life. Compared to the later *Balzac* scandal, these accusations were not of great consequence to anyone but Rodin: the sculpture was, after all, accepted by the jury to the Paris Salon without incident, and the rumors seem not to have been taken seriously by many of Rodin's contemporaries, who expressed their admiration for this work.[49] The persistence of this rumor nevertheless proved to be a deflating experience for him, for he had banked great hopes on the effect that this sculpture would have on his reputation. Instead of winning him praise as a *statuaire*, it brought him the stigma of association with life-casting, with its implications of a deficiency in both skill and imagination. This must have been the more painful owing to Rodin's devastating rejection from the Ecole des Beaux-Arts some 20 years before. The aspersions cast on his abilities therefore fed on his insecurities, along with the concomitant sense of injustice he must have felt, and reinforced the perception of a pattern of organized discrimination against his work in the official Salon, aided by critics unsympathetic to his achievement. A critic for the *Gazette des Beaux-Arts* described Rodin's sculpture as a "sickly nude fellow," and found its title, *The Age of Bronze*, pretentious. The critic Charles Tardieu, writing in the periodical *L'Art*, actually praised the sculpture for its quality of "life," but also found it to be "a slavish likeness of a model with neither character nor beauty, an astonishingly exact copy of a most commonplace individual."[50]

The sparse yet unfavorable reaction by critics to *The Age of Bronze* reflected the widely shared view that sculpture should improve upon nature, and should be ennobling to its beholder. The greatest achievement of *The Age of Bronze* rests in the naturalism of its modeling, its fastidious observation of detail, and the refinement of its surface transitions. Arguably, it is among Rodin's most "finished" sculptures, yet ironically this feature appears to have contributed to its unfavorable critical reception. Critics also found fault with the sculpture's ambiguous meanings. It had been exhibited under the title *The Vanquished* in Brussels, and the figure was originally supposed to support two spears in its raised left hand, transparently alluding to the vanquishing of the French in the Franco-Prussian War. Believing that these props spoiled the sculpture's profiles, Rodin exhibited his sculpture without them in Brussels. When it was shipped to Paris he renamed it *The Age of Bronze*, suggesting an awakening, as opposed to the previous title, which had suggested defeat.

Although he aspired to hold his own in the Salon alongside sculptors who enjoyed a more privileged academic pedigree, Rodin did not have the benefit or carry the burden of a Classical education. "He read a great deal," Rilke tells us,[51] but this sculpture, like many that followed, did not employ a traditional rhetoric of the human figure as a vehicle for narration or symbolic meaning, with clear origins in literature, history, or biography. Clarity of identity and expression at this moment in the history of sculpture were understood as necessary prerequisites of a sculpture's completeness. This was especially important for works that aspired to a monumental purpose. By removing the props, ostensibly for formal reasons, Rodin in essence made the sculpture's meaning incomplete,[52] abrogating its connection to traditional narrative or symbolism while cultivating ambiguity in the vacuum that remained. Rodin's comment to Bartlett, echoing his remarks on *The Man with the Broken Nose*, that he aspired "to make a simple sculpture without reference to subject," seems intended, as in this earlier example, to distance his work from a confining association with Realist subject-matter.[53] We should not assume from such statements, however, that Rodin was pursuing a form of *l'art pour l'art*. As he emerged in the public eye during the decade that followed, critics were drawn to him as much because of the expressive power and psychological legitimacy of his work, and a concomitant receptivity to its modernity, as to his robust handling of material and innate formal confidence.

137. Rodin, Auguste
St. John the Baptist Preaching
c. 1880. Musée Rodin cast in 1962
Bronze
Georges Rudier
19¾ × 11 × 9⅛ in.
(50.2 × 27.9 × 23.2 cm)
Iris and B. Gerald Cantor
Foundation

The malleability and indeterminacy of his subject-matter, resulting from his willingness to divest this sculpture of its props or to allow for the coexistence of potentially conflicting identities, corresponds to his broader disregard for "finish," which was its own form of indeterminacy. This figure's ineffable expression of pathos and its complex emotional character ranging between awakening and acquiescence, élan and inertia, required methods of interpretation at odds with the functional prerequisites of the traditional monument. A new form of criticism was required to interpret meaning on this level, and it is not surprising that some of the most authoritative voices to interpret his work during its emergence—Octave Mirbeau, Gustave Geffroy, Georges Rodenbach, and, not least of all, Rilke—were either poets themselves, or more broadly receptive to the undercurrents of *fin-de-siècle* Symbolism and its connections to a burgeoning embrace of modernity.

138. Unknown photographer
Rodin's *Bust of St. John the Baptist*
in the Salon of the Société des
Artistes français
1879
Albumin print
Paris, Musée Rodin

One of the consequences of the accusations leveled against the perceived naturalism of *The Age of Bronze* was an immediate change in Rodin's working methods and approach to the figure. He would never again aspire to achieve the level of anatomical verisimilitude and refinement of detail that was a dominant feature of this work. *St. John the Baptist Preaching* (pl. 137), begun in 1878 and intended for the Salon of 1879, was larger than life and robustly modeled, foreclosing the possible accusation that it was a life-cast. The statue was not completed in time for the Salon, to which Rodin submitted instead a bust of the figure—in essence, its first fragmentation—which was awarded an honorable mention (pl. 138). Unevenly cut across the chest and shoulders, asymmetrical and rough around the edges, this bust was conspicuously a fragment of a larger whole, as distinguished from a self-contained entity. When the statue was submitted to the Salon in the following year, it stood alongside a bronze cast of *The Age of Bronze* that had been commissioned by the French state and which would stand for many years thereafter in the Jardin du Luxembourg.[54] The statue of *St. John the Baptist Preaching*, alongside *The Age of Bronze*, suggested a complementary relationship in which the ambiguity of the latter was replaced with a degree of narrative and iconographic clarity in the former that is uncharacteristic of Rodin's future development. *St. John's* robust modeling was complemented by its representation in full stride,

139. Freuler, E.
Rodin's *Torso of the Walking Man*
("*First Impression*")
c. 1878
Albumin print
Paris, Musée du Petit Palais

asserting the subject's evangelical identity. It is an affirmative and confident work, the fulfillment of Rodin's maturity as a *statuaire*, and an important step away from *The Age of Bronze*, which is arguably more tentative and labored, if also more prophetic of the open-endedness that become a defining characteristic of Rodin's modernity.

These two statues standing side by side in the first Salon of the decade—one representing Rodin's first official commission, the award of a 3rd Class Medal, and a vindication of his work's integrity, the other, the fulfillment of an honorable mention awarded to the bust the year before—must have signaled to Rodin, as to the contemporary art world in Paris, that he had arrived, a mature talent approaching his fortieth year in full possession of his powers. Few would doubt that he would remain thereafter in the forefront of the public's attention, but for the remainder of the decade this would play out at some remove from the official Salon. Confident and complete in its own right, *St. John* also prefigures the germination of the partial figure in Rodin's sculpture. Ruth Butler observes that while he was at work on *St. John*, he developed an approach that would become his standard procedure of fragmenting segments of the body, working on each part separate from the whole, which he would recombine.[55]

In addition to the fragmentary bust of *St. John the Baptist* submitted to the Salon of 1879, Rodin developed an independent torso that has endured a fairly tortured identity regarding both its origins and its subsequent place in his sculpture (pl. 139).[56] Although not precisely the same torso as the one used in the final version of *St. John*, it seems certain that it was modeled in conjunction with it, was possibly a study for it, and was most likely based on the same model, Pignatelli, whom Rodin described much later in his reminiscences to Dujardin-Beaumetz:

One morning ... a peasant from Abruzzi ... had come to me to offer himself as a model. Seeing him, I was seized with admiration: that rough, hairy man, expressing in his bearing and physical strength all the violence, but also all the mystical character of his race.

I thought immediately of St. John the Baptist; that is, a man of nature, a visionary, a believer, a forerunner come to announce one greater than himself.

The peasant undressed, mounted the model stand as if he had never posed; he planted himself, head up, torso straight, at the same time supported on his two legs, opened like a compass. The movement was so right, so determined, and so true that I cried: "But it's a walking man!" I immediately resolved to make what I had seen.[57]

Rodin may have combined this torso with the legs of *St. John* only around 1900 when, according to Judith Cladel, he struggled with their fusion, no longer having the model before him, and making no attempt to conceal the traces of their attachment.[58] The *Walking Man* (pls. 134, 141) is therefore a late although uniquely important example of the partial figure in Rodin's sculpture, but it is intriguing to consider that it existed in a "potential" state at the time its components were modeled around 1879. There is, however, nothing to prepare us for a leap of this magnitude at this early stage of Rodin's development. Although he may have worked on components of the figure independently, he continued at this stage of his career to approach the human form as an integrated entity possessed of all its parts, harmoniously arranged in the ensemble. The

torso combined with the legs suggests a figure in motion: the fulfillment of that motif originally required its completion and resolution as an organic whole, which is precisely what occurred with the realization of the statue of *St. John* shortly before the Salon of 1880.

The later-named *Torso of the Walking Man* (pl. 139)[59] may be considered the earliest true expression of the partial figure in Rodin's œuvre. Although it is more a fragment than its namesake, it also represents a more imaginable origin of the partial figure for two fundamental reasons: first, it refers to the antique fragment and therefore can be related to a specific iconographic tradition; and second, it is more demonstrably identifiable as a study or preparatory sketch than is the composite *Walking Man*. The torso's antiquarian influences and allusions were prefigured by Rodin's copy of the Belvedere *Torso* for the Palais des Académies in Brussels. Unlike this earlier work, however, the *Torso of the Walking Man* did not originate as a pastiche. It is an original work modeled from life and probably preparatory to the finished *St. John the Baptist Preaching*. The tortured abrasions of its surface, which prompted Elsen to speculate that it was not modeled from life, are probably the result of later reworkings, combined with the vestiges of accidents that may have occurred as this sculpture lay around his studio.[60] The *Walking Man*, on the other hand, is not a preparatory study, but a later synthesis that brings this torso together with the legs from the 1880 statue, deliberately preserving the rough seam that traces its composite identity.[61]

The designation of the *Torso of the Walking Man* as an autonomous work of art calls into question the relationship of a study to a finished work, and the mechanisms by which the contingency of a preparatory work could be displaced by its perceived self-sufficiency. Fundamentally, such distinctions may rest in the eye of the beholder, or in the designs of the maker: might a sculpture not be perceived as "finished" when it is designated as such by its author? As we shall see, beginning at about this time in his career, Rodin would blur the distinctions between sketch and finished work with increasing confidence and independence, focusing on the common thread of the creative act that ties together myriad stages of a sculpture's development.

In traditional practice, there was a clear hierarchical relationship between the various stages of *esquisse* (sketch), *étude* (study), *ébauche* (preliminary stages of the final work), and *maquette* (a refined anticipatory model), as distinguished from the finished work of art that was the synthesis of these forms of preparatory thinking in order to produce a work that was the result of a more deliberate and reflective process and a more careful and resolved technique.[62] The realization of a work of art was understood to be divisible into two distinct stages: the spontaneous creative act, followed by its mechanical transformation into a "finished" form. Distinguishing between these stages and highlighting the value placed on the former, Denis Diderot observed in the *Encyclopédie*: "A fine sketch is the work of genius, and genius cannot be acquired. Technique is the fruit of time, patience and hard work, and this men can acquire if they will."[63]

Conservative artistic theory saw "finish" (*le fini*) as the indispensable condition of a successful work of art, and understood it quite literally as a moral imperative. Progressives, on the other hand, favored the more spontaneous, generative aspects of the creative process, reflecting the values associated with individuality, spontaneity,

inspiration, and artistic and intellectual freedom. Ernest Chesneau (1833–1890), a liberal critic and voice for reform in art education, characterized the differences in these competing points of view in this way: the method of certain artists, he wrote, is driven by their passion (he cites Shakespeare, Rembrandt, and Beethoven). Artists of this kind invite constant analysis, presenting an inexhaustible resource that never leaves you without something new to discover. Artists of this "privilege," he continues, are not the same as those whose talent most closely approaches "perfection," which requires the qualities of finish, precision, and clarity. Artists of this kind (he cites Phidias and Raphael) do not lend themselves to a sustained analysis that always has more to offer. Although such artists are not to be undervalued, there is little that one can interject into their work; they have abandoned nothing to ambiguous interpretation; their meanings are precise, clear, and straightforward: "they bring nothing mysterious to our experience of them."[64] The so-called sketch–finish controversy was rooted in the Romantic movement and in the value it placed on individual "genius" as opposed to "rule" and technique.

Rodin was clearly influenced by Romantic views regarding genius and spontaneity, and the notion of "mystery" (the fluid and open-ended potential of work to reveal new meanings) would become a *sine qua non* of his work in its maturity. In 1880, however, he was still a relative newcomer to the ways of the Salon, an aspiring *statuaire* who subscribed to the primacy of the full-sized figure, and his ideas regarding the fragment were less advanced than they would become in the ensuing decade when he began to work on *The Gates of Hell*.

No single project in Rodin's career was more integral to the development of the partial figure in his work than the commission he received in 1880 to execute a monumental portal for a proposed museum of the decorative arts. As is well known, this museum was never begun, and the *Gates* were never properly finished by Rodin or cast in his lifetime, remaining disassembled in his studio at the time of his death in 1917.[65] Nevertheless, according to Professor Elsen, by 1884 Rodin had probably completed much of what we see today in the *The Gates of Hell*.[66] By 1887, when the project for the proposed Museum of Decorative Arts was no longer viable,[67] the *Gates* had taken on a life of its own, becoming a fountainhead for the seemingly endless stream of figures and groups that Rodin had begun to exhibit almost exclusively in commercial galleries; in particular, at the new and upscale Galerie Georges Petit.

The working methods that Rodin employed when modeling *St. John the Baptist* expanded to encompass the simultaneous production of vast quantities of individual figures and groups that Rodin conceived for the *Gates*, which developed apart from it as free-standing individual subjects. By 1885, when the first articles on "the door" (as it was then called) began to appear, Octave Mirbeau estimated "more than 300 figures, each portraying a different attitude or feeling, each expressing in powerful synthesis a form of human passion, pain, and malediction."[68]

An analysis of Rodin's submissions to the Salon in this decade reveals a two-tiered presentation of his work in which mostly portraits were sent to the Salon and more experimental works—many of them offspring of *The Gates of Hell*—were exhibited within commercial galleries.[69] There is some irony in this, for although the busts presented a sort of "who's who" of important players in the world of arts and letters and were individually works of impressive accomplishment, the *Gates* was a major public

142. Rodin, Auguste
Fallen Caryatid with Stone
1880–81
Marble
17⅜ × 12 × 12 in.
(43.9 × 30.5 × 30.5 cm)
Iris and B. Gerald Cantor Collection,
promised gift to the Iris and
B. Gerald Cantor Foundation

commission, elevating Rodin's public profile and status, while having the practical effect of providing him with a studio in the state-run Dépôt des Marbres on the rue de l'Université. Rodin may have been holding out until the *Gates* was completed and its destination secured before he was ready to feature it in the official Salon; his reticence to bring it into public display may also have been influenced by politics concerning the realization of the museum itself.[70] The most likely reason, however, may be found in the remarkable character of the works that emerged in conjunction with the *Gates*: sculptures whose body language, sexuality, fragmentation, and assemblage would not have passed muster with the Salon juries of the 1880s and possibly not until after his private, one-man exhibition at the place d'Alma during the 1900 Exposition Universelle.

The first public appearance of progeny from the *Gates* occurred in 1883 at the Cercle des Arts Libéraux on the rue Vivienne, which included a figure called *The Age of Stone*, later reincarnated as the *Fallen Caryatid with Stone* (pl. 142), and *Torso of a Contorted Nude Female Figure*, which, although unidentified, represents Rodin's first documented exhibition of a genuine, unmediated partial figure. Charles Frémine, who had written favorably about *The Age of Bronze* and *St. John*, commented that these two works made him "tremble before Rodin's talent," but he continued to offer the following advice: "... that is, that contortion no more creates character than a grimace creates expression, and the originality that one might sometimes go to great lengths to achieve often is nothing other, after all, than frankness (*"la franchise"*) and simplicity."[71]

Rodin's real breakthrough occurred in 1886 when he exhibited three groups: *I am Beautiful* (pl. 143), two unidentified "couples," and five female figures, including the *Crouching Woman, Andromeda*, a version of the *Fallen Caryatid, Eve* (pl. 1), and the *Tempest*, at the Galerie Georges Petit. Although none of these works, technically, is a partial figure, and although at least some of them were exhibited in marble (a material characteristically understood as the paragon of "finish"), they were ostensibly fragments from the door, characterized by Gustave Geffroy with a deliberate oxymoron as *"esquisses realisées en marbre"* ("sketches carved in marble").[72] This constituted the largest collective group of works from *The Gates of Hell* to be exhibited in public at one time, and it reflects an important shift in Rodin's work on many levels: from the Salon statue to the "apartment sculpture" (what Eméric-David denigrated as sculpture of the "boudoir"), from the autonomous figure to work extracted from a larger context, and from work of apparent resolution and finality to work that—regardless of medium—was open to future modification. This display served to bring Rodin to the attention of a group of critics who were favorably disposed toward the originality of this work, and set the stage for a sequel, three years later, when in conjunction with the Exposition Universelle of 1889, he exhibited more than 36 works with Petit in an exhibition shared with the painter Claude Monet.[73]

As in the 1886 show, there were in the Monet–Rodin exhibition relatively few works that were technically partial figures: a torso sometimes known as *Marsyas* (pl. 144), another, unidentified torso, an *Ugolino* study, as well as a handful of wax *"études,"* the identity of which are unknown. The overall impression that one draws from a comprehensive survey of these works recalls contemporary descriptions of the artist's studio, where one saw:

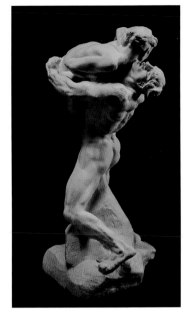

143. Rodin, Auguste
I am Beautiful
1882
Plaster
27½ × 13 × 13⅔ in.
(69.8 × 33.2 × 34.5 cm)
Paris, Musée Rodin

144. Rodin, Auguste
Marsyas (Torso of Falling Man, Enlargement)
c. 1882–89, Musée Rodin cast 4/12 in 1970
Bronze
Georges Rudier
40½ × 27½ × 18½ in.
(102.9 × 69.9 × 47 cm)
Iris and B. Gerald Cantor Collection, promised gift to the Iris and B. Gerald Cantor Foundation

145. Rodin, Auguste
Dried-up Springs
c. 1880
Plaster
26¼ × 21⅔ × 24 in.
(66.5 × 55 × 61 cm)
Paris, Musée Rodin

scattered pell-mell statuettes of every dimension, upturned faces, twisted arms, contorted legs. Behind the Gate ... stretches a vista as of some phantasmagoric cemetery, peopled by a mute yet eloquent crowd, each unit of which we feel impelled to examine, as in the conning of a book that has to be deciphered page by page, paragraph by paragraph, sentence by sentence, word by word.[74]

A somewhat less awestruck Edmond de Goncourt alternatively saw in the collective abundance of Rodin's work from these years: "a man of projects, of sketches, who fragments himself into a thousand imaginings, a thousand dreams, but who brings nothing to its final realization."[75] While there is ample evidence to dispute this latter assertion, one can also observe a demonstrable shift in emphasis from the singular "masterpiece" (evidenced by Rodin's submissions to the Salons of 1880 and 1881) to the image that he had begun to convey of his creative process laid bare. The display of works that one saw at Galerie Georges Petit were in dramatically different states of advancement and varied in orders of identity, ranging from a life-sized plaster of *The Burghers of Calais*, to a marble *Severed Head of St. John the Baptist* (pl. 125), to the enigmatic plaster "relief" *Dried-up Springs* (pl. 145), to the diminutive but powerful *Misery* (pl. 146). These works reflect in their range a deliberate blurring of the lines between the private world of the studio and the public world of display, in which the discrete and perfected object—what the public normally saw in isolation—has been superseded by an emphasis on the creative process of the artist.

The prominence of the partial figure, the fragment, the *non-finito* detail, and the *étude* coincides, of course, with this emerging emphasis on process that seems to have grown out of *The Gates of Hell*. The works seen variously at Petit, or in Rodin's studio by the privileged few, were understood by all who beheld them as part of an organic process of creation stimulated by the doors. Individual works, therefore, were to some extent understood as components of this larger process, and Rodin's increasingly experimental technique further reinforced this perception. The *Marsyas* torso (pl. 144), a particularly robust and expressive *morceau*, was derived from the figure known as the *Falling Man* (pl. 102) on the tympanum of the *Gates*. Like the *Torso of the Walking Man*, it refers to antique fragments such as the Belvedere *Torso*, especially because of its exaggerated muscularity, which places it in Rodin's Michelangelesque mode. Rodin also exhibited a plaster cast of *I am Beautiful* (pl. 143) with Petit, a reprise of the same group exhibited in 1886,[76] which is comprised of the *Falling Man* and a version of the *Crouching Woman*. Connections such as these would presumably have been observed by attentive visitors to the gallery.

Rounding out the variety of works shown with Petit, finally, is a figure such as *Misery* (pl. 146), which conforms in size and facture to what might traditionally have been understood as an *esquisse* or an *étude*—that element of the creative process, as Diderot observed, that was the purest reflection of the artist's inspiration. Rodin's exhibition of such works reflects an uncommon willingness to place on display genres of work that were not traditionally part of an artist's public persona, and which for Rodin, at this moment in his career, became one of his defining attributes. Edmond de Goncourt, ever the astute observer, recognized the uniqueness of Rodin's achievement: "almost always with extremities that are not fully executed. In the midst of this Impressionist craze, where everything is in the state of an *esquisse*, [Rodin] will have achieved, himself, the first, his name and his glory in sculpture with *esquisses*."[77]

Not all of the works exhibited with Petit fit into the familiar categories of torso-fragment or *esquisse*. In addition to works such as *Marsyas*, and quite different in feeling, Rodin exhibited an eerily beautiful marble *Severed Head of St. John the Baptist* (pl. 125) that may be his most literal realization of the partial figure as a by-

146. Rodin, Auguste
Misery
1889
Patinated plaster
3½ × 10 × 6 in.
(9 × 25.5 × 15.5 cm)
Paris, Musée Rodin

product of amputation. This sculpture coincides with the widespread contemporary fascination with the subject of St. John's martyrdom at the whim of Salome (it is variously treated by Gustave Flaubert, Gustave Moreau, Odilon Redon, and Jean-Jacques Henner, and was the subject of a notorious play by Oscar Wilde published three years later). John Tancock has suggested its possible relationship to devotional images (*Andachtsbilder*) that had been popular in the Northern Renaissance.[78] Whatever its sources, this work clearly refers to Rodin's vital *Bust of St. John the Baptist* (pl. 138) that had been awarded an honorable mention at the Salon a decade before, and seems designed at least in part to explore alternatives to the conventions of the traditional bust.

Rodin's explorations of the partial figure around this time are directly related to a complementary technique, called *marcottage*, which involved the construction of figures or groups from pre-existing sculptures.[79] The technique of making a new work from pre-existing components originated from Rodin's experience as a decorative sculptor, in which press-molds were commonly used to originate a new work. *Marcottage*, as it had been employed by Rodin in the 1860s and 1870s, enabled the mass-production of multiples that could be customized once they had been removed from the mold. In the groups exhibited with Petit in 1889, this technique was given a creative role inspired less by the commercial possibilities of prefabrication than by the possibilities for sculptural invention that might result from this technique. *I am Beautiful* (pl. 143), *Fugitive Love* (pl. 80; called *The Dream* in 1889), the doppelgänger *Dried-up Springs* (pl. 145), and the work that came to be known as *The Three Shades* (pl. 95; identified as *Etudes* in the Petit catalogue) from *The Gates of Hell*, were each the by-product of this process in which, as he commented to Dujardin-Beaumetz many years later, the figures seem to "approach one another and group themselves by themselves."[80]

These groups are a fulfillment of the fragment's potential. One traces through them an internal conversation between Rodin's individual fragments and figures—the progeny of the *Gates*—and their deployment as elements of construction in the unfolding of his works. One immediate consequence of this methodology was a fairly radical reversal of a sculpture's traditional narrative structure and development. Rather than beginning with a subject of literary origin that the artist worked up into a finished and resolved narrative, Rodin took individual characters with separate and unrelated identities and brought them together, so that the subject, as Rilke observed, "transforms itself into reality during the process of work." Rilke compared the artist to the custodian of a museum (by which we assume he means a "keeper" or "curator") who continuously evolved new meanings from his work: "One learns much from his interpretations," he cautions, referring to Rodin's habit of assigning multiple titles to his sculptures, "but in [their] contemplation ... alone and undisturbed, one gathers a still fuller and richer understanding of them."[81]

Rodin crossed a threshold in 1889 that had previously separated the private work of the studio from work in the public domain. At an earlier stage in his career, sculptures such as the *Torso of the Walking Man* remained securely in that private domain. This sculpture was germane to the development of his work of the moment, *St. John the Baptist Preaching*, but was relegated to a secondary status as part of its generative subtext. By 1889 it was no longer clear where, if at all, the public and private aspects of

147. Rodin. Auguste
Mme. Morla Vicuña
1888
Marble
22¼ × 19½ × 14½ in.
(56.5 × 49.5 × 36.8 cm)
Paris. Musée d'Orsay

his work diverged.[82] Rodin's submissions to the Salon of 1890 seem to have augured well for an increasing boldness in this privileged arena, for in addition to the marble *Danaïd* (not listed in the catalogue, but purchased from the Salon for the Musée du Luxembourg), and a silver-plated bust of Mrs. Russell, he included an unspecified torso, *esquisses*, a bronze of *She Who Was the Helmet-maker's Beautiful Wife* (pl. 98) "*dans une grotte*" (in a grotto), and possibly the rather animated group called *Entwined Women*.[83] Throughout the 1890s, Rodin continued to send products of *The Gates of Hell* to the annual Salons, but characteristically in more advanced states of "finish." It was not until the Exposition Rodin of 1900 that he again identified the partial figure so indelibly with his œuvre and its focus on the artist's generative hand.

There were, however, two important and very different works exhibited in the Salons of these years that expanded the scope and identity of Rodin's uses of the partial figure. In the Salon of 1895, following the definitive rupture of his on-off relationship with the sculptor Camille Claudel, he submitted a marble bust, identified simply as a "*Tête*" (Head), later called *Thought* (pl. 131), that was developed from an earlier portrait of Camille in a Breton cap dating from the preceding decade.[84] Rodin had pursued a *non-finito* style in earlier marbles from this period, notably in the bust of *Mme. Morla Vicuña* (pl. 147) exhibited in the 1888 Salon and purchased for the Luxembourg, and in the *Danaïd*, exhibited first with Petit in 1889 and then in the Salon of 1890 (from which it was also purchased for the Luxembourg). Never previously had Rodin treated the raw material of a marble sculpture so abstractly or with such evident symbolic intent. In spite of later anecdotal evidence suggesting that the sculptor left the block beneath the head as an afterthought, there is strong empirical evidence to suggest that this concept was entirely deliberate.[85]

The subject-matter of *Thought* is compelling for autobiographical reasons alone. It may be associated with a significant number of figural groups that Rodin developed around this time exploring the theme of tragic love, many of them carved in marble.[86] Independent of its autobiographical context, *Thought* is a remarkable inversion of the torso fragment, in which the body is missing its head. The symbolism of this work, by comparison, depends upon our heightened awareness that the head is missing its body. It may be compared in this regard to the somewhat earlier *Severed Head of St. John the Baptist*, but in *Thought* the conception does not rely on a pre-existing narrative and the outcome is less grotesque. In a traditional bust, the viewer participates in the work's fiction, reading it as an abbreviation of the greater subject, without a heightened awareness of what is not there. The meanings that might be taken from the symbolism of this portrait—themes of loss, separation, isolation, and disengagement—derive specifically from our reading of the figure's immersion in the block. This block is not simply a pedestal or a support. It is a dominant expressive feature that takes on associations with a world beyond our reach. It should be noted that this conception, which refers to Michelangelo's *non-finito* and unfinished marbles, does so by opposition: Rodin's figure (achieved by indirect carving, and developed from an external model) is subsumed into the block, whereas in Michelangelo the figure (carved directly) is understood to be emerging from it.

A critic for *Le Figaro*, reviewing the Salon, described this *Tête* as "an exquisite study" ("*une étude exquise*"), "an evocation more than the bust of a woman."[87] These qualities—the work as an *étude* (always an odd characterization for a marble) and an

148. Druet, Eugène
Rodin's *Monument to Victor Hugo* at
the Salon of the Société Nationale
des Beaux-Arts
1897
Photograph
Paris, Musée Rodin

"evocation" (as distinguished from a "representation")—led another reviewer, who was an important supporter of Rodin and an admirer of his work, to express his reservations about the indeterminacy of Rodin's sculpture in a well-considered critique. That critic was Gustave Larroumet, who had been director of the Fine Arts ministry and was instrumental in awarding Rodin both commissions for the monuments to Victor Hugo. Larroumet expressed his admiration for Rodin's sincerity and conviction; however, he continued, "it is impossible to concede in principle that sculpture can borrow from poetry, even music, that which they have reserved for themselves until now. In the domain of the vague and the imprecise, how can sculpture preserve the clarity of its forms and its contours? Sculpture of this kind risks being limited to the maquette, of indicating everything and finishing nothing."[88] Larroumet may well have had the troubled Hugo project for the Panthéon in mind when he offered these words of caution. But one might nevertheless observe in these remarks, from a well-intentioned supporter, the identification of characteristics that were linked with an increasingly open-ended sculptural language, and a propensity to blur the distinctions as they were understood at that time between a sketch and a "finished" work.[89]

A second noteworthy advancement of the partial figure in the public sphere appeared in the Salon of 1897, in which the *Monument to Victor Hugo* (pl. 148), attended by two "muses" later to be called *Meditation Without Arms* (pl. 53) and *Tragic Muse* (pl. 59), occupied the place of honor under the central dome of the exhibition hall. This project had a rather tortuous past. It had been commissioned in 1889 by Larroumet as part of a grand scheme of works for the Panthéon celebrating the Revolution and the great heroes of France's Republican past, including monuments to Hugo in one transept and to Mirabeau in the other. From the inception, Rodin envisioned a figure of Hugo in exile, seated on the rock at Guernsey, surrounded by three muses whose identities changed frequently throughout the genesis of the project.

In 1890 the committee that had been constituted by Larroumet to oversee the project, including the sculptors Jules Dalou, Jules Chaplain, Eugène Guillaume, and Henri Chapu, reviewed Rodin's project and rejected it unanimously, finding that it lacked clarity and did not harmonize with the architectural milieu. Larroumet, snatching victory from the jaws of defeat, removed this version from the Panthéon's program, sanctioning Rodin to develop a new maquette. He awarded Rodin a second commission that would relocate this monument to an unspecified outdoor site (it was first designated for the Luxembourg and then the Jardin du Palais Royal, where it was inaugurated in 1909).[90]

Hugo was an enormously popular figure in late nineteenth-century France—larger than life, prodigious in his achievement, a symbol of the most cherished values of the Republic, and as close to a god as any mortal could become in secular *fin-de-siècle* France. The work enjoyed the benefit of excited expectation. As soon as it was brought into the Champ de Mars, Geffroy observed: "there was nothing other than a cry of admiration among the workers."[91] Rodin's conception of the poet, "nude like a god,"[92] tapped this deep reservoir of affection. In the following description of the sculpture by Thiébault-Sisson, one can feel the excitement that Rodin's embodiment of the poet aroused, as he conceived him:

on a rock pounded by the tide, the poet-dreamer, seated, his right leg folded, his left leg extended in a movement that produces the most imperious majesty. His powerful head rests on his folded right arm in the attitude popularized by the photograph. Beneath him the sonorous roar of the waves, the steady tremor of the tide, [while] he seeks the perception of something else; he attempts to probe the unfathomable, tear mystery away from the unknown and, as if he could be instructed by what he hears, he cups his hand around his ear, while his extended left arm imposes silence upon everything that might distract him from his goal, the uprooting of the interior vision that he pursues.

The author praised the directness of the gesture: "No trace of rhetoric ... no grandiloquence, no triviality," comparing it to the greatest achievements of Hellenistic sculpture.[93]

The reception of the monument in the Salon of 1897 proved to be one of Rodin's greatest public successes. It is more remarkable considering the state of advancement and condition of the plaster that he put on display. Henri Lebossé, Rodin's master *mouleur*, had trouble completing the casts in time, and Rodin, who was a vice-president of the sculpture section of the Salon, decided to exhibit them anyway.[94] Eugène Druet's photographs of the plaster *in situ* reveal a work that was cobbled together with visible rivets and unevenly matched seams. A network of rods supported the suspended *Tragic Muse* and the poet's outstretched arm, and the figure of *Meditation*, armless, was laced with traces of the piece mold that had not been filed down. It was standard procedure for sculptors to submit works in plaster to the Salon in anticipation of their later transformation into marble or bronze, but the tentativeness of this confection would have tested the limits of public acceptance, were it not for the power of the ensemble overshadowing these details.

By the time the monument was again exhibited, in a marble that was the centerpiece of the 1901 Salon (pl. 149), the ancillary figures had been removed, leaving the magisterial Hugo alone among his thoughts in the grand, domed center of the exhibition hall.

150. Rodin, Auguste
Meditation Without Arms
1883–84 (?)
Plaster
21¼ × 7½ × 6¼ in.
(54 × 18.8 × 15.9 cm)
Paris, Musée Rodin

151. Rodin, Auguste
Tragic Muse
1908–10
Marble (unfinished)
36¼ × 57¾ × 37¾ in.
(92 × 146.5 × 96 cm)
Paris, Musée Rodin

The two muses enjoyed their own afterlife as individual figures. *Meditation Without Arms* (pls. 53, 150), which fragments the figure further by removing her draperies, leaving the legs in a more aggressively unfinished state, has become one of the most poignant modern expressions of Rodin's use of the partial figure. In this isolated figure, Rodin articulated one of the most compelling discourses in his work between the fleshy reality of the female figure, her inward-spiraling, highly abstract gesture, and the near-lustful relationship with raw material that Rodin conveys in its many *non-finito* passages.

Rodin initiated the task of transforming the plaster *Tragic Muse* (pl. 151) into a carved version independent from the ensemble in 1901, and work on it was sporadically undertaken by the practitioner Mathet between 1908 and 1910.[95] Technically, a work in a transitory material such as plaster that anticipates translation into the more durable materials of bronze or marble would fall within a broad definition of "unfinished." An important distinction must be made, however, between a work that only remained to be cast or carved, and a work "in progress"—that is to say, unresolved in its final arrangement or detail. It was widely assumed among Rodin's contemporaries that plaster was not a condition of a work's finality but of its potential, and the transformation of this *Muse* into marble represents in its unfinished state a playing-out of this potential.[96]

The head of the *Tragic Muse* in particular reveals the least-advanced stage of carving known as the *ébauche*: it has been blocked out to conform to the general proportions and placement of the head, but the *mise-au-point*—the marks of a further-advanced stage of the "pointing" technique, visible on the arms and legs—has not yet been applied here. Judging from the molten appearance of the original head, it may be conjectured that Rodin intended to adapt the head in its marble execution, accommodating the differences of material, and possibly instructed his assistant to leave it in this state for his later interpretation. As suggested by the photograph of Rodin carving the marble *Ariadne* (pl. 153), he would occasionally carve "directly" (that is, without the *mise-au-point*), which would make sense when interpreting a prototype that was itself in a highly transitive form.

We will never know precisely why this marble was not carried to completion, but in the context of Rodin's late marbles—many of which exist in some state of "non-completion"—it is arguable that this work, as it is, was as Rodin intended it to be. It is also striking that while certain passages of this marble have been left in a primitive state of advancement, other areas such as the feet and buttocks reveal a greater development. We can observe with some certainty that this sculpture fulfilled Rodin's ambition to display the practice of his studio, and in particular his authority over it, through his "unfinished" works in the collection he gave to France to form the Musée Rodin.[97] But it also seems imaginable that Rodin left this sculpture in this state because he liked it this way. In the broad planes ("*grandes lignes*") and salient expression ("*caractère*") of this sculpture in its present form of completion, and in the so-called *non-finito* carving with its references to Michelangelo, he found the expressive qualities that were sufficient to consider this work "complete," if not "finished" in the traditional sense.

There is, however, a fundamental difference between the *non-finito* employed by Rodin and its appearance in Michelangelo's work, which undoubtedly influenced Rodin. Herbert von Einem, the Michelangelo scholar, observes that the Florentine sculptor proceeded from traditional attitudes regarding the wholeness of the human figure. He regards Michelangelo's incomplete works as "fragments," reflecting a chasm between his conception of the figure (his pure idea) and its execution (the incomplete fulfillment of the idea). Rodin's "fragments," on the other hand, he regards as "completed" sculptures, intended conceptually to represent a formal and objective unity.[98] Ironically, whereas the unfinished figure in the case of Michelangelo may be seen as a fragment of a greater whole (the unfulfilled material realization of his idea), for Rodin the part was intended, and in fact is rightly perceived, as a whole.[99] Thus he commented to his English biographer, Frederick Lawton: "analysis and synthesis balance each other out in the artist; but the analysis is not a tearing to pieces. [The artist] thinks ... of the whole, even in the part, and his study of the part is for him a way towards more nearly grasping the whole."[100]

The modern viewer, perhaps desensitized to the roughness of Rodin's sculpture in other materials, may observe in this figure an analogous expression of vigor and spontaneity that became hallmarks of his modeled sculpture, as seen in the Hugo ensemble exhibited in the Salon of 1897. The *Tragic Muse* (pl. 151), called the *Modern Muse* by Rodin's assistant in 1908 (in all probability echoing Rodin's own change of title), may be no less "finished" in Rodin's sense of the word than the beautiful figure of *Meditation Without Arms* from this same ensemble. We may be less comfortable accepting degrees of "unfinish" when they are manifested in marble, but this should also call attention to the extent to which our expectations are influenced by material and to the general fluidity of this concept in Rodin's sculpture as a whole.

In spite of the near-unanimous praise for the *Monument to Victor Hugo* in 1897, not all critics were mute on the issue of its condition. Georges Lafenestre, a conservator at the Louvre and professor at the Ecole du Louvre, described it as "a dislocated and incoherent maquette," and as "a colossal ébauche."[101] Another critic quipped: "we do not understand the necessity of this unformed block [*sic*] ... . Soon, if this error continues, someone will present us with a stone or a marble barely extracted from the quarry, without the slightest blow of the chisel, [but] with the simple inscription: 'for the indication of the artist's thought.'"[102] And Louis Gonse, offering what seems to have become the requisite acknowledgement that Rodin was a "master" of modern sculpture, proceeded nevertheless to ask rhetorically: "What had he hoped to accomplish by encouraging the public to discuss a work in the process of being born into the world? Did he wish to affirm the public's right to transgress the secret of the atelier? Did he wish ... to declare by this submission [to the Salon] that the work seemed just right and had arrived at that psychological moment where it suited him not to touch it further?"[103]

Gonse's questions, which transcend the *Hugo* monument, deserve to be taken seriously, for they reflect the chasm that separated the sum implications of Rodin's methods from the traditional and widely-shared belief that a work of art was the culmination of a process: the resolution of a set of ideas, their synthesis and refinement, reflecting an Aristotelian vision of artistic wholeness that saw the work as complete and self-contained. It is fair to observe that this had been the unspoken understanding of the essential nature of a work of art throughout its history. From these isolated examples and commentaries it becomes evident that Rodin was perceived by both friend and foe

152. Rodin, Auguste
Head of the Tragic Muse
1890–96
Bronze
11⅜ × 7¼ × 9⅞ in.
(29.5 × 18.4 × 25.1 cm)
Brooklyn Museum of Art, Gift of the Iris and B. Gerald Cantor Foundation

153. Unknown photographer
Rodin carving the marble sculpture *Ariadne*
c. 1909
Photograph
Paris, Musée Rodin

154. Unknown photographer
The Rodin Pavilion in the Place de
l'Alma
1900

to have fundamentally altered this understanding, and much of the discourse unfolding at this moment in his career represents an effort to wrestle with its implications as well as its consequences.

In this regard, the Exposition Rodin, coinciding with the 1900 Exposition Universelle (the swan-song of these enormous international World's Fairs), represented for Rodin, and for the droves of international admirers who came to see it, the fullest affirmation of his achievement and his uncontested place as the "patriarch" of modern sculpture.[104] Many visitors to the Exposition may have been unaware that this retrospective of the artist's achievements, installed in its own pavilion on the Place de l'Alma (the site of previous retrospectives of Courbet and Manet), was privately funded and not a part of the official enterprise. Rodin's achievement with this exhibition is all the more remarkable considering that he had been virtually unknown a mere 25 years before when he submitted his first statue to the Salon, that *The Gates of Hell* remained unfulfilled (and before this exhibition had never been seen in public), and that his most ambitious monument, the towering *Balzac*, had been ignominiously removed from the Salon just two years before.

All three of these works were included in this retrospective exhibition, along with such other key achievements—all in plaster casts—as *The Burghers of Calais* and the *Monument to Victor Hugo*. These works were the "anchors" of the exhibition: the crowning achievements, whatever their individual circumstances, that punctuated Rodin's extraordinarily compressed and prolific career during the two preceding decades. But what may have most adroitly symbolized the character of this show stood at the entrance, out on the street, where Rodin had placed a cast of the solitary, nude figure of *Pierre de Wiessant*, headless and without hands, summoning visitors to have a look at much more of the same inside (pl. 154). What one found there, among the 165 works listed in the catalog, was the most remarkable and unprecedented assortment of plaster casts, maquettes, fragments, and rough figural groupings that had ever been assembled from the work of a living artist, many of these displayed on tall Corinthian columns that bestowed on the whole a certain improvisatory elegance.

What had been intimated in the exhibition with Monet at the Galerie Georges Petit a decade before, the image of the work in progress—not the individual, discrete work, but the collective, integrated work of the artist—was here presented as a defining statement of purpose, and the significance of this gesture was not lost on visitors to the pavilion. One critic observed at length that the exhibition presented the impression of a sculptor's studio, which we have intruded, as though surprising the artist "in the course of his work":

This general impression, we think, is deliberate; if it is surprising at first, the viewer quickly understands. The artist is not content simply to present several finished works, in their definitive state, ripe for private collections or museums; but he has also aspired, above all, to show the public his work in progress, his researches [*sic*], as well as his projects, his sketches, and if you will, his intentions.[105]

The exhibition was an unqualified success. Almost without dissent, critics and the public embraced the work along with the gesture that was at the core of this remarkable exhibition. In a contemporary article, Rodin made a comment on the nature of "finish" in his work that provides a fairly accurate description of his views and the implications of this exhibition. Interviewed for the prestigious English-language *Art Journal*, he explained:

> There is no finish possible in a work of art, since it is Nature, and Nature knows no finish, being infinite; therefore one stops at some stage or another, when one has put into one's work all one sees, all one has sought for, all one cares to put, or all one particularly wants; *but one could really go on forever and see more to do.*[106]

The perception of the collective work as an extension of nature's infinite variability became the leitmotif of sensitive interpretations of Rodin that gelled around this time, and remained his defining attribute thereafter. In a famous article on the sculptor published just in advance of the Exposition, George Rodenbach likened Rodin to "a force of Nature."[107] Charles Morice argued that his many fragments and partial figures were not "unfinished," and not "*ébauches.*" They are more finished, he argued, than the polished works of many Academicians in that they are "susceptible to development: like life itself. In this one may find the single true definition ... of the verb 'to finish.' It is: to rejoin life, that does not begin, and never ends, and is in perpetual development."[108] The superiority of Rodin's method, Adrien Farge wrote, was that it "opens a vast landscape to the imagination,"[109] and Camille Mauclair characterized the "indefinite continuation" of the work as its most singular characteristic. Among these myriad examples, we might cite the observations of Arthur Symons, the distinguished British art historian and critic. The art of Rodin, he wrote:

> competes with nature rather than with the art of other sculptors. Other sculptors turn life into sculpture, he turns sculpture into life. His clay is part of the substance of the earth, and the earth still clings about it as it comes up and lives. It is at once the flower and the root, that of others is the flower only, and the plucked flower. The link with the earth, which we find in the unhewn masses of rock from which his finest creations of pure form can never quite free themselves, is the secret of his deepest force. It links his creations to nature's, in a single fashion of growth.[110]

155. Druet, Eugène
Rodin's *The Earth*
No date
Photograph
Paris, Bibliothèque Nationale

The consistency of this imagery collectively conveys the importance of a work like *The Earth* (pl. 155), in which Rodin pushed the limits of the partial figure to its greatest extreme. With the partial figure, Rodin rendered obsolete the normative standards of finish as they were understood in the late nineteenth century, and introduced an entirely new meaning of "life" into the work of art. It was as though, at the very onset of the new century, Rodin stepped forth like his *Walking Man*, bridging the nineteenth-century figural tradition with the incipient abstraction that would be developed by a generation of younger sculptors who emerged at some remove from Rodin's shadow. The partial figure, which evolves in Rodin's sculpture from the influence of the antique fragment, became the embodiment of his modernity.

Mimesis (from the Greek verb "to imitate") posed a special problem in the art of sculpture, which as Baudelaire trenchantly observed, was closer to nature, and "as brutal and positive as nature herself."[111] Rodin's exploration of the partial figure, his persistent acknowledgement of raw material in every medium and state of his œuvre, his uses of fragmentation, and the suggestion of his work's seemingly endless potential for transformation, seem not to have been so much an affirmation of sculpture's abstraction *per se*, as they were counterpoints that he played against the organic rhythms of his modeling and his figures' animation. In the wake of this achievement, modern sculpture would never again be the same.

Notes

1   Judith Cladel, *Rodin. Sa vie glorieuse, sa vie inconnue*, Paris: Bernard Grasset, 1936, p. 141.

2   *The Partial Figure in Modern Sculpture*, Baltimore: The Baltimore Museum of Art, December 2, 1969 – February 1, 1970. The author was an undergraduate at The Johns Hopkins University in Baltimore at the time, and had the privilege of revisiting this exhibition regularly. To this impressionable undergraduate, Professor Elsen's exhibition revealed the possibilities of an imaginative study of the history of art that linked the past to the present, offering up still-exciting possibilities for modernism in our own time. I proceeded to Stanford in the following year to pursue graduate study with Professor Elsen, eventually writing a thesis on "Rodin's Carved Sculpture" that evolved from research I had begun as an assistant for Elsen's exhibition *The Pioneers of Modern Sculpture*, London: Hayward Gallery, July 20 – September 23, 1973, organized for the Arts Council of Great Britain. B. Gerald Cantor provided a grant that enabled my travel abroad for this project, which focused on the recreation of a "salon" of late nineteenth-century sculpture, and which opened my eyes to the locus of Rodin's modernity in this period. The relationship that grew between Albert Elsen and Mr. Cantor was one of the most eventful collaborations between a scholar and collector to occur in our time, and the symbiosis of their shared passion for Rodin has had a singular influence on Rodin's renown internationally, but especially in America. Albert Elsen's work on the partial figure seems as fresh today as it did some 30 years ago, and I dedicate this essay to his memory and influence.

3   See in particular Rainer Maria Rilke, *Auguste Rodin*, Leipzig: Insel-Verlag, 1913, reprinted in an English translation by Jesse Lamont and Hans Trausil, New York: Fine Editions Press, 1945, and also by Robert Firmage, Salt Lake City: Peregrine Smith, Inc., 1979. Elsen cited the importance of recent German scholarship on the fragment in J.A. Schmoll gen. Eisenwerth, *Der Torso als Symbol und Form: Zur Geschichte des Torso-Motivs im Werk Rodins*, Baden-Baden: Bruno Grimm, 1954, and *Das Unvollendete als künstlerische Form*, ed. J.A. Schmoll gen. Eisenwerth, Bern and Munich: Francke Verlag, 1959. He also acknowledged the importance of Leo Steinberg's work on both Michelangelo and Rodin. See Leo Steinberg, "Michelangelo's Florentine Pietà: The Missing Leg," in *The Art Bulletin*, L, 1968, pp. 343–53; and *Rodin: Sculptures and Drawings*, New York: Charles E. Slatkin Galleries, May 1963, republished as "Rodin," in *Other Criteria: Conversations with Twentieth-Century Art*, New York: Oxford University Press, 1972, pp. 322–403.

4   Albert E. Elsen, *The Partial Figure in Modern Sculpture*, exhib. cat., Baltimore: The Baltimore Museum of Art, 1969, p. 15.

5   Of singular importance to recent scholarship on the partial figure as an art-historical phenomenon up to and including the work of Rodin is *Le Corps en morceaux*, exhib. cat., Paris: Musée d'Orsay, 1990.

6   Ruth Butler, *Rodin: The Shape of Genius*, New Haven, Connecticut and London: Yale University Press, 1993.

7   Regarding the influence of ancient Greek and Hellenistic art upon the art of the West since the Renaissance, see *D'après l'antique*, exhib. cat., Paris: Musée du Louvre, 2000.

8   The term "*non-finito*" means literally "not completed" or "not finished" (as distinguished from "unfinished"), and is used to describe details of Michelangelo's carving that remain rough and unpolished. See, for example, Charles de Tolnay, *Michelangelo: Sculptor, Painter, Architect*, Princeton, New Jersey and London: Princeton University Press, 1975, p. 109.

9   Elsen, *op. cit.* note 4, pp. 13–15.

10 The proliferation of plaster casts, as well as bronze and marble copies of antique "originals" (though these "originals" were often themselves later revealed to be copies of lost works), was a central condition of the dissemination of Classical taste that Francis Haskell and Nicholas Penny take as their subject in *Taste and the Antique*, New Haven, Connecticut and London: Yale University Press, 1981;

see, in particular, "The Proliferation of Casts and Copies," pp. 79–91, and "Epilogue," pp. 117–24, which trace the industry of reproductions in the nineteenth century.

11   Typical of the iconography of the sculptural fragment is a poem by Samuel Rogers, "To the Fragment of a Statue of Hercules, Commonly Called the Torso," (1805) inspired by the Belvedere *Torso* in the Vatican Museum in Rome: "And dost thou still, thou mass of breathing stone,/ (Thy giant limbs to night and chaos hurled)/ Still sit as on the fragment of a world:/ Surviving all, majestic and alone?" See John Hollander, *The Gazer's Spirit: Poems Speaking to Silent Works of Art*, Chicago and London: The University of Chicago Press, 1995, pp. 127–28. For a discussion of the "cult of ruins" in French literature of the late eighteenth century, see Roland Mortier, *La Poétique des ruines en France*, Geneva: Librairie Droz, 1974. Regarding the symbolism of the fragment, especially in the imagery of Fuseli, see Jonah Siegel, *Desire and Excess: The Nineteenth-Century Culture of Art*, Princeton, New Jersey and Oxford: Princeton University Press, 2000, pp. 28–39.

12   Regarding the preference for the restoration of antique fragments see Haskell and Penny, *op. cit.* note 10, pp. 102–03.

13   Haskell and Penny, *op. cit.* note 10, p. 105, observe that William Pars's drawings of the Parthenon reliefs, commissioned by the Society of Dilettanti, were not published until after Winckelmann's premature death in 1768, and that the first casts of these sculptures were not distributed until 1795.

14   Siegel, *op. cit.* note 11, p. 60.

15   Both are quoted in Siegel, *op. cit.* note 11, p. 61, note 30.

16   Although he collected antique fragments when his income made this possible, Rodin was least prone to the Positivist impulse. His periodic writings on ancient sculpture make clear, however, the blend of Romanticism and Naturalism that drew him to this work. Regarding Rodin's frequent expressions of admiration in his later years for Greek art, see Auguste Rodin, *Rodin on Art*, ed. Paul Gsell, trans. Romilly Fedden, New York: Horizon Press, 1971, published originally as *L'Art. Entretiens réunis par Paul Gsell*, Paris: Bernard Grasset, 1911; see also Rodin's "La Leçon de l'Antique," in *Le Musée. Revue de l'art antique*, I, no. 1, January–February 1904, pp. 15–18; "Une statuette de femme au Musée de Naples," in *Le Musée. Revue de l'art antique*, I, no. 3, May–June, 1904, pp. 116–20; and "Vénus. A la Vénus de Milo," in *L'Art et les artistes*, X, March 1910. Regarding his collection of antiquities see *Rodin collectionneur*, exhib. cat., Paris: Musée Rodin, 1967.

17   Marcel Proust, *Du côté de chez Swann* [1913], Paris: Pléiade, I, p. 255.

18   Haskell and Penny, *op. cit.* note 10, p. 333.

19   See Rodin, *L'Art*, *cit.* note 16, p. 278; and F.T. Marinetti, "The Founding and Manifesto of Futurism [1909]," in *Futurist Manifestos*, ed. Umbro Apollonio, New York: Viking Press, 1973, p. 21.

20   Haskell and Penny, *op. cit.* note 10, pp. 328–30. The authors point out the iconographical problems that precluded the restoration of this figure, which was perceived alternately as a Venus Victrix, originally holding the apple awarded to her by Paris; as a Muse holding a lyre; as the guardian deity of Milos, holding an attribute of the island or a shield; or as part of a grouping with her companion Mars. See also "La Vénus de Milo," in *D'après l'antique*, *cit.* note 7, pp. 432ff.

21   For the historical adaptations of this torso in later works of art see Raimunde Wünsche, *Der Torso, Ruhm und Rätsel*, Munich: Staatlichen Antikensammlungen und Glyptothek, 1998; Antoinette Le Normand-Romain, "Torso de Belvédère," in *Le corps en morceaux*, *cit.* note 5, pp. 99–115; Haskell and Penny, *op. cit.* note 10, p. 313; and Schmoll gen. Eisenwerth, *op. cit.* note 3, p. 125 and pl. 47.

22   William Hogarth, *The Analysis of Beauty*, London, 1753, quoted in Haskell and Penny, *op. cit.* note 10, pp. 312–13.

23   Cladel, *op. cit.* note 1, p. 112. All translations from the French by the author unless otherwise noted.

24   Rodin, "Vénus. A la Vénus de Milo," *cit.* note 16; reprinted as *A La Vénus de Milo*, Paris: La Jeune Parque, 1945, pp. 2–3. Italics added for emphasis.

25   Albert E. Elsen, *In Rodin's Studio: A Photographic Record of Sculpture in the Making*, Ithaca, New York: Phaidon in association with the Musée Rodin, 1980, p. 174.

26   For the identification of this hand with this Burgher of Calais see Athena Tacha Spear, *Rodin Sculpture in the Cleveland Museum of Art*, Cleveland: Cleveland Museum of Art, 1967, pp. 79, 82.

27   Albert E. Elsen, *The Gates of Hell by Auguste Rodin*, Stanford, California: Stanford University Press, 1985, p. 146.

28   See Léonce Bénédite, "Les Salons de 1898. La Sculpture," in *Gazette des Beaux-Arts*, August 1, 1898, pp. 140ff.; and Camille Mauclair, "L'Art de M. Auguste Rodin," in *Revue des revues*, June 15, 1898, pp. 604ff.

29 Mauclair, *op. cit.* note 28, p. 607.

30 Paul Gsell, "Propos d'Auguste Rodin sur l'art et les artistes," in *La Revue*, November 1, 1907, pp. 105–06.

31 Francis Haskell, "Enemies of Modern Art," in *Past and Present in Art and Taste: Selected Essays*, New Haven, Connecticut and London: Yale University Press, 1987, pp. 207–21.

32 Gustave Geffroy, "Deux Figures de Rodin," in *La Vie artistique*, V, Paris: H. Floury, 1897, p. 169.

33 Rodin, *L'Art, cit.* note 16, pp. 244–45.

34 See Truman Bartlett, "Auguste Rodin, Sculptor," in *The American Architect and Building News*, XXV, no. 701, June 1, 1889, p. 261.

35 "Le Style Académique," in *Dictionnaire de l'Académie des Beaux-Arts*, I, Paris: Firmin Didot, frères, fils, et cie., 1858, p. 149.

36 The general tenor of this criticism is established in Charles Baudelaire's trenchant chapter on the Salon of 1846, "Pourquoi la sculpture est ennuyeuse," in *Curiosités esthétiques. L'Art romantique et autres œuvres critiques*, p. 187. See also Henry Jouin, *Esthétique du sculpteur*, Paris: Henri Laurens, 1888, pp. 3–4: "The division of fortunes confines statuary, which in earlier times populated the cathedrals and chateaux with its masterpieces, to the execution of a few iconic statues, tomb sculptures, busts, and medallions. Glyptic art is obsolete. Great sculpture has faltered"; Ernest Chesneau, *L'Education de l'artiste*, Paris: Charavay Frères, 1880, p. 180: "I have observed—as everybody else has—that the art of statuary is a dead language." Gustave Larroumet, *L'Art et l'état en France*, Paris: Hachette, 1895, pp. 41–45, notes that the "statuomanie" that has overtaken France since 1870 has produced more than its share of grotesques among the few sublimities: "Triumphs of the Republic without grandeur, and images of the Resistance without energy" that the state is committed to purchase, in spite of their mediocrity. Translations from the French by the author, unless otherwise noted.

37 Etienne Falconet, *Reflections sur la sculpture*, Paris: Prault, 1761, pp. 7–8.

38 Charles Blanc, *Grammaire des arts du dessin*, Paris: Henri Laurens, n.d. (1880), p. 333.

39 T.-B. Eméric-David, *Recherches sur l'art statuaire considéré chez les anciens et chez les modernes*, Paris: Jules Renouard, 1863, pp. 332–39.

40 Blanc, *op. cit.* note 38, p. 372. The term "character" as it is used here refers not to the concept of "personality" as understood in behavioral psychology, but rather to a sculpture's "aspect" and expression. It was used widely in the critical language of the period, including by Rodin: "Character is the essential truth of any natural object ... it is the inner truth translated by the outer truth; it is the soul, the feelings, the ideas, expressed by the features of a face, by the gestures and actions of a human being, by the tones of a sky, by the lines of a horizon." Rodin, *Rodin on Art, cit.* note 16, pp. 45–46.

41 Rodin, *Rodin on Art, cit.* note 16, pp. 58–59.

42 H.-C.-E. Dujardin-Beaumetz, *Entretiens avec Rodin*, Paris: published privately, 1913. Translated by Ann McGarrell in Albert E. Elsen, ed., *Auguste Rodin: Readings on His Life and Work*, Englewood Cliffs, New Jersey: Prentice-Hall, 1965, p. 148. Although this late account does not appear in the earlier literature on Rodin, there is no reason to doubt its veracity. A similar fate befell a figure known as the *Bacchante* that Rodin created around the same time, which was destroyed when it froze in his studio.

43 Bartlett, *op. cit.* note 34. Reprinted in Elsen, *op. cit.* note 42, pp. 20–21.

44 Butler, *op. cit.* note 6, p. 46, note 15, persuasively argues that the bust was submitted to the Salon of 1865 and not, as all of the previous literature maintains, to the Salon of the previous year.

45 Bartlett in Elsen, *op. cit.* note 42, pp. 20–21. Italics added for emphasis.

46 Butler, *op. cit.* note 6, pp. 44–45, notes that the "fine race" to which Rodin refers was Greek, adding that a large portion of the marble heads that Rodin studied in the Louvre around this time literally had their noses broken off.

47 Elsen, *op. cit.* note 4, p. 16. The defense of a work's "purity" as a justification for its artistic legitimacy, in the face of demonstrably challenging aspects of its subject-matter, recalls the arguments for *Olympia* offered by Manet's allies, which attempted somewhat disingenuously to present the work as an exercise in color, line, and form.

48 Bartlett in Elsen, *op. cit.* note 42, p. 21.

49 The sculptor Falguière, who was a successful prodigy of the Ecole, seems to have been particularly supportive of Rodin at this time. For a full account of the sculpture's reception, first in Brussels and then in Paris, see Butler, *op. cit.* note 6, pp. 99–112.

50 Quoted in Butler, *op. cit.* note 6, p. 112.

51 Rainer Maria Rilke, "Auguste Rodin," in Elsen, *op. cit.* note 42, p. 116.

52 Elsen, *op. cit.* note 4, pp. 18–19.

53 Bartlett, *op. cit.* note 34, p. 285.

54 Reproduced *in situ* in Butler, *op. cit.* note 6, p. 121. Butler's account of this phase of the sculpture's history (pp. 118–20) reveals Rodin's relentlessness in pursuit of vindication against the accusations that this sculpture was a life cast.

55 *Ibid.*, pp. 116–17.

56 John Tancock, *The Sculpture of Auguste Rodin*, Philadelphia: David R. Godine in association with the Philadelphia Museum of Art, 1976, pp. 357–67, provides a cogent summary of the conflicting accounts of this sculpture's origins and identity.

57 Dujardin-Beaumetz in Elsen, *op. cit.* note 42, p. 166.

58 The figure not yet known as the *Walking Man* was exhibited in this form for the first time in the 1900 exhibition at the Place d'Alma (no. 63 in catalogue). Alain Beausire, *Quand Rodin exposait*, Paris: Editions Musée Rodin, 1988, p. 185, notes that it was exhibited on a high column, which can be seen in a reproduction from the catalogue for the IXe Vienna Secession in 1901. An enlargement of the *Walking Man* was exhibited for the first time in 1907 in Strasbourg, and in the Paris Salon of that year. See also Tancock, *op. cit.* note 56, pp. 360, 364, n. 10. It is noteworthy that the early appearances of the *Walking Man* are designated as "studies" for *St. John the Baptist*. Its independent identity as the *Walking Man* did not emerge, according to Beausire, until 1907. See Beausire, *op. cit.*, pp. 185–86 and 284–85.

59 Beausire, *op. cit.* note 58, pp. 70–71, without specifying the source, indicates that the torso may originally have been called *Première impression* (First Impression). Its identity as the *Torso of the Walking Man* would obviously postdate Rodin's first use of this title, which, according to Beausire, occurred in 1907, two years after the composite was enlarged.

60 Albert E. Elsen, "Rodin's 'Walking Man' as seen by Henry Moore," in *Studio International*, 174, July–August 1967, p. 27, identifies this torso as the fulfillment of an "antiquarian" impulse that is tied to the revival of antiquity in the Late Renaissance and the seventeenth century. The author also argues (incorrectly in this writer's opinion) that this torso was created after an antique sculpture, and not after the living model.

61 Beausire, *op. cit.* note 58, p. 71, is able to date the original cast of this torso, now in the Petit Palais, Paris, only to sometime before 1890, based upon inscriptions on a vintage photograph. Regrettably, we do not know precisely when Rodin designated this torso a self-sufficient and autonomous work, or what adaptations preceded that decision, and speculation as to whether it was exhibited with Georges Petit in 1889 has not been satisfactorily confirmed by documentary evidence, although it makes sense to suppose that Rodin's willingness to cast a work of this status emerged in the context of the Petit show.

62 A summary of the issues at play in these distinctions in nineteenth-century theory can be found in Albert Boime, *The Academy and French Painting in the Nineteenth Century*, London: Phaidon, 1971, pp. 81–93. The distinction between these stages of a sculpture's development can be seen in the work of Rodin's predecessor Carpeaux, and was the subject of the exhibition *Sur les traces de Jean-Baptiste Carpeaux*, Paris: Grand Palais, March 11 – May 5, 1975. A contemporary interest in issues of "seriality," which focused more on the states of a sculpture than on its generative process, is explored in Jeanne L. Wasserman, ed., *Metamorphoses in Nineteenth-Century Sculpture*, Cambridge, Massachussets: Fogg Art Museum, 1975.

63 From the *Encyclopédie*, III, p. 298, quoted by Boime, *op. cit.* note 62, p. 201, n. 35.

64 Chesneau, *op. cit.* note 36, pp. 231–34. Chesneau, who was sympathetic to the work of the Impressionists, also wrote on the education of the *métiers* and the importance of the individual hand in an age of the machine. The value of an object, he argued, lies in its individuality, which, he continues, "is a product of spontaneity, which must not be suppressed by too much precision of execution." Quoted in Robert L. Herbert, *Impressionism: Art, Leisure, and Parisian Society*, New Haven, Connecticut, and London: Yale University Press, 1988, pp. 192–93.

65 Elsen, *op. cit.* note 27, pp. 143–48. From a purely legal point of view, Elsen seems to have believed that Rodin never exercised his "right of divulgation," which was usurped by his executor, Léonce Bénédite, in 1917—although he brings substantial evidence to bear on his belief that Rodin would have been prepared to cast the *Gates* in bronze in 1900 (at the time of its exhibition in a partially disassembled state at the Exposition Rodin), in 1889 (for the Exposition Universelle), or even in 1885, "with or without modifications," if the government had pressed for its completion.

66 Elsen, *op. cit.* note 27, p. 62.

67 Butler, *op. cit.* note 6, p. 187, and pp. 214–19.

68 Octave Mirbeau, "Chronique Parisiennes," in *La France*, February 18, 1885, trans. John Anzalone in Ruth Butler, *Rodin in Perspective*, Englewood Cliffs, New Jersey: Prentice-Hall, 1980, pp. 45–48. The first description of the *Gates of Hell* by this title appears to have been in Paul Guigou, "La Sculpture moderne," in *La Revue moderne*, September 30, 1885, p. 75.

69 In the Salon of 1881 he exhibited a bronze version of *St. John the Baptist Preaching* (commissioned by the state) along with a figure of Adam (called *The Creation*)—the first and only figure related to the *Gates* to be seen in the official Salon throughout the remainder of the decade. Thereafter, until the Exposition Universelle of 1889, he exhibited only busts: *Henri Laurens* and *Albert-Ernest Carrier-Belleuse* in 1882; *J. Danielli* and *Alphonse Legros* in 1883; *Victor Hugo* and *Jules Dalou* in 1884; *Antonin Proust* in 1885; nothing at all in 1886 and 1887; *Mme. Vicuña* in 1888; and then, in the large Exposition Universelle of 1889, the *Age of Bronze* and *St. John the Baptist Preaching* (which then belonged to the Musée du Luxembourg), busts of *Proust*, *Hugo*, and *Dalou*, and one of the *Burghers of Calais* (the only work among this grouping not seen before in the Salons).

70 Butler, *op. cit.* note 6, pp. 214–19ff.

71 Charles Frémine, *Le Rappel*, November 28, 1883, in Beausire, *op. cit.* note 58, pp. 82–83.

72 Gustave Geffroy, "Chronique Rodin," in *La Justice*, Paris, July 11, 1886, p. 1.

73 A reconstruction of this exhibition was organized by the Musée Rodin on the occasion of its centenary. See *Claude Monet – Auguste Rodin. Centenaire de l'exposition de 1889*, exhib. cat., Paris: Musée Rodin, 1989.

74 Gustave Geffroy, "The Sculptor Rodin," in *Arts and Letters*, London 1889, p. 295, quoted in Butler, *op. cit.* note 68, pp. 66–67.

75 Edmond de Goncourt, *Journal. Mémoires de la vie littéraire*, Monaco: Editions de l'Imprimerie Nationale de Monaco, 1956, XIV [April 17, 1886], p. 116.

76 *Claude Monet – Auguste Rodin*, cit. note 73, p. 184 (no. 29).

77 Edmond de Goncourt, *op. cit.* note 75, III [July 11, 1889], p. 1005.

78 John Tancock, *op. cit.* note 56, p. 205.

79 See Paris, Ministère de la Culture et de la Communication, *La Sculpture française au XIXe siècle*, exhib. cat., ed. Anne Pingeot, Paris: Galeries nationales du Grand Palais, 1986, pp. 95–109.

80 H.-C.-E. Dujardin-Beaumetz, "Rodin's Reflections on Art," in Elsen, *op. cit.* note 42, p. 159.

81 Rilke, *op. cit.* note 51, p. 131.

82 It is widely accepted that in making a gift of his œuvre to the French state, along with its *droits de suivre*, Rodin ceded to his heirs his rights of divulgation. A challenge of Rodin scholarship, however, is to try to determine when this right was in fact exercised by Rodin himself: when, in what context, and in what condition or state did he first exhibit a work? What, in addition to the original plaster, are the states in which a work was realized by Rodin in his lifetime, according to what chronology? When, in what physical state, and under what circumstances did he let a work go (by sale, gift, or exchange)? In what instances was a work signed by Rodin? None of these questions is easy to answer, nor are the answers always definitive when one can, but it is only by posing them that one can begin to identify the boundaries of Rodin's intentions for his work in his own time.

83 Beausire, *op. cit.* note 58, p. 109.

84 The now familiar title *Thought (La Pensée)* was later given to the work—under what circumstances it is not known—when it was exhibited in the 1900 Exposition Rodin. See Beausire, *op. cit.* note 58, p. 189 (no. 96).

85 This anecdote is recorded in later notes by Léonce Bénédite. See Nicole Barbier, *Marbres de Rodin. Collection du musée*, Paris: Editions du Musée Rodin, 1987, p. 256. Petit's receipts for this work, however, list this as "*tête d'étude*," which would indicate that it was never intended as a full bust. It does not seem that the width of the block could have accommodated the figure's shoulders, and the evidence of the many unfinished marbles in the Musée Rodin reveals that figures were carved holistically and not one section at a time. Rodin would develop a significant number of marble portraits that continued to explore the symbolic possibilities of the head immersed in a matrix of stone, but the dating of any of these earlier than *Thought* is highly problematic. See Barbier, *op. cit.* note 85, pp. 32, 34, 36, 62, 88.

86 Some of these, such as *Fugitive Love*, may have originated in the *Gates of Hell*, while others, such as *Man and his Thought*, *Orpheus and Eurydice*, or the tormented *Sculptor and his Muse*, seem to have been created out of some internal necessity independent of the portal. Camille also developed a sculp-

ture around this time, called *Maturity*, that poses her own reaction to the sad conclusion of this affair. See Butler, *op. cit.* note 6, pp. 268–84.

87 Philippe Gille, *Le Figaro*, April 24, 1895.

88 Larroumet, *op. cit.* note 36, p. 142.

89 Larroumet left the Ministry of Fine Art in 1891 and returned to the Sorbonne as a lecturer in French literature. Although his remarks are addressed to the *"Tête"* in the Salon of 1895, it is possible to find in this critique a commentary on the ill-fated outcome of the Panthéon monument. See Jane Mayo Roos, "Rodin's Monument to Victor Hugo: Art and Politics in the Third Republic," in *The Art Bulletin*, LXVIII, no. 4, December, 1986, p. 655.

90 Jane Mayo Roos, "Steichen's Choice," in Ruth Butler, Jeanine Parisier Plottel, and Jane Mayo Roos, *Rodin's Monument to Victor Hugo*, London: Merrell Holberton in association with the Iris and B. Gerald Cantor Foundation, 1998, pp. 68–85; Ruth Butler, *op. cit.* note 6, pp. 239–51, 308–15.

91 Gustave Geffroy, "Le Salon du Champ de Mars," in *Le Journal*, April 23, 1897.

92 Gustave Geffroy, "La Sculpture, Rodin: Victor Hugo," in *Le Matin*, April 21, 1901.

93 [Albert] Thiébault-Sisson, "Le Salon du Champ-de-Mars," in *Le Petit Temps*, April 23, 1897.

94 Butler, *op. cit.* note 6, pp. 311–12.

95 Barbier, *op. cit.* note 85, p. 228.

96 For a discussion of the role of plasters in Rodin's work, see Albert E. Elsen, "When the Sculptures were White: Rodin's Work in Plaster," in Albert E. Elsen, ed., *Rodin Rediscovered*, Washington, D.C.: National Gallery of Art, 1981, pp. 127–50. The author notes that Rodin made frequent gifts of his work in plaster to friends, suggesting that they were sometimes intended as the final condition of a sculpture. However, these *moulages* were, in all likelihood, not unique, and the original molds were conserved by Rodin, enabling their future transformation.

97 Eugène Lintilhac, *Rapport fait au nom de la commission chargée d'examiner le projet de loi, adopté par la chambre des deputés, portant acceptation définitive de la donation consentie à l'état par M. Auguste Rodin*, Sénat de la République Française, no. 387, October 26, 1916, p. 14.

98 Herbert von Einem, *Michelangelo*, trans. Ronald Taylor, London: Methuen & Co. Ltd., 1973, pp. 262–63; first published in German (Stuttgart: Verlag W. Kohlhammer, 1959).

99 Elsen calls this tendency in Rodin the *"pars pro toto"* (the part for the whole), referring somewhat ambiguously to two different instances of segmentation: in one, which he describes as "parturition" (literally, the term means to "give birth"), a figure isolated from a group is left to symbolize the whole; in the other, a self-sufficient partial figure stands in for the whole human body, physically as well as in its mood or spirit. A third deviation from this category, it seems, might be the *pars pro part*, in which a fragment stands just for itself, with no necessary reference to a greater whole. See Elsen, *op. cit.* note 4, pp. 19–20.

100 Frederick Lawton, *The Life and Work of Auguste Rodin*, London: T. Fisher Unwin, 1906, p. 170.

101 Cladel, *op. cit.* note 1, p. 176.

102 Argus Cortès-Gaillard, "La Sculpture au Salon du Champ-de-Mars," in *Le Journal des artistes*, May 9, 1897.

103 Louis Gonse, "Les Salons de 1897," in *Le Monde moderne*, July 1897, pp. 90–92.

104 The fullest analyses of this exhibition are provided by Beausire, *op. cit.* note 58, pp. 159–206, and Butler, *op. cit.* note 6, pp. 349–61.

105 Marcel Nicolle, "L'Exposition Rodin," in *Journal de Rouen*, July 11, 1900.

106 Charles Quentin, "The Musée Rodin," in *The Art Journal*, 52, 1900, p. 216. Italics added for emphasis.

107 Georges Rodenbach, "M. Rodin," in *L'Elite*, Paris: Charpentier, 1899, p. 277.

108 Charles Morice, *Rodin*, Paris: H. Floury, 1900, pp. 16–17.

109 Adrien Farge, "Rodin," in *Art et littérature*, February 5, 1901, p. 2.

110 Arthur Symons, "Rodin," in *The Fortnightly Review*, June, 1902, p. 957.

111 "Brutale et positive comme la nature": Baudelaire, *op. cit.* note 36, p. 188.

Checklist

Works are grouped by theme and listed chronologically. Those works illustrated are followed by the relevant plate numbers.

A. *THE GATES OF HELL* AND DERIVATIVES

Rodin, Auguste
Adam with Pillar
1878–80, Musée Rodin cast 10/12 in 1978
Bronze
Georges Rudier
16½ × 4¾ × 5 in.
(41.9 × 12.1 × 12.7 cm)
Signed and numbered *A. Rodin* and N^{o} *10* and inscribed *.Georges Rudier.Fondeur.Paris.* and © *by: musée Rodin 1978.*
Iris and B. Gerald Cantor Foundation
1604

Rodin, Auguste
Adam with Pillar
1878–80, Musée Rodin cast 11/12 in 1978
Bronze
Georges Rudier
16½ × 4¾ × 5 in.
(41.9 × 12.1 × 12.7 cm)
Signed and numbered *A. Rodin* and *No. 11* and inscribed © *By musée Rodin 1978* and *Georges Rudier/ .Fondeur.Paris.*
Iris and B. Gerald Cantor Foundation
1485

Rodin, Auguste
Eve with Pillar
1878–80, Musée Rodin cast 8/12 about 1977
Bronze
Georges Rudier
16½ × 5½ × 6 in.
(41.9 × 14 × 15.2 cm)
Signed and numbered *A.Rodin/ No 8* and inscribed *.Georges.Rudier.Fondeur.Paris* and © *by musée Rodin 1977.*
Iris and B. Gerald Cantor Foundation
1486

Rodin, Auguste
The Gates of Hell, 2nd Maquette
1880, Musée Rodin cast 1/8 in 1995
Bronze
Godard
6⅔ × 5½ × 1⅛ in.
(16.9 × 14.1 × 2.8 cm)
Signed and numbered *A. Rodin* N^{o} *1/8* and inscribed *E. GODARD FOND*^{r} and © *By MUSEE Rodin 1995*
Iris and B. Gerald Cantor Collection, promised gift to the Iris and B. Gerald Cantor Foundation
1725

Rodin, Auguste
The Gates of Hell, 2nd Maquette
1880, Musée Rodin cast II/IV in 1995
Bronze
Godard
6⅔ × 5½ × 1⅛ in.
(16.9 × 14.1 × 2.8 cm)
Signed and numbered *A. Rodin No II/IV* and inscribed *E. GODARD Fond*^{r} and © *By MUSEE Rodin 1995.*
Iris and B. Gerald Cantor Foundation
1686 (plate 69)

Rodin, Auguste
The Gates of Hell, 3rd Maquette
1880, Musée Rodin cast 1/8 in 1991
Bronze
Godard
43⅜ × 29 × 11¾ in.
(110.1 × 73.8 × 29.8 cm)
Numbered *No 1/8* and inscribed *E. GODARD Fond*^{r} and © *By MUSEE Rodin 1991.*
Iris and B. Gerald Cantor Collection, promised gift to the Iris and B. Gerald Cantor Foundation
1511

Rodin, Auguste
The Gates of Hell, 3rd Maquette
1880, Musée Rodin cast IV/IV in 1992
Bronze
Godard
43⅜ × 29 × 11¾ in.
(110.1 × 73.8 × 29.8 cm)
Signed *A. Rodin* and inscribed © *By MUSEE Rodin 1992* and *E. GODARD Fond*^{r}
Iris and B. Gerald Cantor Foundation
1626 (plate 70)

Rodin, Auguste
The Thinker
1880, date of cast unknown
Bronze
Alexis Rudier
28 × 20¼ × 23 in.
(71.1 × 51.4 × 58.4 cm)
Signed and numbered *A. Rodin/2* and inscribed *Alexis Rudier/ Fondeur.Paris.*
Iris and B. Gerald Cantor Collection, promised gift to the Iris and B. Gerald Cantor Foundation
1120

Rodin, Auguste
The Thinker
1880, enlarged in 1902–03, this bronze cast about 1960
Bronze
Georges Rudier
79 × 51¼ × 55¼ in.
(200.7 × 130.2 × 140.3 cm)
Signed *A. Rodin* and inscribed *Georges Rudier/ Fondeur. Paris.*
Iris and B. Gerald Cantor Foundation, promised gift to the Iris and B. Gerald Cantor Center for Visual Arts at Stanford University
6440 (frontispiece)

Rodin, Auguste
The Thinker
1880, reduced in 1903, cast about 1931
Bronze
Alexis Rudier
14¾ × 7⅞ × 11⅜ in.
(37.5 × 20 × 28.9 cm)
Signed *A. Rodin* and inscribed *Alexis Rudier/ Fondeur Paris* with special plaque on marble base that reads: *Le Conseil du Musee Rodin a son colleague M. Paul Doumer, en souvenir de sa precieuse collaboration et avec ses voeux les plus ardents pour son septannat. 20 November 1931.*
Iris and B. Gerald Cantor Collection, promised gift to the Iris and B. Gerald Cantor Foundation
11100

Rodin, Auguste
The Thinker
1880, reduced in 1903, date of cast unknown
Bronze
Alexis Rudier
14¾ × 7⅞ × 11⅜ in.
(37.5 × 20 × 28.9 cm)
Signed *A. Rodin* and inscribed *Alexis Rudier, Fondeur, Paris.*
Iris and B. Gerald Cantor Foundation
1499

Rodin, Auguste
Head of a Shade
c. 1880, Musée Rodin cast 1/8 in 1988
Bronze
Godard
13 × 9⅞ × 12¼ in.
(33 × 25.1 × 31.1 cm)
Signed and numbered *A. Rodin/* N^{o} *1/8* and inscribed *E. GODARD Fond*^{r} and © *BY MUSEE Rodin 1988.*
Iris and B. Gerald Cantor Foundation
1449

Rodin, Auguste
Head of a Shade
c. 1880, Musée Rodin cast II/IV in 1995
Bronze
Godard
26½ × 14¼ × 15½ in.
(67.3 × 36.2 × 39.4 cm)
Signed and numbered *A.Rodin* N^{o} *II/IV* and inscribed *E. GODARD Fond*^{r} and © *by MUSEE Rodin 1995.*
Iris and B. Gerald Cantor Foundation
1681

Rodin, Auguste
Adam
1880–81, Musée Rodin cast 7/8 in 1984
Bronze
Coubertin
75½ × 29½ × 29½ in.
(191.8 × 74.9 × 74.9 cm)
Signed and numbered *Rodin No. 7/8* and inscribed © *By Musee Rodin/ 1984* with Coubertin foundry mark.
Iris and B. Gerald Cantor Collection, promised gift to the Iris and B. Gerald Cantor Foundation
1383 (plate 84)

Rodin, Auguste
Fallen Caryatid with Stone
1880–81
Marble
17⅜ × 12 × 12 in.
(44.1 × 30.5 × 30.5 cm)
Signed *A. Rodin.*
Iris and B. Gerald Cantor Collection, promised gift to the Iris and B. Gerald Cantor Foundation
1597 (plate 142)

Rodin, Auguste
Fallen Caryatid with Stone
1880–81, date of cast unknown
Bronze
Alexis Rudier
17⅜ × 12 × 12 in.
(44.1 × 30.5 × 30.5 cm)
Signed *A. Rodin* and inscribed *Alexis Rudier Fondeur Paris.*
Iris and B. Gerald Cantor Collection, promised gift to the Iris and B. Gerald Cantor Foundation
1387

Rodin, Auguste
Fallen Caryatid with Stone
1880–81, enlarged 1911–17, Musée Rodin
cast 2/8 in 1982
Bronze
Coubertin
52½ × 33 × 39 in.
(133.4 × 83.8 × 99.1 cm)
Signed and numbered A. *Rodin* Nº *2/8*
and inscribed © *Musée Rodin 1982* with
Coubertin foundry mark.
Iris and B. Gerald Cantor Collection,
promised gift to the Iris and B. Gerald
Cantor Foundation
1207

Rodin, Auguste
Fallen Caryatid with Stone
1880–81, enlarged 1911–17, Musée Rodin
cast II/IV in 1988
Bronze
Coubertin
52½ × 33 × 39 in.
(133.4 × 83.8 × 99.1 cm)
Signed and numbered A. *Rodin/* Nº *II/IV*
and inscribed *Musée Rodin 1988* with
Coubertin foundry mark.
Iris and B. Gerald Cantor Foundation
1563 (plate 74)

Rodin, Auguste
The Three Shades
1880–1904, single figure conceived about
1880, group composition by 1904, Musée
Rodin cast 9 in 1980
Bronze
Coubertin
38¼ × 37½ × 20½ in.
(97.2 × 95.3 × 52.1 cm)
Signed and numbered A. *Rodin* Nº *9* with
Coubertin foundry mark and inscribed ©
by Musée Rodin 1980.
Iris and B. Gerald Cantor Collection,
promised gift to the Iris and B. Gerald
Cantor Foundation
1163

Rodin, Auguste
The Three Shades
1880–1904, single figure conceived about
1880, group composition by 1904, Musée
Rodin cast 10 in 1981
Bronze
Coubertin
38¼ × 37½ × 20½ in.
(97.2 × 95.3 × 52.1 cm)
Signed and numbered A. *Rodin No. 10*
with Coubertin foundry mark and
inscribed © *by Musée Rodin, 1981.*
Iris and B. Gerald Cantor Collection,
promised gift to the Iris and B. Gerald
Cantor Foundation
1492

Rodin, Auguste
The Three Shades
1880–1904, single figure conceived about
1880, enlarged individually in 1904, group
composition by 1904, Musée Rodin cast
3/8 in 1983
Bronze
Coubertin
75½ × 75½ × 42 in.
(191.8 × 191.8 × 106.7 cm)
Signed A. *Rodin* with Coubertin foundry
mark and inscribed © *By Musée Rodin
1983.*
Iris and B. Gerald Cantor Collection,
promised gift to the Iris and B. Gerald
Cantor Foundation
1343

Rodin, Auguste
The Three Shades
1880–1904, single figure conceived about
1880, enlarged individually in 1901, group
composition by 1904, Musée Rodin cast
II/IV in 1991
Bronze
Coubertin
75½ × 75½ × 42 in.
(191.8 × 191.8 × 106.7 cm)
Signed and numbered A.*Rodin/* Nº *II/IV*
and inscribed © *BY MUSEE RODIN 1991*
with Coubertin foundry mark.
Iris and B. Gerald Cantor Foundation
1628 (plate 95)

Rodin, Auguste
Eve
c. 1881, Musée Rodin cast 8/12 in 1970
Bronze
Georges Rudier
68 × 23¾ × 30 in.
(172.7 × 60.3 × 76.2 cm)
Signed A. *Rodin* and inscribed *Georges
Rudier.Fondeur. Paris* and © *By Musee
Rodin 1970.*
Iris and B. Gerald Cantor Collection,
promised gift to the Iris and B. Gerald
Cantor Foundation
1179 (plate 111)

Rodin, Auguste
The Kiss
c. 1881–82, date of cast unknown
Bronze
Alexis Rudier
34 × 17 × 22 in.
(86.4 × 43.2 × 55.9 cm)
Signed A. *Rodin* and inscribed *Alexis.
RUDIER Fondeur. PARIS* with raised
signature A. *Rodin* inside.
Iris and B. Gerald Cantor Foundation
1689 (plate 83)

Rodin, Auguste
The Kiss
c. 1881–82, Musée Rodin cast 6/12 in 1958
Bronze
Georges Rudier
34 × 17 × 22 in.
(86.4 × 43.2 × 55.9 cm)
Signed A. *Rodin* and inscribed *Georges
Rudier Fondeur.Paris* and
© *by Musée Rodin 1958.*
Iris and B. Gerald Cantor Collection,
promised gift to the Iris and B. Gerald
Cantor Foundation
1410O

Rodin, Auguste
The Kiss (Reduction)
c. 1881–82, date of cast unknown
Bronze
Barbedienne
9½ × 5⅞ × 6¼ in.
(24.1 × 14.9 × 15.9 cm)
Signed *Rodin* and inscribed F. *BARBEDI-
ENNE Fondeur.*
Iris and B. Gerald Cantor Collection,
Promised Gift to the Iris and B. Gerald
Cantor Foundation
3720

Rodin, Auguste
Ugolino and Sons
c. 1881–82, date of cast unknown
Bronze
No foundry mark
16⅛ × 16⅞ × 19⅞ in.
(41 × 42.9 × 50.5 cm)
Signed *Rodin* and inscribed 2ème *épreuve.*
Iris and B. Gerald Cantor Foundation
1550 (plate 108)

Rodin, Auguste
Despairing Adolescent
1882, Museé Rodin cast 3/12 in 1975
Bronze
Godard
16¼ × 5½ × 5¾ in.
(41.3 × 14 × 14.6 cm)
Signed and numbered A. *Rodin* Nº *3* and
inscribed E. *GODARD Fond^{r}*
and © *BY MUSÉE RODIN 1975.*
Iris and B. Gerald Cantor Collection,
promised gift to the Iris and B. Gerald
Cantor Foundation
583 (plate 85)

Rodin, Auguste
Falling Man
1882, Musée Rodin cast 5 in 1974
Bronze
Susse
23¼ × 17 × 10 in.
(59 × 43.2 × 25.4 cm)
Signed and numbered A. *Rodin No 5* and
inscribed *Susse Fondeur Paris* and © *BY
MUSEE RODIN 1974.*
Iris and B. Gerald Cantor Collection,
promised gift to the Iris and B. Gerald
Cantor Foundation
657

Rodin, Auguste
Falling Man
1882, Musée Rodin cast 8 in 1979
Bronze
Godard
23¼ × 17 × 10 in.
(59 × 43.2 × 25.4 cm)
Signed and numbered A *Rodin No. 8* and
inscribed E. *Godard Fondeur* and © *by
Musee Rodin, 1979.*
Iris and B. Gerald Cantor Foundation
1606 (plate 102)

Rodin, Auguste
Small Torso of Falling Man
c. 1882, Musée Rodin cast II/IV in 1984
Bronze
Godard
10½ × 7¾ × 6½ in.
(26.7 × 19.7 × 16.5 cm)
Signed and numbered A. *Rodin/ No. II/IV*
and inscribed © *By musée Rodin 1984* and
E. *Godard Foundeur.*
Iris and B. Gerald Cantor Foundation
1571

Rodin, Auguste
Head of Sorrow
c. 1882, Musée Rodin cast in 1956
Bronze
Georges Rudier
9½ × 7⅞ × 10 in.
(24.1 × 20 × 25.4 cm)
Signed A. *Rodin* and dated *1956.*
Iris and B. Gerald Cantor Foundation
1467

Rodin, Auguste
Torso of Despairing Adolescent
c. 1882–87, Musée Rodin cast 1/8 in 1992
Bronze
Godard
10½ × 4¼ × 5⅛ in.
(26.7 × 10.8 × 13 cm)
Signed and numbered A.*Rodin* Nº *1/8* and
inscribed E. *GODARD Fond^{r}* and © *BY
MUSEE Rodin 1992.*
Iris and B. Gerald Cantor Collection,
promised gift to the Iris and B. Gerald
Cantor Foundation
1577

Rodin, Auguste
Marsyas (Torso of Falling Man, Enlargement)
c. 1882–89, Musée Rodin cast 4/12 in 1970
Bronze
Georges Rudier
40½ × 27½ × 18½ in.
(102.9 × 69.9 × 47 cm)
Signed and numbered *A. Rodin No 4* and inscribed *Georges Rudier. Fondeur. Paris* and © *by musée Rodin 1970.*
Iris and B. Gerald Cantor Collection, promised gift to the Iris and B. Gerald Cantor Foundation
4070 (plate 144 and front jacket/cover)

Rodin, Auguste
Eve (Small Version)
1883, cast 7/12, date of cast unknown
Bronze
Georges Rudier
28 × 10 × 10½ in.
(71.1 × 25.4 × 26.7 cm)
Signed *A. Rodin* and stamped with raised signature inside base, and inscribed *Georges Rudier Fondeur Paris.*
Iris and B. Gerald Cantor Foundation
1500

Rodin, Auguste
Eve (Small Version)
1883, Musée Rodin cast 12/12 in 1967
Bronze
Georges Rudier
28 × 10 × 10½ in.
(71.1 × 25.4 × 26.7 cm)
Signed *A. Rodin* and inscribed © *by Musee Rodin 1967.*
Iris and B. Gerald Cantor Collection, promised gift to the Iris and B. Gerald Cantor Foundation
1100

Rodin, Auguste
Fallen Caryatid with Urn
1883, Musée Rodin cast 8/12 in 1969
Bronze
Georges Rudier
15¾ × 11⅜ × 10⅝ in.
(40 × 28.9 × 27 cm)
Signed *A.Rodin* and inscribed *GEORGES.RUDIER.FONDEUR.PARIS* and © *BY Musée Rodin 1969.*
Iris and B. Gerald Cantor Collection, promised gift to the Iris and B. Gerald Cantor Foundation
109

Rodin, Auguste
Fallen Caryatid with Urn
1883, enlarged 1911–17, Musée Rodin cast 4/8 in 1982
Bronze
Coubertin
45¼ × 36¾ × 31⅛ in.
(114.9 × 93.3 × 79.1 cm)
Signed and numbered *A. Rodin No 4* and inscribed © *By Musee Rodin 1982* with Coubertin foundry mark.
Iris and B. Gerald Cantor Foundation, promised gift to the Iris and B. Gerald Cantor Foundation
1221

Rodin, Auguste
Women Damned
c. 1885, Musée Rodin cast 2/12 about 1978
Bronze
Coubertin
8 × 10¾ × 5 in.
(20.3 × 27.3 × 12.7 cm)
Signed and numbered *A. Rodin 2/12* and inscribed © *musée Rodin 2/12* with Coubertin foundry mark.
Iris and B. Gerald Cantor Foundation
1603 (plate 68)

Rodin, Auguste
Women Damned
c. 1885, Musée Rodin cast 10/12 in 1979
Bronze
Coubertin
8 × 10¾ × 5 in.
(20.3 × 27.3 × 12.7 cm)
Signed and numbered *A. Rodin No. 10* and inscribed © *by Musee Rodin 1979* with Coubertin foundry mark.
Iris and B. Gerald Cantor Collection, promised gift to the Iris and B. Gerald Cantor Foundation
138000

Rodin, Auguste
Danaïd
1885–89, Musée Rodin cast 5/12 in 1969
Bronze
Georges Rudier
12¾ × 28¾ × 22½ in.
(32.4 × 73 × 57.2 cm)
Inscribed © *Musee Rodin 1969* and *Georges Rudier Fondeur Paris.*
Iris and B. Gerald Cantor Collection, promised gift to the Iris and B. Gerald Cantor Foundation
11700

Rodin, Auguste
Danaïd
1885–89, Musée Rodin cast 8 in 1979
Bronze
Godard
12¾ × 28¾ × 22½ in.
(32.4 × 73 × 57.2 cm)
Signed and numbered *A. Rodin Nº 8* and inscribed *E. GODARD Fondr* and © *BY MUSÉE RODIN 1979*
Iris and B. Gerald Cantor Foundation
1600 (plate 99)

Rodin, Auguste
Ovid's Metamorphoses
c. 1885–89, date of cast unknown
Bronze
Perzinka
13⅛ × 15¾ × 10¼ in.
(33.3 × 40 × 26 cm)
Signed on base with raised signature *A. Rodin* inside.
Iris and B. Gerald Cantor Foundation
1192

Rodin, Auguste
Ovid's Metamorphoses
c. 1885–89, Musée Rodin cast 10 in 1979
Bronze
Georges Rudier
13⅛ × 15¾ × 10¼ in.
(33.3 × 40 × 26 cm)
Signed and numbered *A.Rodin Nº 10* and inscribed *.Georges Rudier.Fondeur.Paris* and © *by musée Rodin 1979.*
Iris and B. Gerald Cantor Foundation
483

Rodin, Auguste
I am Beautiful
Before 1886, date of cast unknown
Bronze
Alexis Rudier
27¾ × 12 × 12½ in.
(70.5 × 30.5 × 31.7 cm)
Signed and stamped inside with raised signature *A. Rodin* and inscribed *Alexis Rudier Fondeur Paris* and the following quotation from Charles Baudelaire's *Les Fleurs du mal*:
Je suis belle o mortels, comme un rêve de pierre
Et mon sein où chacun s'est meurtri tour à tour
Est fait pour inspirer au poète un amour
Eternel et muet ainsi que la matière
Iris and B. Gerald Cantor Foundation
1714 (plate 81)

Rodin, Auguste
Toilette of Venus
c. 1886, Musée Rodin cast 4/12 in 1967
Bronze
Georges Rudier
18 × 9½ × 8½ in.
(45.7 × 24.1 × 21.6 cm)
Signed and inscribed *A. Rodin* © *by Musée Rodin 1967* and *Georges Rudier/ Fondeur Paris.*
Iris and B. Gerald Cantor Collection, promised gift to the Iris and B. Gerald Cantor Foundation
126000 (plate 9)

Rodin, Auguste
Fugitive Love
Before 1887, date of cast unknown
Bronze
No foundry mark
10½ × 22 × 11½ in.
(26.7 × 55.9 × 29.2 cm)
Signed *Rodin.*
Iris and B. Gerald Cantor Foundation
1106

Rodin, Auguste
Fugitive Love
Before 1887, cast 2, date of cast unknown
Bronze
Alexis Rudier
20¾ × 33 × 15 in.
(52.7 × 83.8 × 38.1 cm)
Signed and numbered *A. Rodin* and *No 2.* and inscribed *Alexis Rudier/ Fondeur PARIS.*
Iris and B. Gerald Cantor Foundation
1305 (plate 80)

Rodin, Auguste
Eve
c. 1887
Marble
30¼ × 11½ × 13 in.
(76.8 × 29.2 × 33 cm)
Signed *A. RODIN.*
Iris and B. Gerald Cantor Collection, promised gift to the Iris and B. Gerald Cantor Foundation
1242 (plate 1)

Rodin, Auguste
Gates of Hell, Right Pilaster
c. 1887, Musée Rodin cast 5/8 in 1982
Bronze
Godard
10¾ × 2¼ × 1¼ in.
(27.3 × 5.7 × 3.2 cm)
Signed *A.Rodin* and inscribed *E. GODARD Fondr* and © *MUSEE RODIN 1982.*
Iris and B. Gerald Cantor Collection, promised gift to the Iris and B. Gerald Cantor Foundation
1291

Rodin, Auguste
Paolo and Francesca
1889. Musée Rodin cast 5 in 1983
Bronze
Georges Rudier
12⅛ × 22¼ × 14¾ in.
(30.7 × 56.5 × 37.5 cm)
Signed and numbered *A. Rodin No 5* and
inscribed *.GeorgesRudier.Fondeur.Paris.*
and © *by Musée Rodin 1983*
Iris and B. Gerald Cantor Collection,
promised gift to the Iris and B. Gerald
Cantor Foundation
1299 (plate 79)

Rodin, Auguste
Sorrow
1889. Musée Rodin cast 2/8 in 1983
Bronze
Coubertin
11½ × 6½ × 6¾ in.
(29.2 × 16.5 × 17.1 cm)
Signed and numbered *A. Rodin/ № 2/8*
and inscribed © *By MUSEE RODIN 1983*
with Coubertin foundry mark.
Iris and B. Gerald Cantor Collection,
promised gift to the Iris and B. Gerald
Cantor Foundation
1346

Rodin, Auguste
*She Who Was the Helmet-maker's
Beautiful Wife*
1889–90. date of cast unknown
Bronze
Perzinka
19¾ × 11½ × 10¼ in.
(50.1 × 29.2 × 26 cm)
Signed and inscribed *A. Rodin* and *L
Perzinka/ Fondeur.*
Iris and B. Gerald Cantor Collection,
promised gift to the Iris and B. Gerald
Cantor Foundation
1224 (plate 98)

Rodin, Auguste
Despair
1890. cast 12, date of cast unknown
Bronze
Georges Rudier
9½ × 6½ × 9 in.
(24.1 × 16.5 × 22.9 cm)
Signed *A.Rodin* and inscribed
Georges.Rudier.Fondeur.Paris.
Iris and B. Gerald Cantor Collection,
promised gift to the Iris and B. Gerald
Cantor Foundation
119000

Rodin, Auguste
Study for Despair
1890. date of cast unknown
Bronze
Alexis Rudier
7¾ × 3¾ × 3½ in.
(19.7 × 9.5 × 8.9 cm)
Signed *A. Rodin* and inscribed *Alexis
RUDIER/ Fondeur.PARIS.*
Iris and B. Gerald Cantor Collection,
promised gift to the Iris and B. Gerald
Cantor Foundation
11800

Rodin, Auguste
Embracing Couple
1898. cast in 1967
Bronze
Georges Rudier
4⅜ × 2⅛ × ½ in.
(11.1 × 5.4 × 1.3 cm)
Signed *A. Rodin* and inscribed *Georges
Rudier Foundeur, Paris* and © *by Museé
Rodin 1967.*
Iris and B. Gerald Cantor Collection,
promised gift to the Iris and B. Gerald
Cantor Foundation
373000

Rodin, Auguste
The Creator (Bas-relief)
c. 1900. Musée Rodin cast 1/8 in 1983
Bronze
Coubertin
16 × 14¼ × 2½ in.
(40.6 × 36.2 × 6.4 cm)
Signed and numbered *A. Rodin No 1/8*
with Coubertin foundry mark and
inscribed © *by Musee Rodin 1983.*
Iris and B. Gerald Cantor Collection,
promised gift to the Iris and B. Gerald
Cantor Foundation
1342

Rodin, Auguste
The Creator (Bas-relief)
c. 1900. Musée Rodin cast 3/8 in 1983
Bronze
Coubertin
16 × 14¼ × 2½ in.
(40.6 × 36.2 × 6.4 cm)
Signed and numbered *A. Rodin № 3/8*
with Coubertin foundry mark and
inscribed © *By Musee Rodin 1983.*
Iris and B. Gerald Cantor Collection,
promised gift to the Iris and B. Gerald
Cantor Foundation
1353

Rodin, Auguste
The Creator (Bas-relief)
c. 1900. Musée Rodin cast II/IV in 1984
Bronze
Coubertin
16 × 14¼ × 2½ in.
(40.6 × 36.2 × 6.4 cm)
Signed and numbered *A. Rodin No II/IV*
with Coubertin foundry mark and
inscribed © *by Musee Rodin 1984.*
Iris and B. Gerald Cantor Foundation
1568

Rodin, Auguste
Eve with Long Hair
1912. Musée Rodin cast 1 in 1973
Bronze
Godard
13½ × 5 × 5¼ in.
(34.3 × 12.7 × 13.3 cm)
Signed and numbered *A.Rodin № 1* and
inscribed *E. Godard. Fond.F* and © *BY
MUSÉE RODIN 1973.*
Iris and B. Gerald Cantor Collection,
promised gift to the Iris and B. Gerald
Cantor Foundation
1140

Rodin, Auguste
Toilette of Venus and Andromede
No date. Musée Rodin cast 1/8 in 1987
Bronze
Godard
20 × 14½ × 23½ in.
(50.8 × 36.8 × 59.7 cm)
Signed and numbered *A.Rodin No 1/8* and
inscribed *E. GODARD Fond.F* and © *By
MUSEE RODIN 1987.*
Iris and B. Gerald Cantor Collection,
promised gift to the Iris and B. Gerald
Cantor Foundation
1435

Rodin, Auguste
Toilette of Venus and Andromede
No date. Musée Rodin cast II/IV in 1987
Bronze
Godard
20 × 14½ × 23½ in.
(50.8 × 36.8 × 59.7 cm)
Signed and numbered *A. Rodin/ No. II/IV*
and inscribed *E. Godard Fondeur* and ©
by musée Rodin 1987.
Iris and B. Gerald Cantor Foundation
1510

B. STUDIES FOR *THE BURGHERS OF
CALAIS*

Rodin, Auguste
The Burghers of Calais, 1st Maquette
1884. date of cast unknown
Bronze
Godard
13⅜ × 13¾ × 9½ in.
(34 × 35 × 24.1 cm)
Signed and numbered *A. Rodin no. 5* and
inscribed *E. Godard Fondeur.*
Iris and B. Gerald Cantor Foundation
1498 (plate 33)

Rodin, Auguste
The Burghers of Calais, 1st Maquette
1884. Musée Rodin cast 7/8 in 1987
Bronze
Godard
23¾ × 14⅞ × 13 in.
(60.3 × 37.7 × 33 cm)
Signed and numbered *A. Rodin/ № 7/8*
and inscribed *E. Godard Fond.F* and © *By
Musee Rodin 1987.*
Iris and B. Gerald Cantor Foundation
1450

Rodin, Auguste
Andrieu d'Andres
c. 1886–87. Musée Rodin cast 11 in 1966
Bronze
Georges Rudier
18½ × 7¾ × 8½ in.
(47 × 19.7 × 21.6 cm)
Signed *A. Rodin* and inscribed *Georges
Rudier, Fondeur, Paris* and © *by Musée
Rodin 1966.*
Iris and B. Gerald Cantor Foundation
1497 (plate 36)

Rodin, Auguste
Small Head of Andrieu d'Andres
No date. Musée Rodin cast 1/6 in 1985
Bronze
Godard
3 × 2⅓ × 2¾ in.
(7.6 × 5.8 × 7 cm)
Signed and numbered *A. Rodin/ № 1/6*
and inscribed © *BY MUSEE Rodin 1985*
and *E. GODARD/ Fond.F*
Iris and B. Gerald Cantor Collection,
promised gift to the Iris and B. Gerald
Cantor Foundation
1399

Rodin, Auguste
Eustache de Saint-Pierre, Vêtu
1886–87, Musée Rodin cast III/IV in 1987
Bronze
Coubertin
85 × 30 × 48 in.
(215.9 × 76.2 × 121.9 cm)
Signed and numbered *A. Rodin* and *Nº III/IV* and inscribed © *By Musee Rodin 1987* with Coubertin foundry mark.
Iris and B. Gerald Cantor Collection, promised to the Iris and B. Gerald Cantor Foundation
1440 (plate 38)

Rodin, Auguste
Final Head of Eustache de Saint-Pierre
c. 1886, Musée Rodin cast II/IV in 1995
Bronze
Godard
16¼ × 9⅝ × 11½ in.
(41.2 × 24.4 × 29.2 cm)
Signed and numbered *A.Rodin/ Nº II/IV* and inscribed © *By MUSÉE Rodin 1995* and *E. Godard Fondᴱ.*
Iris and B. Gerald Cantor Foundation
1685

Rodin, Auguste
Small Head of Eustache de Saint-Pierre
No date
Bronze
Georges Rudier
4 × 3½ × 2¼ in.
(10.2 × 8.9 × 5.7 cm)
Signed *A. Rodin* and inscribed *.G.Rudier/ Fondeur.Paris.*
Iris and B. Gerald Cantor Collection, promised gift to the Iris and B. Gerald Cantor Foundation
1672

Rodin, Auguste
Jacques de Wiessant, Vêtu
1885–86, Musée Rodin cast 3/8 in 1989
Bronze
Coubertin
83⅞ × 26⅜ × 49⅝ in.
(213 × 67 × 126 cm)
Signed and numbered *A. Rodin N 3/8* and inscribed © *By MUSEE Rodin 1989* with Coubertin foundry mark.
Iris and B. Gerald Cantor Collection, promised gift to the Iris and B. Gerald Cantor Foundation
1574 (plate 41)

Rodin, Auguste
Monumental Head of Jean d'Aire
c. 1884–86, enlarged 1909–10, date of cast unknown
Bronze
Georges Rudier
26¾ × 19⅞ × 22½ in.
(67.9 × 50.3 × 57.2 cm)
Signed and numbered *A. Rodin No 1* on back and inscribed *Georges Rudier Fondeur Paris.*
Iris and B. Gerald Cantor Foundation
15800 (plate 45)

Rodin, Auguste
Monumental Head of Jean d'Aire
c. 1884–86, enlarged 1909–10, date of cast unknown
Bronze
Georges Rudier
26¾ × 19⅞ × 22½ in.
(67.9 × 50.3 × 57.2 cm)
Signed and numbered *A. Rodin Nº 5* and inscribed *Georges Rudier Fondeur Paris.*
Iris and B. Gerald Cantor Collection, promised gift to the Iris and B. Gerald Cantor Foundation
1363

Rodin, Auguste
Small Head of Jean d'Aire
No date
Bronze
Georges Rudier
5¾ × 4⅜ × 4¾ in.
(14.6 × 11.1 × 12.1 cm)
Signed and inscribed *A. Rodin* and *G. Rudier/ Fondeur. PARIS.*
Iris and B. Gerald Cantor Collection, promised gift to the Iris and B. Gerald Cantor Foundation
1547

Rodin, Auguste
Jean d'Aire, 2nd Maquette
1885–86, Musée Rodin cast 1/12 in 1970
Bronze
Susse
27½ × 9½ × 9¾ in.
(69.8 × 24.1 × 24.8 cm)
Signed and inscribed *A. Rodin* and © *by Musee Rodin 1970* and *Susse Fondeur Paris.*
Iris and B. Gerald Cantor Foundation
16100 (plate 34)

Rodin, Auguste
Jean d'Aire, Nude
1885–86, Musée Rodin cast 4 in 1976
Bronze
Georges Rudier
41¾ × 13¾ × 11⅞ in.
(106.1 × 34.9 × 30.2 cm)
Signed and numbered *A. Rodin/ Nº 4* and inscribed *Georges Rudier/ Fondeur Paris.*
Iris and B. Gerald Cantor Foundation
1554

Rodin, Auguste
Jean d'Aire, Nude
1885–86, Musée Rodin cast 5 in 1981
Bronze
Coubertin
82 × 30 × 24 in.
(208.3 × 76.2 × 61 cm)
Signed and numbered *A. Rodin No 5* and inscribed © *By Musée Rodin 1981* with Coubertin foundry mark.
Iris and B. Gerald Cantor Collection, promised gift to the Iris and B. Gerald Cantor Foundation
1490

Rodin, Auguste
Jean de Fiennes, Vêtu
1885–86, Musée Rodin cast 2 in 1981
Bronze
Coubertin
82 × 48 × 38 in.
(208.3 × 121.9 × 96.5 cm)
Signed and numbered *A. Rodin/ Nº 2* and inscribed © *By Musee Rodin 1981* with Coubertin foundry mark.
Iris and B. Gerald Cantor Collection, promised gift to the Iris and B. Gerald Cantor Foundation
1294

Rodin, Auguste
Jean de Fiennes, Vêtu
1885–86, Musée Rodin cast 5/8 in 1983
Bronze
Coubertin
82 × 48 × 38 in.
(208.3 × 121.9 × 96.5 cm)
Signed and numbered *A. Rodin* and *No 5/8* and inscribed © *By Musée Rodin 1983* with Coubertin foundry mark.
Iris and B. Gerald Cantor Foundation
1330 (plate 40)

Rodin, Auguste
Monumental Head of Pierre de Wiessant
c. 1884–85, enlarged about 1909, date of cast unknown
Bronze
Godard
32 × 19 × 20½ in.
(81.3 × 48.3 × 52.1 cm)
Signed and inscribed *A. Rodin* and *Godard-Fondeur, Paris.*
Iris and B. Gerald Cantor Foundation
775 (plate 44)

Rodin, Auguste
Monumental Head of Pierre de Wiessant
c. 1884–85, enlarged in 1909, Musée Rodin cast 10 in 1980
Bronze
Godard
32 × 19 × 20½ in.
(81.3 × 48.3 × 52.1 cm)
Signed and inscribed *A. Rodin* and *E.GODARD Fondᵉ* and © *BY MUSEE Rodin 1980.*
Iris and B. Gerald Cantor Collection, promised gift to the Iris and B. Gerald Cantor Foundation
1252

Rodin, Auguste
Small Head of Pierre de Wiessant
No date, date of cast unknown
Bronze
Alexis Rudier
4⅛ × 3 × 2⅛ in.
(10.5 × 7.6 × 5.4 cm)
Signed *A. Rodin* and inscribed *Alexis Rudier/ .Fondeur.Paris.*
Iris and B. Gerald Cantor Collection, promised gift to the Iris and B. Gerald Cantor Foundation
1360

Rodin, Auguste
Pierre de Wiessant, Vêtu
c. 1886–87, Musée Rodin cast 7/8 in 1983
Bronze
Coubertin
81 × 40 × 48 in.
(205.7 × 101.6 × 121.9 cm)
Signed *A.Rodin* and inscribed © *BY MUSEE Rodin 1983* with Coubertin foundry mark.
Iris and B. Gerald Cantor Collection, promised gift to the Iris and B. Gerald Cantor Foundation
1331 (plate 42)

Rodin, Auguste
Pierre de Wiessant (*Reduction*)
c. 1886–87, reduction made in either 1895 or 1899, date of cast unknown
Bronze
Alexis Rudier
18¾ × 6½ × 6⅜ in.
(47.6 × 16.5 × 16.2 cm)
Signed and inscribed *A. Rodin* and *Alexis Rudier Fondeur. Paris* and marked with raised signature *A. Rodin* inside.
Iris and B. Gerald Cantor Collection, promised gift to the Iris and B. Gerald Cantor Foundation
1715

C. STUDIES FOR THE *MONUMENT TO BALZAC*

Rodin, Auguste
Balzac in a Frockcoat
c. 1891–92
Bronze
Godard
23½ × 8 × 10¼ in.
(59.6 × 20.3 × 26 cm)
Signed and inscribed *A. Rodin* and © *By Musee Rodin 1980* and *E. Godard Fond^r^*
Iris and B. Gerald Cantor Collection, promised gift to the Iris and B. Gerald Cantor Foundation
1219

Rodin, Auguste
Nude Study of Balzac (*Type "C"*)
Probably 1892, Musée Rodin cast 12 in 1976
Bronze
Georges Rudier
50¼ × 27¾ × 22¾ in.
(127.6 × 70.5 × 57.8 cm)
Signed and numbered *A. Rodin N° 12* and inscribed © *by Musée Rodin 1976* and *Georges Rudier Fondeur. Paris.*
Iris and B. Gerald Cantor Collection, promised gift to the Iris and B. Gerald Cantor Foundation
16900

Rodin, Auguste
Nude Study of Balzac (*Reduction, Type "C"*)
Probably 1892, Musée Rodin cast 10/12 in 1970
Bronze
Georges Rudier
30 × 16¾ × 13½ in.
(76.2 × 42.5 × 34.3 cm)
Signed *Auguste Rodin* and inscribed © *Musee Rodin 1970* and *Georges Rudier, Fondeur, Paris.*
Iris and B. Gerald Cantor Collection, promised gift to the Iris and B. Gerald Cantor Foundation
171000

Rodin, Auguste
Nude Study of Balzac (*Reduction, Type "C"*)
Probably 1892, Musée Rodin cast 11/12 in 1972
Bronze
Georges Rudier
30 × 16¾ × 13½ in.
(76.2 × 42.5 × 34.3 cm)
Signed *A. Rodin* and inscribed © *Musee Rodin 1972* and *Georges Rudier, Fondeur, Paris.*
Iris and B. Gerald Cantor Foundation
16800 (plate 62)

Rodin, Auguste
Head of Balzac
1892–93, Musée Rodin cast 1/8 in 1985
Bronze
Godard
10 × 10¼ × 9¾ in.
(25.4 × 26 × 25 cm)
Signed and numbered *A. Rodin* and *N° 1/8* and inscribed © *By MUSEE Rodin 1985.*
Iris and B. Gerald Cantor Collection, promised gift to the Iris and B. Gerald Cantor Foundation
1401

Rodin, Auguste
Head of Balzac
1892–93, Musée Rodin cast 4/8 in 1985
Bronze
Godard
10 × 10¼ × 9¾ in.
(25.4 × 26 × 25 cm)
Signed and numbered *A. Rodin* and *N° 4/8* and inscribed © *by Musee Rodin 1985.*
Iris and B. Gerald Cantor Collection, promised gift to the Iris and B. Gerald Cantor Foundation
1400

Rodin, Auguste
Balzac in a Dominican Robe
1893–94, Musée Rodin cast 9 in 1981
Bronze
Georges Rudier
41¾ × 20⅛ × 20 in.
(106 × 51.2 × 50.8 cm)
Inscribed © *by Musee Rodin, 1981.*
Iris and B. Gerald Cantor Collection, promised gift to the Iris and B. Gerald Cantor Foundation
1491 (plate 63)

Rodin, Auguste
Bust of Young Balzac
1893, Musée Rodin cast 1/8 in 1983
Bronze
Godard
28⅛ × 13⅜ × 14⅝ in.
(71.4 × 34 × 37.1 cm)
Inscribed © *by Musee Rodin 1983* and *E. Godard/ Fondeur.*
Iris and B. Gerald Cantor Collection, promised gift to the Iris and B. Gerald Cantor Foundation
1456

Rodin, Auguste
Bust of Young Balzac
1893, Musée Rodin cast II/IV in 1988
Bronze
Godard
28⅛ × 13⅜ × 14⅝ in.
(71.4 × 34 × 37.1 cm)
Signed and numbered *A. Rodin/ N° II/IV* and inscribed *E. Godard Fond^r^* and © *BY Musée Rodin 1988.*
Iris and B. Gerald Cantor Foundation
1579

Rodin, Auguste
Study for Balzac (*Type "B"*)
1896, Musée Rodin cast 8 in 1963
Bronze
Georges Rudier
11⅛ × 3½ × 4 in.
(28.2 × 8.9 × 10.2 cm)
Signed *A. Rodin* and indistinctly dated *1963*. Inscribed and numbered *Georges Rudier./ .Fondeur Paris* and *No 8.*
Iris and B. Gerald Cantor Foundation
1476

Rodin, Auguste
Nude Study of Balzac as an Athlete (*Type "F"*)
c. 1896, Musée Rodin cast 5 in 1974
Bronze
Georges Rudier
37 × 16 × 15½ in.
(94 × 40.6 × 39.4 cm)
Signed and numbered *A. Rodin No 5* and inscribed *Georges Rudier/ Fondeur–Paris.*
Iris and B. Gerald Cantor Foundation
1555 (plate 64)

Rodin, Auguste
Penultimate Study for the Head of Balzac
1897
Bronze
Alexis Rudier
6¼ × 6 × 7 in.
(15.9 × 15.2 × 17.8 cm)
No inscriptions
Iris and B. Gerald Cantor Collection, promised gift to the Iris and B. Gerald Cantor Foundation
1208

Rodin, Auguste
Monumental Head of Balzac (*Enlargement*)
1897, Musée Rodin cast 9/12 in 1980
Bronze
Georges Rudier
20 × 17½ × 16 in.
(50.8 × 44.5 × 40.6 cm)
Signed and numbered *A. Rodin No. 9* and inscribed *Georges Rudier Fondeur* and © *Musee Rodin 1980*
Iris and B. Gerald Cantor Foundation
1301 (plate 65)

Rodin, Auguste
Final Study for the Monument to Balzac
c. 1897–98, Musée Rodin cast 1/8 in 1983
Bronze
Godard
41¾ × 17¾ × 15 in.
(106 × 45.1 × 38.1 cm)
Signed and numbered *A. Rodin N° 1/8* and inscribed © *by MUSEE Rodin 1983* and *E. GODARD FOND^r^.*
Iris and B. Gerald Cantor Collection, promised gift to the Iris and B. Gerald Cantor Foundation
1352

D. WORK RELATED TO *THE MONUMENT TO VICTOR HUGO*

Rodin, Auguste
Meditation Without Arms
Originally conceived for *The Gates of Hell*, 1880s; enlarged about 1896, Musée Rodin cast 6/8 in 1983
Bronze
Coubertin
57½ × 28 × 22⅛ in.
(146 × 71.1 × 56.2 cm)
Signed and numbered *A. Rodin/ N° 6/8* and inscribed © *By Musée Rodin 1983* with Coubertin foundry mark.
Iris and B. Gerald Cantor Collection, promised gift to the Iris and B. Gerald Cantor Foundation
1325 (plate 53)

Rodin, Auguste
Meditation With Arms
Originally conceived for *The Gates of Hell*, 1880s; enlarged about 1896, Musée Rodin cast 8/12 in 1979
Bronze
Coubertin
61 × 25 × 25 in.
(154.9 × 63.5 × 63.5 cm)
Signed and numbered *A. Rodin N° 8* and inscribed *FONDERIE DE COUBERTIN* and © *by Musee Rodin 1979.*
Iris and B. Gerald Cantor Collection, promised gift to the Iris and B. Gerald Cantor Foundation
6540 (plate 52)

Rodin, Auguste
Meditation With Arms
Originally conceived for *The Gates of Hell*, 1880s; enlarged about 1896. Musée Rodin cast 9 in 1980
Bronze
Coubertin
61 × 25 × 25 in.
(154.9 × 63.5 × 63.5 cm)
Signed and numbered *A. Rodin/ No. 9* and inscribed © *by musee Rodin 1980* with Coubertin foundry mark.
Iris and B. Gerald Cantor Foundation
1618

Rodin, Auguste
Heroic Bust of Victor Hugo
1890–97 or 1901–02, Musée Rodin cast 7/12 in 1981
Bronze
Coubertin
29¼ × 23½ × 21¼ in.
(74.3 × 59.7 × 54 cm)
Signed and numbered *A. Rodin/ N⁰ 7* and inscribed © *by Musée Rodin 1981* with Coubertin foundry mark.
Iris and B. Gerald Cantor Collection, promised gift to the Iris and B. Gerald Cantor Foundation
1181 (plate 50)

Rodin, Auguste
Mask of Iris
1891, Musée Rodin cast 6 in 1964
Bronze
Georges Rudier
4½ × 2¾ × 2¼ in.
(11.4 × 7 × 5.7 cm)
Signed and numbered *A. Rodin N⁰ 6* and inscribed © *by MUSÉE Rodin 1964* and *G. Rudier F. Paris* with raised signature *A Rodin* inside.
Iris and B. Gerald Cantor Foundation
1506

Rodin, Auguste
Mask of Iris
1891, Musée Rodin cast 12 in 1967
Bronze
Georges Rudier
4 × 3 × 3 in.
(10.2 × 7.6 × 7.6 cm)
Signed and numbered *A. Rodin No. 12* and inscribed *G. Rudier/ Fond.Paris.* and © *by Musee Rodin 1967* with raised signature *A. Rodin* inside.
Iris and B. Gerald Cantor Collection, promised gift to the Iris and B. Gerald Cantor Foundation
374000

Rodin, Auguste
Iris, Messenger of the Gods
1891, date of cast unknown
Bronze
Georges Rudier
18 × 18¼ × 7½ in.
(45.7 × 46.4 × 19.1 cm)
Signed *A. Rodin* and inscribed *Georges.Rudier.Fondeur. Paris.*
Iris and B. Gerald Cantor Collection, promised gift to the Iris and B. Gerald Cantor Foundation
1607

Rodin, Auguste
Tragic Muse
1894–96, Musée Rodin cast 1/8 in 1986
Bronze
Godard
13 × 25½ × 15¼ in.
(33 × 64.8 × 38.7 cm)
Signed and numbered *A. Rodin No 1/8* and inscribed *E. GODARD Fond⁻* and © *BY MUSEE Rodin 1986*.
Iris and B. Gerald Cantor Collection, promised gift to the Iris and B. Gerald Cantor Foundation
1445

Rodin, Auguste
Tragic Muse
1894–96, Musée Rodin cast 3/8 in 1986
Bronze
Godard
13 × 25½ × 15¼ in.
(33 × 64.8 × 38.7 cm)
Signed and numbered *A Rodin No 3/8* and inscribed *E. GODARD FONDEUR* and © *BY MUSEE Rodin 1986*.
Iris and B. Gerald Cantor Foundation
1446

Rodin, Auguste
Tragic Muse
1894–96, Musée Rodin cast 5/8 in 1986
Bronze
Godard
13 × 25½ × 15¼ in.
(33 × 64.8 × 38.7 cm)
Signed and numbered *A. Rodin/ N⁰ 5/8* and inscribed *E. Godard Fondr* and © *BY MUSEE Rodin 1986*
Iris and B. Gerald Cantor Foundation
1504 (plate 59)

Rodin, Auguste
Iris, Messenger of the Gods
1895, Musée Rodin cast 1969
Bronze
Georges Rudier
38 × 32½ × 15½ in.
(96.5 × 82.5 × 39.4 cm)
Signed *A. Rodin* and inscribed *Georges Rudier/ Fondeur.Paris* and © *by musee Rodin 1969*.
Iris and B. Gerald Cantor Collection, promised gift to the Iris and B. Gerald Cantor Foundation
1229 (plate 51)

Rodin, Auguste
Monument to Victor Hugo
Large model incomplete 1897, definitive model completed shortly after 1900. Musée Rodin cast 1/8 in 1996
Bronze
Coubertin
72¾ × 112⅛ × 63¾ in.
(184.8 × 284.8 × 161.9 cm)
Signed and numbered *A. Rodin 1/8* and inscribed *Fonderie de Coubertin France* © *By musee Rodin 1996*
Iris and B. Gerald Cantor Foundation
1762 (plate 47)

E. MONUMENTS, PORTRAITS, AND SYMBOLIC FIGURES

Rodin, Auguste
Bust of Jean-Baptiste Rodin
1860, Musée Rodin cast 2/12 in 1980
Bronze
Godard
16⅛ × 11¼ × 9½ in.
(41 × 28.6 × 24.1 cm)
Signed and numbered *A. Rodin No. 2* and inscribed *E. Godard Fondr* and © *by Musee Rodin 1980*.
Iris and B. Gerald Cantor Foundation
1139 (plate 14)

Rodin, Auguste
Mask of the Man with the Broken Nose
1863–64, date of cast unknown
Bronze
Coubertin
12¼ × 7⅜ × 6½ in.
(31.1 × 18.7 × 16.5 cm)
Inscribed *DON A MR CANTOR* and © *Musée Rodin*.
Iris and B. Gerald Cantor Collection, promised gift to the Iris and B. Gerald Cantor Foundation
148000

Rodin, Auguste
Mask of the Man with the Broken Nose
1863–64, date of cast unknown
Bronze
Georges Rudier
3¾ × 2¼ × 2½ in.
(9.5 × 5.7 × 6.4 cm)
Signed *A. Rodin* and inscribed *G. Rudier/ Fond. Paris.*
Iris and B. Gerald Cantor Collection, promised gift to the Iris and B. Gerald Cantor Foundation
606

Rodin, Auguste
Mask of the Man with the Broken Nose
1863–64, Musée Rodin cast 12/12 in 1979
Bronze
Coubertin
18¼ × 7⅜ × 6½ in.
(46.4 × 18.7 × 16.5 cm)
Signed and numbered *A. Rodin N⁰ 12* with Coubertin foundry mark and inscribed © *By Musée Rodin 1979*.
Iris and B. Gerald Cantor Collection, promised gift to the Iris and B. Gerald Cantor Foundation
1368

Rodin, Auguste
Mask of the Man with the Broken Nose
1863–64, Musée Rodin cast 3/12 probably in the 1970s
Bronze
Coubertin
12½ × 7¼ × 6 in.
(31.8 × 18.4 × 15.2 cm)
Signed and numbered *A. Rodin N⁰ 3* with Coubertin foundry mark.
Iris and B. Gerald Cantor Foundation
1605 (plate 107)

Rodin, Auguste
Head of the Call to Arms
1878, Musée Rodin cast 12 in 1980
Bronze
Godard
6½ × 5¾ × 5⅞ in.
(16.5 × 14.6 × 14.9 cm)
Signed and numbered *A. Rodin No 12* and inscribed *E. Godard Fond⁻* and © *BY MUSEE Rodin 1980*.
Iris and B. Gerald Cantor Collection, promised gift to the Iris and B. Gerald Cantor Foundation
1135

Rodin, Auguste
The Call to Arms
1879, date of cast unknown
Bronze
Alexis Rudier
44½ × 22½ × 15 in.
(113 × 57.2 × 38.1 cm)
Signed *A. Rodin* and inscribed *Alexis RUDIER/ FOUNDEUR PARIS.*
Iris and B. Gerald Cantor Foundation
1546

Rodin, Auguste
Bust of St. John the Baptist
c. 1879, Musée Rodin cast II/IV in 1985
Bronze
Godard
21⅝ × 14½ × 10¼ in.
(54.9 × 36.8 × 26 cm)
Signed and numbered *A. Rodin Nº II/IV* and inscribed © *By MUSEE RODIN 1985.*
Iris and B. Gerald Cantor Foundation
1562

Rodin, Auguste
Monumental Head of St. John the Baptist
c. 1879, Musée Rodin cast 4/8 in 1986
Bronze
Godard
21½ × 20¾ × 15¼ in.
(54.6 × 52.7 × 38.6 cm)
Signed and numbered *A. Rodin Nº 4/8* and inscribed *E. GODARD Fondr* and © *BY MUSEE RODIN 1986.*
Iris and B. Gerald Cantor Collection, promised gift to the Iris and B. Gerald Cantor Foundation
1426 (plate 115)

Rodin, Auguste
Monumental Head of St. John the Baptist
c. 1879, Musée Rodin cast II/IV in 1985
Bronze
Godard
21½ × 20¾ × 15¼ in.
(54.6 × 52.7 × 38.6 cm)
Signed *A. Rodin* and inscribed *E. GODARD Fondr* and © *By Musee Rodin 1985.*
Iris and B. Gerald Cantor Collection, promised gift to the Iris and B. Gerald Cantor Foundation
1427

Rodin, Auguste
Monumental Head of St. John the Baptist
c. 1879, Musée Rodin cast III/IV in 1988
Bronze
Godard
21½ × 20¾ × 15¼ in.
(54.6 × 52.7 × 38.6 cm)
Signed *A. Rodin* and inscribed *E. GODARD Fondr III/IV* and © *By Musée Rodin 1988.*
Iris and B. Gerald Cantor Foundation
1451

Rodin, Auguste
The Man with the Broken Nose
c. 1882, date of cast unknown
Bronze
Alexis Rudier
5 × 3¼ × 3⅞ in.
(12.7 × 8.3 × 9.8 cm)
Signed *A. Rodin* and inscribed *Alexis Rudier/ Fondeur PARIS.*
Iris and B. Gerald Cantor Collection, promised gift to the Iris and B. Gerald Cantor Foundation
1623

Rodin, Auguste
Small Head of the Man with the Broken Nose
c. 1882, date of cast unknown
Bronze
Georges Rudier
4¾ × 3 × 3¾ in.
(12.1 × 7.6 × 9.5 cm)
Signed *A. Rodin* and inscribed *Georges Rudier, Fondeur, Paris.*
Iris and B. Gerald Cantor Collection, promised gift to the Iris and B. Gerald Cantor Foundation
1177

Rodin, Auguste
The Spirit of War
1883
Bronze
Griffoul & Lorge
44½ × 22½ × 15 in.
(113 × 57.2 × 38 cm)
Signed *Rodin* and inscribed *GRIFFOUL & LORGE/ FONDEURS A PARIS/ 6 PASSAGE DOMBASLE.*
Iris and B. Gerald Cantor Foundation
1454 (plate 15)

Rodin, Auguste
Maquette of General Lynch
1886, Musée Rodin cast 5 in 1981
Bronze
Godard
17¾ × 13¾ × 7⅞ in.
(45.1 × 34.9 × 20 cm)
Signed and numbered *A. Rodin/ Nº 5* and inscribed *E. Godard/ Fondr* and © *By Musée Rodin 1981.*
Iris and B. Gerald Cantor Foundation
1567

Rodin, Auguste
Bust of Mrs. Russell
1888, Musée Rodin cast 11 in 1993
Bronze
Georges Rudier
13¾ × 10 × 10¼ in.
(34.9 × 25.4 × 26 cm)
Signed and numbered *A. Rodin Nº 11* and inscribed *Georges Rudier.Fondeur.Paris.*
Iris and B. Gerald Cantor Collection, promised gift to the Iris and B. Gerald Cantor Foundation
1611

Rodin, Auguste
Study for the Monument to Claude Lorrain
1889, Musée Rodin cast 5/8 in 1992
Bronze
Godard
19⅞ × 8 × 8 in.
(50.5 × 20.3 × 20.3 cm)
Signed and numbered *A. Rodin No 5/8* and inscribed © *by Musee Rodin 1992.*
Iris and B. Gerald Cantor Foundation
1570

Rodin, Auguste
Claude Lorrain
1889, Musée Rodin cast 5/8 in 1992
Bronze
Coubertin
84½ × 42½ × 46 in.
(214.6 × 108 × 116.8 cm)
Signed and numbered *A. Rodin Nº 5/8* with Coubertin foundry mark and inscribed © *By Musée Rodin 1992.*
Iris and B. Gerald Cantor Collection, promised gift to the Iris and B. Gerald Cantor Foundation
1572

Rodin, Auguste
Claude Lorrain
1889, Musée Rodin cast III/IV in 1993
Bronze
Coubertin
84½ × 42½ × 46 in.
(214.6 × 108 × 116.8 cm)
Signed and numbered *A. Rodin Nº II/IV* with Coubertin foundry mark and inscribed © *By Musée Rodin 1992.*
Iris and B. Gerald Cantor Foundation
1564

Rodin, Auguste
Jules Bastien-Lepage
1889, Musée Rodin cast 4/8 in 1988
Bronze
Coubertin
69 × 36 × 33½ in.
(175.3 × 91.4 × 85.1 cm)
Signed and numbered *A. Rodin Nº 4/8* with Coubertin foundry mark and inscribed © *by Musee Rodin 1988.*
Iris and B. Gerald Cantor Foundation
1565

Rodin, Auguste
Tragic Head
c. 1890–96, Musée Rodin cast 6/12 in 1963
Bronze
Georges Rudier
6½ × 5 × 4¾ in.
(16.5 × 12.7 × 12.1 cm)
Signed and numbered *A. Rodin/ No 6* and inscribed *G. Rudier Fondeur. Paris* and © *by Musée Rodin 1963.*
Iris and B. Gerald Cantor Foundation
1472

Rodin, Auguste
Tragic Head
c. 1890–96
Bronze
Alexis Rudier
6½ × 5 × 4¾ in.
(16.5 × 12.7 × 12.1 cm)
Signed *A. Rodin* and inscribed *Alexis Rudier/ Fondeur.Paris.*
Iris and B. Gerald Cantor Collection, promised gift to the Iris and B. Gerald Cantor Foundation
1842

Rodin, Auguste
La France
c. 1904
Bronze
No foundry mark
23½ × 21½ × 12 in.
(59.7 × 54.6 × 30.5 cm)
Stamped *A.Rodin.*
Iris and B. Gerald Cantor Collection, promised gift to the Iris and B. Gerald Cantor Foundation
1105 (plate 32)

Rodin, Auguste
Head of a Muse
c. 1905, date of cast unknown
Bronze
Alexis Rudier
4¼ × 2¾ × 4 in.
(10.8 × 7 × 10.2 cm)
Signed A. *Rodin* and inscribed
Alexis Rudier Fondeur, Paris.
Iris and B. Gerald Cantor Foundation
1507

Rodin, Auguste
Study for the Monument to Whistler
1905–06, Musée Rodin cast 3/8 in 1983
Bronze
Godard
24¾ × 13 × 13½ in.
(62.9 × 33 × 34.3 cm)
Signed and numbered A. *Rodin/ Nº 3/8*
and inscribed *E. Godard/ Fondr* and © *By*
Musée Rodin 1983.
Iris and B. Gerald Cantor Foundation
1560

Rodin, Auguste
Mask of Hanako
1908, date of cast unknown
Bronze
Alexis Rudier
6½ × 4⅞ × 3½ in.
(16.5 × 12.4 × 8.9 cm)
Signed A. *Rodin* and inscribed
Alexis Rudier, fondeur, Paris.
Iris and B. Gerald Cantor Collection,
promised gift to the Iris and B. Gerald
Cantor Foundation
1471

Rodin, Auguste
Mask of Hanako (Type "D")
1908, Musée Rodin cast 8/12 in 1979
Bronze
Godard
7⅞ × 7 × 6 in.
(20 × 17.8 × 15.2 cm)
Signed and numbered A.*Rodin/ No 8* and
inscribed © *MUSÉE RODIN 1979.*
Iris and B. Gerald Cantor Foundation
4140

Rodin, Auguste
Head of Hanako
1908–11, Musée Rodin cast 1962
Bronze
Georges Rudier
12¼ × 10 × 10 in.
(31.1 × 25.4 × 25.4 cm)
Signed A. *Rodin* and inscribed *Georges*
Rudier. Fondeur. Paris. and © *by Musee*
Rodin 1962.
Iris and B. Gerald Cantor Collection,
promised gift to the Iris and B. Gerald
Cantor Foundation
1412

Rodin, Auguste
Gustav Mahler
1909, cast at a later date
Bronze
Alexis Rudier
13 × 13½ × 12 in.
(33 × 34.3 × 30.5 cm)
Signed A. *Rodin* and inscribed
Alexis.Rudier.Fondeur.Paris.
Iris and B. Gerald Cantor Collection,
promised gift to the Iris and B. Gerald
Cantor Foundation
1444

Rodin, Auguste
Head of Malvina
After 1910, Musée Rodin cast 1/8 in 1988
Bronze
Godard
8¼ × 5½ × 5½ in.
(21 × 14 × 14 cm)
Signed and numbered A. *Rodin No 1/8*
and inscribed *E. GODARD Fondr* and ©
By MUSEE Rodin 1988.
Iris and B. Gerald Cantor Collection,
promised gift to the Iris and B. Gerald
Cantor Foundation
1312

Rodin, Auguste
Head of Nijinsky
1912
Bronze
Georges Rudier
2⅞ × 1⅛ × 1½ in.
(7.3 × 2.9 × 3.8 cm)
Signed and numbered A. *Rodin Nº 11* and
inscribed *G. Rudier Fond. Paris.*
Iris and B. Gerald Cantor Collection,
promised gift to the Iris and B. Gerald
Cantor Foundation
607

Rodin, Auguste
Head of Pope Benedict XV
1915, Musée Rodin cast 10 in 1978
Bronze
Georges Rudier
10 × 7 × 9½ in.
(25.4 × 17.8 × 24.1 cm)
Signed and numbered A. *Rodin/ Nº 10*
and inscribed *Georges Rudier*
Fondeur.Paris.
Iris and B. Gerald Cantor Foundation
1608

F. GROUP FIGURES

Rodin, Auguste
Idyll of Ixelles
1885, Musée Rodin cast 3/8 in 1980
Bronze
Coubertin
21 × 14⅝ × 14⅝ in.
(53.3 × 37.1 × 37.1 cm)
Signed and numbered A. *Rodin 1881 (sic)*
and *No 3/8* with Coubertin foundry mark
and inscribed © *by Musée Rodin 1980.*
Iris and B. Gerald Cantor Collection,
promised gift to the Iris and B. Gerald
Cantor Foundation
1364

Rodin, Auguste
Idyll of Ixelles
1885, Musée Rodin cast 4/8 in 1981
Bronze
Coubertin
21 × 14⅝ × 14⅝ in.
(53.3 × 37.1 × 37.1 cm)
Signed and numbered A. *Rodin No. 4* with
Coubertin foundry mark and inscribed ©
by Musée Rodin 1981.
Iris and B. Gerald Cantor Foundation
1682 (plate 13)

Rodin, Auguste
Amour and Psyche
c. 1885, cast c. 1901
Bronze
No foundry mark
9 × 28¼ × 18½ in.
(22.9 × 71.8 × 47 cm)
Signed A. *Rodin.*
Iris and B. Gerald Cantor Collection,
promised gift to the Iris and B. Gerald
Cantor Foundation
13400

Rodin, Auguste
Amour and Psyche
c. 1885, cast at a later date
Bronze
Coubertin
9 × 28¼ × 18½ in.
(22.9 × 71.8 × 47 cm)
Signed and numbered A. *Rodin*
Nº 9.
Iris and B. Gerald Cantor Collection,
promised gift to the Iris and B. Gerald
Cantor Foundation
782

Rodin, Auguste
Eternal Idol
c. 1889, Musée Rodin cast 6/12 in 1970
Bronze
Georges Rudier
29 × 21 × 15 in.
(73.7 × 53.3 × 38.1 cm)
Signed A. *Rodin* and inscribed *Georges*
Rudier Fondeur Paris and
© *by Musée Rodin 1970.*
Iris and B. Gerald Cantor Collection,
promised gift to the Iris and B. Gerald
Cantor Foundation
14000

Rodin, Auguste
Eternal Idol
c. 1889, Musée Rodin cast 7 in 1971
Bronze
Georges Rudier
29 × 21 × 15 in.
(73.7 × 53.3 × 38.1 cm)
Signed A. *Rodin* and inscribed *Georges*
Rudier. Fondeur. Paris. and © *by Musée*
Rodin 1971.
Iris and B. Gerald Cantor Collection,
promised gift to the Iris and B. Gerald
Cantor Foundation
1289 (plate 10)

Rodin, Auguste
Amour and Psyche
Before 1893
Marble
9 × 27½ × 17¾ in.
(22.9 × 69.9 × 45.1 cm)
Signed A. *RODIN.*
Iris and B. Gerald Cantor Collection,
promised gift to the Iris and B. Gerald
Cantor Foundation
1658 (plate 12)

Rodin, Auguste
The Benedictions
1894, Musée Rodin cast in 1955
Bronze
Georges Rudier
35½ × 24 × 19 in.
(90.2 × 61 × 48.3 cm)
Signed A. *Rodin* and inscribed *Georges*
Rudier Fondeur Paris and
© *by Musée Rodin 1955.*
Iris and B. Gerald Cantor Foundation
1386

Rodin, Auguste
Illusions Received by the Earth
(The Fallen Angel)
1895, Musée Rodin cast 1/8 in 1983
Bronze
Coubertin
15½ × 27 × 15½ in.
(39.4 × 68.6 × 39.4 cm)
Signed and numbered *A. Rodin/*
Nº 1/8 and inscribed © *by Musée Rodin*
1983.
Iris and B. Gerald Cantor Collection,
promised gift to the Iris and B. Gerald
Cantor Foundation
1341

Rodin, Auguste
Three Faunesses
Before 1896, date of cast unknown
Bronze
No foundry mark
9¼ × 11½ × 6½ in.
(23.5 × 29.2 × 16.5 cm)
Signed *A. Rodin*.
Iris and B. Gerald Cantor Collection,
promised gift to the Iris and B. Gerald
Cantor Foundation
13900

Rodin, Auguste
Three Faunesses
Before 1896, cast in 1959
Bronze
Georges Rudier
9¼ × 11½ × 6½ in.
(23.5 × 29.2 × 16.5 cm)
Signed *A. Rodin* and inscribed *G. Rudier*
Fondeur Paris. and
© *by musée Rodin 1959*.
Iris and B. Gerald Cantor Foundation
1596

Rodin, Auguste
The Night (Double Figure)
After 1898, Musée Rodin cast 1 in 1980
Bronze
Godard
10¼ × 5½ × 6⅞ in.
(26 × 14 × 17.5 cm)
Signed and numbered *A. Rodin/ Nº 1* and
inscribed © *By MUSÉE RODIN 1980* and
E. GODARD FONDᴿ
Iris and B. Gerald Cantor Collection,
promised gift to the Iris and B. Gerald
Cantor Foundation
1161

Rodin, Auguste
The Night (Double Figure)
After 1898, Musée Rodin cast 2 in 1980
Bronze
Godard
10¼ × 5½ × 6⅞ in.
(26 × 14 × 17.5 cm)
Signed and numbered *A. Rodin/ Nº 2* and
inscribed © *by Musée Rodin 1980* and *E.*
GODARD Fondr.
Iris and B. Gerald Cantor Collection,
promised gift to the Iris and B. Gerald
Cantor Foundation
1162

Rodin, Auguste
The Night (Double Figure)
After 1898, Musée Rodin cast I/IV in 1983
Bronze
Godard
10¼ × 5½ × 6⅞ in.
(26 × 14 × 17.5 cm)
Signed and numbered *A. Rodin Nº I/IV*
and inscribed *E. Godard Fondᴿ* and © *by*
MUSÉE Rodin 1983.
Iris and B. Gerald Cantor Foundation
1340

Rodin, Auguste
Romeo and Juliette
1902, cast before Rodin's death in 1917
Bronze
Alexis Rudier
27 × 20 × 13 in.
(68.6 × 50.8 × 33 cm)
Signed and inscribed *A. Rodin* and *Alexis*
Rudier, Fondeur.Paris.
Iris and B. Gerald Cantor Foundation
1414

Rodin, Auguste
Dance Movement, Pas de Deux "B"
c. 1910–11, Musée Rodin cast 8 in 1965
Bronze
Georges Rudier
13 × 7⅛ × 5 in.
(33 × 18.1 × 12.7 cm)
Signed and numbered *A. Rodin No 8* and
inscribed *G. Rudier/ Fondeur.Paris* and
© *musée/ Rodin.1965*.
Iris and B. Gerald Cantor Collection,
promised gift to the Iris and B. Gerald
Cantor Foundation
768

Rodin, Auguste
Dance Movement, Pas de Deux "B"
c. 1910–11, Musée Rodin cast 10 in 1965
Bronze
Georges Rudier
13 × 7⅛ × 5 in.
(33 × 18.1 × 12.7 cm)
Signed and numbered *A. Rodin/ No 10*
and inscribed © *by musée Rodin 1965* and
Georges Rudier.Fondeur.Paris.
Iris and B. Gerald Cantor Foundation
1559

Rodin, Auguste
Dance Movement, Pas de Deux "G"
c. 1910–13, Musée Rodin cast 6/12 in 1967
Bronze
Georges Rudier
13½ × 6½ × 6½ in.
(34.3 × 16.5 × 16.5 cm)
Signed *A. Rodin* and inscribed *GEORges*
Rudier Fondeur.Paris and © *by Musée*
Rodin 1967.
Iris and B. Gerald Cantor Collection,
promised gift to the Iris and B. Gerald
Cantor Foundation
14200

G. SINGLE FIGURES

Rodin, Auguste
The Age of Bronze (Reduction)
1876, reduction c. 1903–04, date of cast
unknown
Bronze
Alexis Rudier
26 × 8½ × 7 in.
(66 × 21.6 × 17.8 cm)
Signed *Rodin* and inscribed *Alexis Rudier.*
Fondeur Paris.
Iris and B. Gerald Cantor Foundation
1484 (plate 17)

Rodin, Auguste
St. John the Baptist Preaching
c. 1880, cast in 1925
Bronze
Alexis Rudier
31½ × 19 × 9½ in.
(80 × 48.3 × 24.1 cm)
Signed and inscribed *A. Rodin* and *Alexis*
RUDIER..Fondeur PARIS with raised
signature *A. Rodin* inside.
Iris and B. Gerald Cantor Collection,
promised gift to the Iris and B. Gerald
Cantor Foundation
1726

Rodin, Auguste
St. John the Baptist Preaching
c. 1880, Musée Rodin cast in 1962
Bronze
Georges Rudier
19¾ × 11 × 9⅛ in.
(50.2 × 27.9 × 23.2 cm)
Signed *A. Rodin* and inscribed *Georges*
Rudier Fondeur Paris and © *Musée Rodin*
1962 with raised signature *A. Rodin*
inside.
Iris and B. Gerald Cantor Foundation
1560 (plate 137)

Rodin, Auguste
St. John the Baptist Preaching
c. 1880, Musée Rodin cast in 1974
Bronze
Georges Rudier
19¾ × 11 × 9⅛ in
(50.2 × 27.9 × 23.2 cm)
Signed *A. Rodin* and inscribed
.Georges.Rudier.fondeur.Paris. and © *by*
Musée Rodin 1974
Iris and B. Gerald Cantor Foundation
1601

Rodin, Auguste
Crying Lion
1881, date of cast unknown
Bronze
No foundry mark
7⅞ × 13¼ × 6 in.
(20 × 33.7 × 15.2 cm)
Signed *A. Rodin* dated *1881* and inscribed
GARDE BIEN.
Iris and B. Gerald Cantor Foundation
14700

Rodin, Auguste
Woman with Crab
c. 1886, date of cast unknown
Bronze
No foundry mark
8½ × 4½ × 4½ in.
(21.6 × 11.4 × 11.4 cm)
Signed *Rodin*.
Iris and B. Gerald Cantor Foundation
12500

Rodin, Auguste
Venus
c. 1888, Musée Rodin cast 1/12 in 1973
Bronze
Godard
40½ × 7½ × 11½ in.
(102.9 × 19.1 × 29.2 cm)
Signed and numbered *A. Rodin/ No 1* and
inscribed © *BY MUSÉE RODIN 1973* and
E. Godard/ Fondr.
Iris and B. Gerald Cantor Collection,
promised gift to the Iris and B. Gerald
Cantor Foundation
127000

Rodin, Auguste
Venus
c. 1888, Musée Rodin cast 9 in 1978
Bronze
Godard
40½ × 7½ × 11½ in.
(102.9 × 19.1 × 29.2 cm)
Signed and numbered *A.Rodin Nº 9* and
inscribed *E.GODARD Fondr* and © *BY*
MUSÉE RODIN 1978.
Iris and B. Gerald Cantor Foundation
1599

Rodin, Auguste
Sphinx on a Column
c. 1889 or later, Musée Rodin cast 1/8 in
1995
Bronze
Godard
36 × 6⅛ × 9 in.
(91.4 × 15.6 × 23 cm)
Signed and numbered *A. Rodin Nº 1/8*
and inscribed *E. GODARD Fond* and ©
BY MUSEE Rodin 1995.
Iris and B. Gerald Cantor Collection,
promised gift to the Iris and B. Gerald
Cantor Foundation
1723

Rodin, Auguste
Sphinx on a Column
c. 1889 or later, Musée Rodin cast III/IV
in 1995
Bronze
Godard
36 × 6⅛ × 9 in.
(91.4 × 15.6 × 23 cm)
Signed and numbered *A. Rodin No III/IV*
and inscribed *E.Godard Fondr* and ©
MUSEE Rodin 1995.
Iris and B. Gerald Cantor Foundation
1684

Rodin, Auguste
The Night (Single Figure)
After 1898, Musée Rodin cast 5/12 in 1973
Bronze
Georges Rudier
10¼ × 5½ × 6⅞ in.
(26 × 14 × 17.5 cm)
Signed and numbered *A. Rodin No 5* and
inscribed *.Georges Rudier.Fondeur.Paris*
and © *by musée Rodin 1973* with raised
signature *A. Rodin* inside.
Iris and B. Gerald Cantor Foundation
567

Rodin, Auguste
The Spirit of Eternal Repose
(with Head)
c. 1898–99, Musée Rodin cast 2/8 in 1982
Bronze
Coubertin
76 × 46 × 48 in.
(193 × 116.8 × 121.9 cm)
Signed and numbered *A. Rodin No 2/8*
and inscribed © *By Musee Rodin 1982*
with Coubertin foundry mark.
Iris and B. Gerald Cantor Collection,
promised gift to the Iris and B. Gerald
Cantor Foundation
1295 (plate 29)

Rodin, Auguste
Ecclesiastes
Before 1899, Musée Rodin cast 1/8 in 1995
Bronze
Godard
10½ × 10¼ × 11¾ in.
(26.7 × 26 × 29.8 cm)
Signed and numbered *A. Rodin/ Nº 1/8*
and inscribed *E. GODARD Fondr* and ©
By Musee Rodin 1995
Iris and B. Gerald Cantor Collection,
promised gift to the Iris and B. Gerald
Cantor Foundation
1724

Rodin, Auguste
Ecclesiastes
Before 1899, Musée Rodin cast II/IV in
1995
Bronze
Godard
10½ × 10¼ × 11¾ in.
(26.7 × 26 × 29.8 cm)
Signed and numbered *A. Rodin/
Nº II/IV* and inscribed *E.GODARD Fondr*
and © *By MUSEE Rodin 1995.*
Iris and B. Gerald Cantor Foundation
1683

Rodin, Auguste
Whistler's Muse
1907, Musée Rodin cast IV/IV in 1991
Bronze
Coubertin
88 × 35½ × 42⅞ in.
(223.5 × 90.2 × 108.9 cm)
Signed and numbered *A. Rodin/
Nº IV/IV* and inscribed © *By Musée Rodin
1991* with Coubertin foundry mark.
Iris and B. Gerald Cantor Foundation
1627 (plate 31)

Rodin, Auguste
Crouching Man
c. 1910, Musée Rodin cast 3 in 1963
Bronze
Georges Rudier
5 × 6½ × 3¼ in.
(12.7 × 16.5 × 8.3 cm)
Signed and numbered *A. Rodin No 3* and
inscribed *Georges Rudier. Fondeur. Paris*
and © *by Musee Rodin 1963.*
Iris and B. Gerald Cantor Collection,
promised gift to the Iris and B. Gerald
Cantor Foundation
1594

Rodin, Auguste
Sitting Man, Legs Extended
c. 1910, Musée Rodin cast 6 in 1965
Bronze
Georges Rudier
6 × 6⅛ × 3¾ in.
(15.2 × 15.6 × 9.5 cm)
Signed and numbered *A. Rodin nº 6* and
inscribed *Georges Rudier.Fondeur. Paris*
and © *by musée Rodin 1965* with raised
signature *A. Rodin* inside.
Iris and B. Gerald Cantor Collection,
promised gift to the Iris and B. Gerald
Cantor Foundation
1595

Rodin, Auguste
Dance Movement "B"
c. 1910–11, Musée Rodin cast 7/12 in 1956
Bronze
Georges Rudier
12½ × 5⅛ × 4½ in.
(31.8 × 13 × 11.4 cm)
Signed and numbered *A. Rodin/ No. 7* and
inscribed © *by Musée/ Rodin/ 1956.*
Iris and B. Gerald Cantor Collection,
promised gift to the Iris and B. Gerald
Cantor Foundation
123000

Rodin, Auguste
Dance Movement "D"
c. 1910–11, date of cast unknown
Bronze
No foundry mark
12¾ × 4¼ × 3⅝ in.
(32.4 × 10.8 × 9.2 cm)
Signed and numbered *Rodin/ No. 1.*
Iris and B. Gerald Cantor Foundation
1400

Rodin, Auguste
Dance Movement "D"
c. 1910–11, cast 6/12, date of cast unknown
Bronze
Georges Rudier
12¾ × 4¼ × 3⅝ in.
(32.4 × 10.8 × 9.2 cm)
Signed and numbered *A. Rodin 6/12.*
Iris and B. Gerald Cantor Collection,
promised gift to the Iris and B. Gerald
Cantor Foundation
1000

Rodin, Auguste
Dance Movement "E"
c. 1910–11, Musée Rodin cast 5/12 in 1956
Bronze
Georges Rudier
14 × 4½ × 8 in.
(35.6 × 11.4 × 20.3 cm)
Signed and numbered *A. Rodin No. 5* and
inscribed © *by Musée Rodin 1956.*
Iris and B. Gerald Cantor Collection,
promised gift to the Iris and B. Gerald
Cantor Foundation
124000

Rodin, Auguste
Dance Movement "F"
c. 1910–11, date of cast unknown
Bronze
Coubertin
11 × 10½ × 5½ in.
(27.9 × 26.7 × 14 cm)
Signed and numbered *A. Rodin No. 10*
and stamped ©.
Iris and B. Gerald Cantor Collection,
promised gift to the Iris and B. Gerald
Cantor Foundation
1307

Rodin, Auguste
Dance Movement "H"
c. 1910–11, date of cast unknown
Bronze
Georges Rudier
11 × 5¼ × 5½ in.
(27.9 × 13.3 × 14 cm)
Signed *A. Rodin* and inscribed *Georges
Rudier Fondeur Paris.*
Iris and B. Gerald Cantor Collection,
promised gift to the Iris and B. Gerald
Cantor Foundation
1230

Rodin, Auguste
Dance Movement "I"
1910–11, date of cast unknown
Bronze
Georges Rudier
5 × 2⅝ × 9¼ in.
(12.7 × 6.7 × 23.5 cm)
Signed and numbered *A. Rodin/
No. 1* and inscribed *Georges Rudier
Fondeur. Paris.*
Iris and B. Gerald Cantor Collection,
promised gift to the Iris and B. Gerald
Cantor Foundation
1502

Rodin, Auguste
Young Girl with Serpent
No date, Musée Rodin cast 4/8 in 1988
Bronze
Godard
13⅜ × 4¾ × 5⅝ in.
(34 × 12.1 × 14.3 cm)
Signed and numbered *A. Rodin No 4/8*
and inscribed *E. GODARD Fondr* and ©
BY MUSEE Rodin 1988.
Iris and B. Gerald Cantor Collection,
promised gift to the Iris and B. Gerald
Cantor Foundation
1576 (plate 11)

H. PARTIAL FIGURES

Rodin, Auguste
Torso of the Walking Man
c. 1878–79, Musée Rodin cast 2 in 1979
Bronze
Coubertin
20½ × 10¾ × 8 in.
(52.1 × 27.3 × 20.3 cm)
Signed and numbered *A. Rodin no 2* with
Coubertin foundry mark and inscribed ©
By Musée Rodin 1979.
Iris and B. Gerald Cantor Collection,
promised gift to the Iris and B. Gerald
Cantor Foundation
653

Rodin, Auguste
Torso of the Walking Man
c. 1878–79, Musée Rodin cast 6 in 1979
Bronze
Coubertin
20½ × 10¾ × 8 in.
(52.1 × 27.3 × 20.3 cm)
Signed *A. Rodin* with Coubertin foundry
mark and inscribed © *by musee Rodin
1979.*
Iris and B. Gerald Cantor Collection,
promised gift to the Iris and B. Gerald
Cantor Foundation
1448

Rodin, Auguste
Torso of the Walking Man
c. 1878–79, Musée Rodin cast 10/12 in
1979
Bronze
Coubertin
20½ × 10¾ × 8 in.
(52.1 × 27.3 × 20.3 cm)
Signed and numbered *A. Rodin nº 10* with
Coubertin foundry mark and inscribed ©
By Musee Rodin 1979.
Iris and B. Gerald Cantor Foundation
1516

Rodin, Auguste
Torso of Centauresse
c. 1884–87, Musée Rodin cast II/IV in
1986
Bronze
Godard
8 1/5 × 3¾ × 3 in.
(20.8 × 9.5 × 7.6 cm)
Signed and numbered *A. Rodin No II/IV*
and inscribed *E. GODARD Fondr* and ©
By MUSÉE RODIN 1986.
Iris and B. Gerald Cantor Collection,
promised gift to the Iris and B. Gerald
Cantor Foundation
1425

Rodin, Auguste
Torso of a Young Woman
1886, date of cast unknown
Bronze
Georges Rudier
8⅞ × 5¼ × 3⅞ in.
(22.5 × 13.3 × 9.8 cm)
Signed and numbered *A. Rodin No. 8* and
inscribed *Georges Rudier Fondeur. Paris.*
Iris and B. Gerald Cantor Collection,
promised gift to the Iris and B. Gerald
Cantor Foundation
1548

Rodin, Auguste
Walking Man
c. 1889, date of cast unknown
Bronze
Alexis Rudier
33 × 20¼ × 20 in.
(83.8 × 51.4 × 50.8 cm)
Signed and inscribed *A.R* and *Alexis
Rudier.Fondeur.a.PARIS.*
Iris and B. Gerald Cantor Collection,
promised gift to the Iris and B. Gerald
Cantor Foundation
1070

Rodin, Auguste
Walking Man
c. 1889, date of cast unknown
Bronze
No foundry mark
33 × 20¼ × 20 in.
(83.8 × 51.4 × 50.8 cm)
Inscribed *A.R.*
Iris and B. Gerald Cantor Foundation
1060 (plate 134)

Rodin, Auguste
Cybèle
c. 1890, enlarged in 1904, Musée Rodin
cast 3/8 in 1982
Bronze
Coubertin
65 × 34 × 56 in.
(165.1 × 86.4 × 142.2 cm)
Signed and numbered *A. Rodin Nº 3/8*
with Coubertin foundry mark and © *by
Musee Rodin 1982.*
Iris and B. Gerald Cantor Collection,
promised gift to the Iris and B. Gerald
Cantor Foundation
1189

Rodin, Auguste
Cybèle
c. 1890, enlarged in 1904, Musée Rodin
cast 7/8 in 1987
Bronze
Coubertin
65 × 34 × 56 in.
(165.1 × 86.4 × 142.2 cm)
Signed *A. Rodin* with Coubertin foundry
mark and inscribed © *By Musee Rodin
1987.*
Iris and B. Gerald Cantor Foundation
1473

Rodin, Auguste
Female Torso Clasping her Left Thigh
c. 1890, date of cast unknown
Bronze
Georges Rudier
14⅜ × 9½ × 11 in.
(36.5 × 24.1 × 27.9 cm)
Signed and numbered *A. Rodin
Nº 11.*
Iris and B. Gerald Cantor Collection,
promised gift to the Iris and B. Gerald
Cantor Foundation
10800

Rodin, Auguste
Female Torso Clasping her Left Thigh
c. 1890, Musée Rodin cast 8 in 1957
Bronze
Georges Rudier
14⅜ × 9½ × 11 in.
(36.5 × 24.1 × 27.9 cm)
Signed and numbered *A. Rodin Nº 8* and
inscribed *Georges Rudier Fondeur Paris*
and © *by musee Rodin 1957.*
Iris and B. Gerald Cantor Collection,
promised gift to the Iris and B. Gerald
Cantor Foundation
1375

Rodin, Auguste
Flying Figure
c. 1890–91, date of cast unknown
Bronze
Georges Rudier
20½ × 29½ × 12 in.
(52.1 × 74.9 × 30.5 cm)
Signed *A. Rodin* and inscribed *Georges
Rudier Fondeur Paris © Musée Rodin.*
Iris and B. Gerald Cantor Foundation
1302

Rodin, Auguste
*Half-length Figure of a Woman
(The Martyr)*
Before 1900, Musée Rodin cast in 1966
Bronze
Georges Rudier
31 × 27 × 17 in.
(78.7 × 68.6 × 43.2 cm)
Signed *A.Rodin* and inscribed
.Georges.Rudier.Fondeur.Paris and © *by
musée Rodin 1966.*
Iris and B. Gerald Cantor Foundation
1617

Rodin, Auguste
Monumental Torso of the Walking Man
c. 1905, Musée Rodin cast 1/8 in 1985
Bronze
Godard
43⅓ × 26¾ × 15 in.
(110.1 × 67.9 × 38.1 cm)
Signed and numbered *A. Rodin Nº 1/8*
and inscribed *E. GODARD FONDᴱ* and ©
By MUSEE Rodin 1985.
Iris and B. Gerald Cantor Collection,
promised gift to the Iris and
B. Gerald Cantor Foundation
1394

Rodin, Auguste
Monumental Torso of the Walking Man
c. 1905, Musée Rodin cast 4/8 in 1985
Bronze
Godard
43⅓ × 26¾ × 15 in.
(110.1 × 67.9 × 38.1 cm)
Signed and numbered *A.Rodin/ Nº 4/8*
and inscribed *E.GODARD Fondᴱ* and ©
BY MUSEE Rodin 1985.
Iris and B. Gerald Cantor Foundation
1410 (plate 140)

Rodin, Auguste
Female Torso (V&A)
1909, Musée Rodin cast 3 in 1979
Bronze
Coubertin
24⅞ × 15 × 7⅞ in.
(63.2 × 38.1 × 20 cm)
Signed and numbered *A. Rodin nº 3* with
Coubertin foundry mark and inscribed ©
by musee Rodin 1979.
Iris and B. Gerald Cantor Foundation
1609

Rodin, Auguste
The Prayer
1910, Musée Rodin cast 3/12 in 1977
Bronze
Georges Rudier
49½ × 21⅝ × 19⅝ in.
(125.7 × 54.9 × 49.8 cm)
Signed and numbered *A.Rodin/ N<u>o</u> 3* and inscribed *Georges Rudier Fondeur Paris* and © *by musee Rodin 1977*.
Iris and B. Gerald Cantor Collection, promised gift to the Iris and B. Gerald Cantor Foundation
1050 (plate 110)

Rodin, Auguste
The Prayer
1910, Musée Rodin cast 5 in 1979
Bronze
Godard
49½ × 21⅝ × 19⅝ in.
(125.7 × 54.9 × 49.8 cm)
Signed and numbered *A. Rodin/ No 5* and inscribed *E. GODARD/ Fondr* and © *BY MUSEE Rodin 1979*.
Iris and B. Gerald Cantor Foundation
1553

Rodin, Auguste
Female Nude, Reclining
No date, Musée Rodin cast 1 in 1970
Bronze
Coubertin
20 × 7 × 11 in.
(50.8 × 17.8 × 27.9 cm)
Signed and numbered *A. Rodin no 1.* and inscribed © *by musee Rodin 1970*.
Iris and B. Gerald Cantor Collection, promised gift to the Iris and B. Gerald Cantor Foundation
1369

Rodin, Auguste
Female Torso, Kneeling, Twisting Nude
No date, Musée Rodin cast 7/8 in 1984
Bronze
Godard
23¾ × 12⅝ × 13¾ in.
(60.3 × 32.1 × 34.9 cm)
Signed and numbered *A. Rodin/ No 7/8* and inscribed © *By MUSEE Rodin. 1984*.
Iris and B. Gerald Cantor Collection, promised gift to the Iris and B. Gerald Cantor Foundation
1392

Rodin, Auguste
Female Torso, Kneeling, Twisting Nude
No date, Musée Rodin cast II/IV in 1984
Bronze
Godard
23¾ × 12⅝ × 13¾ in.
(60.3 × 32.1 × 34.9 cm)
Signed and numbered *A. Rodin No II/IV* and inscribed *E. Godard/ Fondr* and © *By MUSEE Rodin 1984*.
Iris and B. Gerald Cantor Collection, promised gift to the Iris and B. Gerald Cantor Foundation
1509

Rodin, Auguste
Small Seated Female Torso
No date, Musée Rodin cast 1 in 1979
Bronze
Coubertin
7½ × 5 × 5⅜ in.
(19.1 × 12.7 × 13.7 cm)
Signed and numbered *A. Rodin No 1* with Coubertin foundry mark and inscribed © *by Musée Rodin 1979*.
Iris and B. Gerald Cantor Collection, promised gift to the Iris and B. Gerald Cantor Foundation
10100

Rodin, Auguste
Narcisse
No date, Musée Rodin cast 8/8 in 1985
Bronze
Godard
32 × 13 × 12¼ in.
(81.3 × 33 × 31.1 cm)
Signed and numbered *A. Rodin/ No 8/8* and inscribed *E. Godard Fondr* and © *By Musée Rodin 1985*.
Iris and B. Gerald Cantor Foundation
1402

Rodin, Auguste
Small Torso of a Woman (Type "A")
No date, Musée Rodin cast 11 in 1978
Bronze
Georges Rudier
6¾ × 3½ × 2½ in.
(17.1 × 8.9 × 6.4 cm)
Signed and numbered *A. Rodin No 11* and inscribed *Georges Rudier.Fondeur Paris.* and
© *by. musée Rodin 1978*.
Iris and B. Gerald Cantor Foundation
1552

Rodin, Auguste
Small Torso of a Woman (Type "A")
No date, date of cast unknown
Bronze
Georges Rudier
6¾ × 3½ × 2½ in.
(17.1 × 8.9 × 6.4 cm)
Signed *A. Rodin.*
Iris and B. Gerald Cantor Collection, promised gift to the Iris and B. Gerald Cantor Foundation
369000

Rodin, Auguste
Torso of a Centauresse & Study for Iris
No date, Musée Rodin cast 4/8 in 1991
Bronze
Godard
9 × 4⅜ × 5¼ in.
(22.9 × 11.1 × 13.3 cm)
Signed and numbered *A. Rodin No 4/8* and inscribed *E. GODARD Fondr* and © *By MUSEE Rodin 1991*.
Iris and B. Gerald Cantor Collection, promised gift to the Iris and B. Gerald Cantor Foundation
1575

I. HANDS, FEET, AND RELATED ASSEMBLAGES

Rodin, Auguste
Left Hand of Pierre de Wiessant
c. 1884–89, date of cast unknown
Bronze
Alexis Rudier
11 × 7½ × 6 in.
(27.9 × 19 × 15.2 cm)
Signed *A. Rodin* and inscribed *ALEXIS.RUDIER.Fondeur.PARIS.*
Iris and B. Gerald Cantor Foundation
1610

Rodin, Auguste
Right Hand of Pierre and Jacques de Wiessant
c. 1884–89, date of cast unknown
Bronze
Alexis Rudier
12½ × 7 × 3 in.
(31.7 × 17.8 × 7.62 cm)
Signed and inscribed *A. Rodin* and *Alexis Rudier Fondeur Paris*.
Iris and B. Gerald Cantor Collection, promised gift to the Iris and B. Gerald Cantor Foundation
4260 (plate 43)

Rodin, Auguste
Large Left Hand of a Pianist
1885, Musée Rodin cast 8/12 in 1969
Bronze
Georges Rudier
7¼ × 10 × 4⅞ in.
(18.4 × 25.4 × 12.4 cm)
Signed and numbered *A. Rodin/ No 8* and inscribed *.Georges Rudier/ .Fondeur. Paris* and © *by musée Rodin 1969*.
Iris and B. Gerald Cantor Collection, promised gift to the Iris and B. Gerald Cantor Foundation
3750

Rodin, Auguste
Large Left Hand of a Pianist
1885, Musée Rodin cast 9/12 in 1969
Bronze
Georges Rudier
7¼ × 10 × 4⅞ in.
(18.4 × 25.4 × 12.4 cm)
Signed and numbered *A. Rodin No 9* and © *by musée Rodin 1969* and inscribed *Georges Rudier. Fondeur.Paris.*
Iris and B. Gerald Cantor Foundation
1488 (plate 123)

Rodin, Auguste
Small Left Hand of a Pianist
No date
Bronze
Georges Rudier
2 × 5 × 2½ in.
(5.1 × 12.7 × 6.4 cm)
Signed *A. Rodin* and inscribed *G. Rudier./ .Fondeur. Paris.*
Iris and B. Gerald Cantor Collection, promised gift to the Iris and B. Gerald Cantor Foundation
2340

Rodin, Auguste
Large Clenched Left Hand
c. 1885, Musée Rodin cast 3/12 in 1966
Bronze
Georges Rudier
18¼ × 10⅜ × 7⅝ in.
(46.4 × 26.4 × 19.3 cm)
Signed *A. Rodin* and inscribed
© *by Musee Rodin 1966.*
Iris and B. Gerald Cantor Foundation
2120 (plate 119)

Rodin, Auguste
Large Clenched Right Hand
c. 1885, Musée Rodin cast 1965
Bronze
Georges Rudier
18½ × 12½ × 6¼ in.
(46.9 × 31.7 × 15.9 cm)
Signed *A. Rodin* and inscribed
© *by musée Rodin 1965* and
Georges.Rudier.Fondeur.Paris. with raised signature *A. Rodin* inside.
Iris and B. Gerald Cantor Collection, promised gift to the Iris and B. Gerald Cantor Foundation
2300

Rodin, Auguste
Small Clenched Right Hand
c. 1885, date of cast unknown
Bronze
Alexis Rudier
5½ × 4½ × 2½ in.
(14 × 11.4 × 6.4 cm)
Signed *A. Rodin.*
Iris and B. Gerald Cantor Collection, promised gift to the Iris and B. Gerald Cantor Foundation
2150

Rodin, Auguste
Small Clenched Right Hand
c. 1885, date of cast unknown
Bronze
Alexis Rudier
5½ × 4½ × 2½ in.
(14 × 11.4 × 6.4 cm)
Signed *A. Rodin* and inscribed *A. RUDIER Fond. PARIS.*
Iris and B. Gerald Cantor Foundation
2160

Rodin, Auguste
Grasping Left Hand
No date
Bronze
No foundry mark
5¾ × 3¾ × 2¼ in.
(14.6 × 9.5 × 5.7 cm)
Signed *A. Rodin.*
Iris and B. Gerald Cantor Collection, promised gift to the Iris and B. Gerald Cantor Foundation
15300

Rodin, Auguste
Clenched Left Hand with Figure
1906 or 1907, Musée Rodin cast 1/12 in 1970
Bronze
Godard
17½ × 11½ × 10⅜ in.
(44.5 × 29.2 × 26.4 cm)
Signed and numbered *A. Rodin/ No 1* and inscribed *Godard Fondeur Paris* and © *by musée Rodin.*
Iris and B. Gerald Cantor Collection, promised gift to the Iris and B. Gerald Cantor Foundation
2240 (plate 121)

Rodin, Auguste
The Hand of God
1898, date of cast unknown
Bronze
Alexis Rudier
12¾ × 11¼ × 11¾ in.
(32.4 × 28.6 × 29.8 cm)
Signed *A. Rodin* and inscribed *Alexis RUDIER Fondeur Paris.*
Iris and B. Gerald Cantor Collection, promised gift to the Iris and B. Gerald Cantor Foundation
15500

Rodin, Auguste
The Hand of God
1898, Musée Rodin cast 11/12 in 1966
Bronze
Georges Rudier
12¾ × 11¼ × 11¾ in.
(32.4 × 26 × 29.8 cm)
Signed *A Rodin* and inscribed © *by musée Rodin 1966* and *.Georges Rudier./ Foundeur.Paris.*
Iris and B. Gerald Cantor Collection, promised gift to the Iris and B. Gerald Cantor Foundation
770 (plate 130)

Rodin, Auguste
The Hand of God
1898, date of cast unknown
Bronze
Alexis Rudier
5¼ × 3½ × 3⅝ in.
(13.3 × 8.9 × 9.1 cm)
Signed *A. Rodin* and inscribed *Alexis Rudier, Fondeur, Paris.*
Iris and B. Gerald Cantor Collection, promised gift to the Iris and B. Gerald Cantor Foundation
604

Rodin, Auguste
The Hand of God
1898, date of cast unknown
Bronze
Alexis Rudier
5¼ × 3½ × 3⅝ in.
(13.3 × 8.9 × 9.1 cm)
Signed *A.Rodin* and inscribed *Alexis Rudier Fondeur PARIS.*
Iris and B. Gerald Cantor Collection, promised gift to the Iris and B. Gerald Cantor Foundation
15200 (plate 133)

Rodin, Auguste
The Cathedral
Original stone version executed in 1908, Musée Rodin cast in 1955
Bronze
Georges Rudier
25¼ × 12¾ × 13½ in.
(64.1 × 32.3 × 34.3 cm)
Inscribed *Georges Rudier Fondeur Paris* © *Musee Rodin 1955* and signed *A. Rodin* inside.
Iris and B. Gerald Cantor Foundation
15600 (plate 116 and back jacket/cover)

Rodin, Auguste
The Cathedral
Original stone version executed in 1908, this bronze version cast at a later date
Bronze
Alexis Rudier
25¼ × 12¾ × 13½ in.
(64.1 × 32.3 × 34.3 cm)
Signed *A. Rodin* and inscribed *Alexis Rudier.Fondeur.Paris.*
Iris and B. Gerald Cantor Collection, promised gift to the Iris and B. Gerald Cantor Foundation
1690

Rodin, Auguste
Study for The Secret
c. 1910, date of cast unknown
Bronze
Alexis Rudier
4¾ × 2⅛ × 2¼ in.
(12.1 × 5.4 × 5.7 cm)
Signed *A. Rodin* and inscribed *ALEXIS RUDIER./ Fondeur.PARIS.*
Iris and B. Gerald Cantor Collection, promised gift to the Iris and B. Gerald Cantor Foundation
15400

Rodin, Auguste
Hand of Rodin Holding Torso
1917, Musée Rodin cast in 1968
Bronze
Georges Rudier
6⅛ × 8¾ × 4⅛ in.
(15.6 × 22.2 × 10.5 cm)
Signed *A. Rodin* and inscribed © *by musée Rodin 1968* and *.Georges Rudier./ Fondeur.Paris.*
Iris and B. Gerald Cantor Collection, promised gift to the Iris and B. Gerald Cantor Foundation
603 (plate 124)

Rodin, Auguste
Blessing Hand
No date
Bronze
No foundry mark
5½ × 4¾ × 2⅞ in.
(14 × 12 × 7.3 cm)
No inscriptions
Iris and B. Gerald Cantor Collection, promised gift to the Iris and B. Gerald Cantor Foundation
1373

Rodin, Auguste
Blessing Hand (called *Hand No. 33*)
No date, Musée Rodin cast 1/12 in 1964
Bronze
Georges Rudier
4¾ × 2⅞ × 6 in.
(12 × 7.3 × 15.2 cm)
Signed *A Rodin* and inscribed © *by musée Rodin 1964* and *G Rudier Fondeur Paris.*
Iris and B. Gerald Cantor Collection, promised gift to the Iris and B. Gerald Cantor Foundation
2210

Rodin, Auguste
Left Hand, Almost Closed
No date
Bronze
No foundry mark
4¾ × 2⅝ × 2¾ in.
(12.1 × 6.7 × 7 cm)
Signed *A Rodin.*
Iris and B. Gerald Cantor Collection, promised gift to the Iris and B. Gerald Cantor Foundation
22500

Rodin, Auguste
Left Hand, Bent Forward
No date
Bronze
Alexis Rudier
4⅛ × 2½ × 3⅝ in.
(10.5 × 6.4 × 9.2 cm)
Signed and inscribed *A. Rodin./ Alexis
Rudier/ Fondeur PARIS.*
Iris and B. Gerald Cantor Collection,
promised gift to the Iris and B. Gerald
Cantor Foundation
1233

Rodin, Auguste
Left Hand (called Hand No. 39)
No date, Musée Rodin cast 1/12 in 1974
Bronze
Godard
5¼ × 3⅛ × 1¾ in.
(13.3 × 8 × 4.4 cm)
Signed and numbered *A. Rodin/ No. 1* and
inscribed *E. GODARD/ FOND* and © *by
musée Rodin 1974.*
Iris and B. Gerald Cantor Collection,
promised gift to the Iris and B. Gerald
Cantor Foundation
2230

Rodin, Auguste
Left Hand, Four Fingers Together
No date
Bronze
No foundry mark
3¼ × 2¼ × 1½ in.
(8.3 × 5.7 × 3.8 cm)
Signed *A. Rodin.*
Iris and B. Gerald Cantor Collection,
promised gift to the Iris and B. Gerald
Cantor Foundation
2190

Rodin, Auguste
Left Hand, Slightly Bent
No date
Bronze
Alexis Rudier
3½ × 1¾ × 1¾ in.
(8.9 × 4.4 × 4.4 cm)
Signed *A. Rodin* and inscribed
A. RUDIER./ Fond. PARIS.
Iris and B. Gerald Cantor Collection,
promised gift to the Iris and B. Gerald
Cantor Foundation
2100

Rodin, Auguste
*Left Hand, Three Fingers Joined, Small
Finger Slightly Extended*
No date
Bronze
No foundry mark
2¾ × 1½ × 1 in.
(7 × 3.8 × 2.5 cm)
Signed *A. Rodin* and inscribed *A. Rudier/
Fond. Paris.*
Iris and B. Gerald Cantor Collection,
promised gift to the Iris and B. Gerald
Cantor Foundation
2110

Rodin, Auguste
Right Hand, Bent at Wrist
No date
Bronze
Alexis Rudier
4¾ × 2½ × 3¼ in.
(12.1 × 6.4 × 8.3 cm)
Signed *A. Rodin* and inscribed *Alexis
Rudier/ Fond. Paris.*
Iris and B. Gerald Cantor Collection,
promised gift to the Iris and B. Gerald
Cantor Foundation
1235

Rodin, Auguste
Right Hand (called Hand No. 12)
No date
Bronze
No foundry mark
2⅝ × 1½ × ¾ in.
(6.7 × 3.8 × 1.9 cm)
Signed *A. Rodin.*
Iris and B. Gerald Cantor Collection,
promised gift to the Iris and B. Gerald
Cantor Foundation
2180

Rodin, Auguste
Right Hand (called Hand No. 15)
No date
Bronze
Alexis Rudier
3 × 1⅝ × ⅞ in.
(7.6 × 4.1 × 2.2 cm)
Signed *A. Rodin* and inscribed
A. RUDIER./ F. PARIS.
Iris and B. Gerald Cantor Collection,
promised gift to the Iris and B. Gerald
Cantor Foundation
760

Rodin, Auguste
Right Hand (called Hand No. 22)
No date
Bronze
Georges Rudier
3½ × 1⅜ × 2 in.
(8.9 × 3.4 × 5.1 cm)
Signed *A. Rodin* and inscribed *G. Rudier/
Fond. Paris.*
Iris and B. Gerald Cantor Collection,
promised gift to the Iris and B. Gerald
Cantor Foundation
1513

Rodin, Auguste
Right Hand (called Hand No. 23)
No date
Bronze
Georges Rudier
4¼ × 2½ × 2½ in.
(10.8 × 6.4 × 6.4 cm)
Signed *A. Rodin.*
Iris and B. Gerald Cantor Collection,
promised gift to the Iris and B. Gerald
Cantor Foundation
1322

Rodin, Auguste
Right Hand (called Hand No. 27)
No date, Musée Rodin cast 4/12 in 1965
Bronze
Georges Rudier
4½ × 3 × 2 in.
(11.4 × 7.6 × 5.1 cm)
Signed *A. Rodin* and inscribed *Georges
Rudier Fondeur* and © *by musée Rodin,
1965.*
Iris and B. Gerald Cantor Collection,
promised gift to the Iris and B. Gerald
Cantor Foundation
2220

Rodin, Auguste
Right Hand (called Hand No. 32)
No date
Bronze
Georges Rudier
3 × 1½ × 1½ in.
(7.6 × 3.8 × 3.8 cm)
Signed *A. Rodin.*
Iris and B. Gerald Cantor Collection,
promised gift to the Iris and B. Gerald
Cantor Foundation
1377

Rodin, Auguste
*Right Hand, Fingers Close Together,
Slightly Bent*
No date
Bronze
Georges Rudier
4¾ × 2⅛ × 1½ in.
(12.1 × 5.4 × 3.8 cm)
Signed and numbered *A. Rodin 6* and
inscribed *G. Rudier Fondeur.Paris.*
Iris and B. Gerald Cantor Collection,
promised gift to the Iris and B. Gerald
Cantor Foundation
1489

Rodin, Auguste
Right Hand, Half Closed
No date
Bronze
No foundry mark
3⅛ × 1¼ × 1⅝ in.
(7.9 × 3.2 × 4.1 cm)
Signed *A. Rodin.*
Iris and B. Gerald Cantor Collection,
promised gift to the Iris and B. Gerald
Cantor Foundation
2350

Rodin, Auguste
Right Hand, Middle Finger Slightly Bent
No date
Bronze
Alexis Rudier
4½ × 2⅛ × 1⅛ in.
(11.4 × 5.4 × 2.8 cm)
Signed *A. Rodin* and inscribed *Alexis
Rudier/ Fondeur Paris.*
Iris and B. Gerald Cantor Collection,
promised gift to the Iris and B. Gerald
Cantor Foundation
2360

Rodin, Auguste
Right Hand, Middle Fingers Together
No date
Bronze
No foundry mark
4 × 2 × 1½ in.
(10.2 × 5.1 × 3.8 cm)
Signed *A. Rodin.*
Iris and B. Gerald Cantor Foundation
4290

Rodin, Auguste
*Right Hand, Small Finger and Thumb
Extended*
No date
Bronze
No foundry mark
4 × 2 × 2 in.
(10.2 × 5.1 × 5.1 cm)
Signed *A. Rodin.*
Iris and B. Gerald Cantor Collection,
promised gift to the Iris and B. Gerald
Cantor Foundation
2310

Rodin, Auguste
Left Foot
No date
Bronze
Eugène Rudier
2⅞ × 2 × 4½ in.
(7.3 × 5 × 11.4 cm)
No inscriptions
Iris and B. Gerald Cantor Collection,
promised gift to the Iris and B. Gerald
Cantor Foundation
2260

Rodin, Auguste
Head of Shade with Two Hands
c. 1910, date of cast unknown
Bronze
Alexis Rudier
7⅞ × 10¾ × 8⅛ in.
(19.4 × 27.3 × 20.6 cm)
Signed and numbered *A.Rodin/ No. 2* and
inscribed *ALEXIS RUDIER/ Fondeur-Paris*
and stamped with a raised signature *A.
Rodin* inside.
Iris and B. Gerald Cantor Foundation
1545 (plate 129)

Rodin, Auguste
Small Head of Jean de Fiennes with Hand
No date, Musée Rodin cast III/IV in 1986
Bronze
Godard
3 × 3 × 3 in.
(7.6 × 7.6 × 7.6 cm)
Signed and numbered *A. Rodin No III/IV*
and inscribed © *BY MUSEE Rodin 1986*
and *E. GODARD Fondr.*
Iris and B. Gerald Cantor Collection,
promised gift to the Iris and B. Gerald
Cantor Foundation
1428

J. PORTRAITS OF RODIN

CLAUDEL, CAMILLE (French, 1864–1943)
Bust of Rodin
1888–92, date of cast unknown
Bronze
Alexis Rudier
15¾ × 9¼ × 11 in.
(40 × 23.5 × 28 cm)
Signed *Camille Claudel.*
Iris and B. Gerald Cantor Foundation
593 (plate 25)

TWEED, JOHN (English, 1869–1933)
Relief Portrait Bust of Rodin
c. 1895
Bronze
No foundry mark
9 × 8 × 1½ in.
(22.9 × 20.3 × 3.8 cm)
Signed *Tweed.*
Iris and B. Gerald Cantor Foundation
1519

PAULIN, PAUL (French, 1850–1932)
Bust of Auguste Rodin
1917
Bronze
Valsuani
15¼ × 11½ × 13 in.
(38.7 × 29.2 × 33 cm)
Signed and inscribed *PPaulin, Rodin,
1917, pour M.A. Rosenthal* and stamped
with Valsuani seal.
Iris and B. Gerald Cantor Foundation
1598

SOUDBININE, SERAPHIN (Russian,
1870–1944)
Bust of Rodin
No date
Bronze
Alexis Rudier
21½ × 11½ × 11 in.
(54.6 × 29.2 × 27.9 cm)
Iris and B. Gerald Cantor Collection,
promised gift to the Iris and B. Gerald
Cantor Foundation
13610

K. WORKS ON PAPER

Rodin, Auguste
The Round
c. 1883
Engraving
11½ × 7¾ in.
(29.2 × 19.7 cm)
Iris and B. Gerald Cantor Foundation
690

Rodin, Auguste
Antonin Proust
1885
Engraving
12 × 8½ in.
(30.5 × 21.6 cm)
Iris and B. Gerald Cantor Foundation
670

Rodin, Auguste
Victor Hugo (Frontal View)
1886
Drypoint
8¾ × 6½ in.
(22.2 × 16.5 cm)
Iris and B. Gerald Cantor Foundation
669 (plate 49)

STEICHEN, EDWARD (American,
1879–1973)
*Portrait of Rodin with The Thinker and
the Monument to Victor Hugo*
1902
Silver print
13¼ × 16⅝ in.
(33.7 × 42.2 cm)
Iris and B. Gerald Cantor Foundation
1110 (plate 55)

Rodin, Auguste
Head Study for Mlle. Jean Simpson
c. 1903
Pencil
12¾ × 9¾ in.
(32.3 × 24.8 cm)
Iris and B. Gerald Cantor Foundation
1422

Rodin, Auguste
Mlle. Jean Simpson, Leaning Over
c. 1903
Watercolor and pencil
12¾ × 9¾ in.
(32.3 × 24.8 cm)
Iris and B. Gerald Cantor Foundation
1281

STEICHEN, EDWARD (American,
1879–1973)
Portrait of Rodin
1910
Photogravure
9½ × 6½ in.
(24.1 × 16.5 cm)
Iris and B. Gerald Cantor Foundation
685

DRUET, EUGENE (French, 1868–1916)
Bronze Bust of T. Ryan
Photograph
15¼ × 10 in.
(38.7 × 25.4 cm)
Iris and B. Gerald Cantor Foundation
1275

L. CASTING PROCESS

Ten-step Lost-wax Casting Process of
Rodin's *Sorrow*
1987
Plaster, clay, wax, ceramic, and bronze
Coubertin
10 pieces, approx. 15 × 10 × 8 in. each
(10 pieces, 38.1 × 25.4 × 20.3 cm each)
Iris and B. Gerald Cantor Collection,
promised gift to the Iris and B. Gerald
Cantor Foundation
1436

Auguste Rodin
Sorrow
1889, Musée Rodin cast 1/8 in 1983
Bronze
Coubertin
11½ × 6½ × 6¾ in.
(29.2 × 16.5 × 17.1 cm)
Signed *A. Rodin* and inscribed © *Musee
Rodin, 1983 No 1/8* and *La Porte de l'enfer
1977–81 don DE B. Gerald Cantor.*
Iris and B. Gerald Cantor Collection,
promised gift to the Iris and B. Gerald
Cantor Foundation
1324

Ten-step Lost-wax Casting Process of
Rodin's *Sorrow*
1994
Plaster, clay, wax, ceramic, and bronze
Coubertin
10 pieces, approx. 15 × 10 × 8 in. each
(10 pieces, 38.1 × 25.4 × 20.3 cm each)
Iris and B. Gerald Cantor Collection,
promised gift to the Iris and B. Gerald
Cantor Foundation
1635

Rodin, Auguste
Sorrow
1889, Musée Rodin cast 6/8 in 1983
Bronze
Coubertin
11½ × 6½ × 6¾ in.
(29.2 × 16.5 × 17.1 cm)
Signed and numbered *A. Rodin/ No 6/8*
and inscribed © *By Musée Rodin 1983*
and *LA PORTE DE L'ENFER 1977–1981/
DON DE B. GERALD CANTOR.*
Iris and B. Gerald Cantor Collection,
promised gift to the Iris and B. Gerald
Cantor Foundation
1354

Ten-step Lost-wax Casting Process of
Rodin's *Sorrow*
1990
Plaster, clay, wax, ceramic, and bronze
Coubertin
10 pieces, approx. 15 × 10 × 8 in. each
(10 pieces, 38.1 × 25.4 × 20.3 cm each)
Iris and B. Gerald Cantor Foundation
1494

Rodin, Auguste
Sorrow
1889, Musée Rodin cast III/IV in 1983
Bronze
Coubertin
11½ × 6½ × 6¾ in.
(29.2 × 16.5 × 17.1 cm)
Signed and numbered *A. Rodin No III/IV*
and inscribed © *By Musée Rodin 1983*
and *LA PORTE DE L'ENFER 1977–1981
DON DE B. GERALD CANTOR.*
Iris and B. Gerald Cantor Foundation
1356

Picture Credits

Pl. 120 © Alinari

Pls. 97, 113 © Berlin Kupferstichkabinett

Pl. 75 © Biblioteca Laurenziana, Florence

Pl. 71 © Biblioteca Nazionale, Turin

Pl. 114 © Bibliothèque de l'Arsenal, Paris

Pl. 58 © Bibliothèque historique de la Ville de Paris

Pls. 91, 92, 94, 155 © Bibliothèque Nationale, Paris

Pl. 104 © Casino Massimo, Rome

Pl. 23 © Ecole Nationale Supérieure des Beaux-Arts, Paris

Pl. 118 © Giraudon

Pls. 2–9, 17, 30, 33, 34, 37, 44, 52, 67, 69, 73, 89, 115, 125, 129, 134, 137, 152 © Iris and B. Gerald Cantor Foundation 2001

Pls. 36, 68 © Iris and B. Gerald Cantor Foundation 2001/Ben Blackwell

Pls. 79, 99 © Iris and B. Gerald Cantor Foundation 2001/Robert Fouts

Pl. 108 © Iris and B. Gerald Cantor Foundation 2001/Thomas Hager

Pls. 40, 45 © Iris and B. Gerald Cantor Foundation 2001/Andrew Moore

Frontispiece, pls. 1, 10, 11, 12, 13, 14, 15 and back jacket/cover, 25, 29, 31, 32, 38, 41, 42, 49, 50, 51, 53, 55, 59, 62, 63, 65, 70, 74, 80, 81, 83, 85, 95, 102, 107, 110, 111, 116, 119, 121, 123, 124, 130, 133, 140, 142, 144 and front jacket/cover © Iris and B. Gerald Cantor Foundation 2001/Steve Oliver

Pls. 43, 84, 98 © Iris and B. Gerald Cantor Foundation 2001/Bruce Schwarz

Pl. 47 © Iris and B. Gerald Cantor Foundation 2001/Meidad Suchowolski

Pl. 88 © Musée des Arts Décoratifs, Paris

Pl. 86 © Musée Condé, Chantilly

Pls. 101, 105, 109 © Musée Goupil, Bordeaux

Pl. 16 © Musée de Nogent-sur-Seine

Pl. 147 © Musée d'Orsay, Paris

Pl. 149 Courtesy of the Archives of the Musée Rodin, Paris

Pls. 18, 19, 20, 21, 22, 24, 26, 27, 28, 39, 46, 48, 54, 56, 57, 61, 64, 76, 87, 90, 93, 100, 103, 106, 112, 128, 132, 135, 136, 138, 139, 143, 148, 153 © Musée Rodin, Paris

Pl. 66 © Musée Rodin, Paris/Jacques-Ernest Bulloz

Pls. 35, 145 © Musée Rodin, Paris/Béatrice Hatala

Pl. 141 © Musée Rodin, Paris/Stephen Haweis and Henry Coles

Pls. 127, 131, 151, 154 © Musée Rodin, Paris/P. Bruno Jarret/ADAGP

Pls. 146, 150 © Musée Rodin, Paris/Adam Rzepka/ADAGP

Pl. 126 © Roger-Viollet

Pl. 60 © Photothèque des Musées de la Ville de Paris

Pl. 82 © Réunion des Musées Nationaux/Art Resource, New York/P. Bernard

Pl. 122 © Vatican Museum, Rome

Index